THE WICKED + THE DIVINE

VOL. 5, IMPERIAL PHASE PART 1

GILLEN

McKELVIE

WILSON

COWLES

KIERON GILLEN
WRITER

JAMIE McKELVIE
ARTIST

MATTHEW WILSON
COLOURIST

CLAYTON COWLES
LETTERER

SERGIO SERRANO
DESIGNER

CHRISSY WILLIAMS
EDITOR

DEE CUNNIFFE
FLATTER

THE WICKED + THE DIVINE, VOL. 5, IMPERIAL PHASE PART 1
First printing. June 2017.
ISBN: 978-1-5343-0185-6
Published by Image Comics Inc.
Office of publication: 2701 NW Vaughn St., Suite 780, Portland, OR 97210.

For information regarding the CPSIA on this printed material call: 203-595-3636 and provide reference # RICH – 738674. Representation: Law Offices of Harris M. Miller II, P.C. (rights.inquiries@gmail.com).

This book was designed by Sergio Serrano, based on a design by Hannah Donovan and Jamie McKelvie, and set into type by Sergio Serrano in Edmonton, Canada. The text face is Gotham, designed and issued by Hoefler & Co. in 2000. The paper is Escanaba 60 matte.

IMAGE COMICS, INC.
Robert Kirkman, CHIEF OPERATING OFFICER
Erik Larsen, CHIEF FINANCIAL OFFICER
Todd McFarlane, PRESIDENT
Marc Silvestri, CHIEF EXECUTIVE OFFICER
Jim Valentino, VICE-PRESIDENT
Eric Stephenson, PUBLISHER
Corey Murphy, DIRECTOR OF SALES
Jeff Boison, DIRECTOR OF PUBLISHING PLANNING & BOOK TRADE SALES
Chris Ross, DIRECTOR OF DIGITAL SALES
Jeff Stang, DIRECTOR OF SPECIALTY SALES

Kat Salazar, DIRECTOR OF PR & MARKETING
Branwyn Bigglestone, CONTROLLER
Sue Korpela, ACCOUNTS MANAGER
Drew Gill, ART DIRECTOR
Brett Warnock, PRODUCTION MANAGER
Meredith Wallace, PRINT MANAGER
Tricia Ramos, TRAFFIC MANAGER
Briah Skelly, PUBLICIST
Aly Hoffman, EVENTS & CONVENTIONS COORDINATOR
Sasha Head, SALES & MARKETING PRODUCTION DESIGNER
David Brothers, BRANDING MANAGER
Melissa Gifford, CONTENT MANAGER

Drew Fitzgerald, PUBLICITY ASSISTANT
Vincent Kukua, PRODUCTION ARTIST
Erika Schnatz, PRODUCTION ARTIST
Ryan Brewer, PRODUCTION ARTIST
Shanna Matuszak, PRODUCTION ARTIST
Carey Hall, PRODUCTION ARTIST
Esther Kim, DIRECT MARKET SALES REPRESENTATIVE
Emilio Bautista, DIGITAL SALES ASSOCIATE
Leanna Caunter, ACCOUNTING ASSISTANT
Chloe Ramos-Peterson, LIBRARY MARKET SALES REPRESENTATIVE
Marla Eizik, ADMINISTRATIVE ASSISTANT
www.imagecomics.com

GILLEN McKELVIE WILSON COWLES

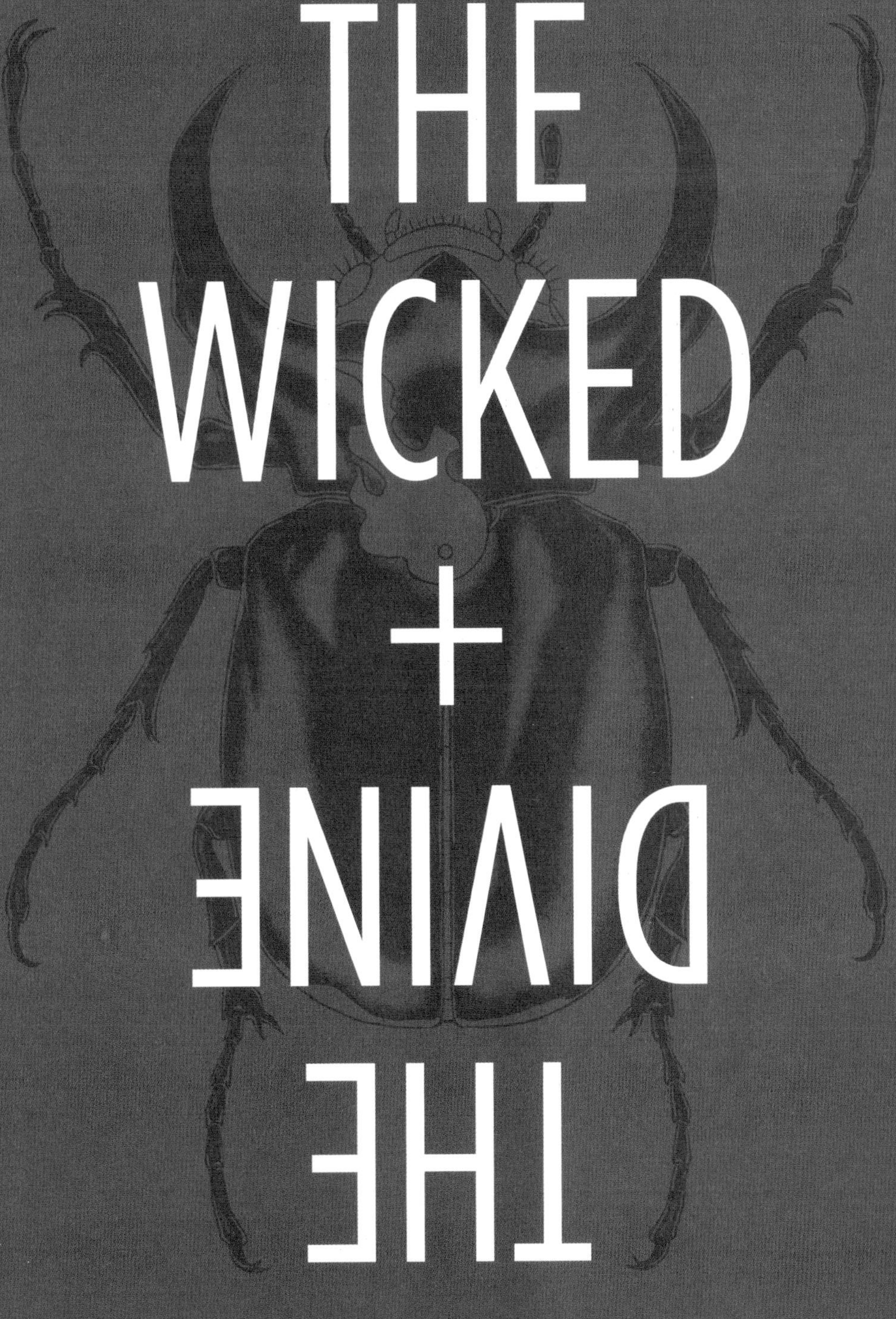

THE WICKED + THE DIVINE

VOL. 5, IMPERIAL PHASE PART 1

PREVIOUSLY...

Every ninety years twelve gods return as young people. They are loved. They are hated. In two years, they are all dead. It's happening now. It's happening again.

Her secrets uncovered, Ananke claimed to have been killing gods to avert "The Great Darkness" for thousands of years. The gods decided to imprison Ananke and question her... but in revenge for the death of her family, Persephone murdered Ananke. The gods agreed to cover it up.

Life goes on.

Persephone. Is in hell. Ascended fangirl Laura. Murdered Ananke.

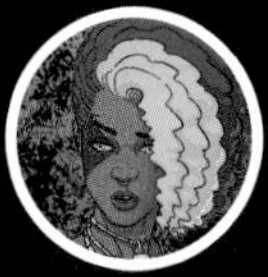

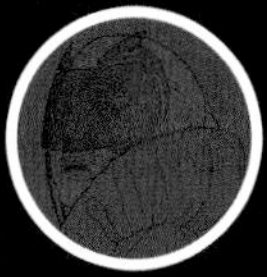

Ananke. Murderous manipulative ~~immortal~~ god of destiny. A bad 'un.

THE PANTHEON

Lucifer. Underworld god. Framed for murder. Killed by Ananke.

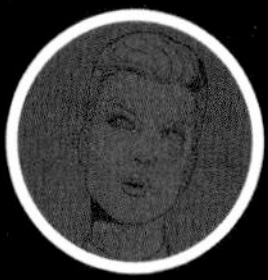

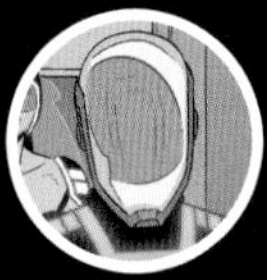

Woden. Shithead god, master of Valkyries. Ananke's secret semi-willing assistant.

Baphomet. Punderworld god. Wanted criminal. The Morrigan's lover. Cheated with Persephone.

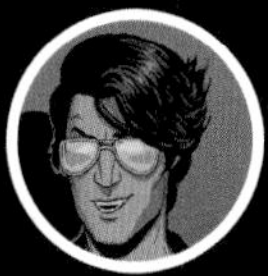

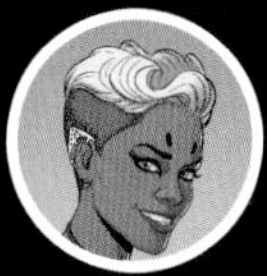

Sakhmet. Feline war god. Emotionally blank hedonist. Ate her dad. No, really.

The Morrigan. Triple-formed underworld god. Previously beaten harshly by Baal when captured.

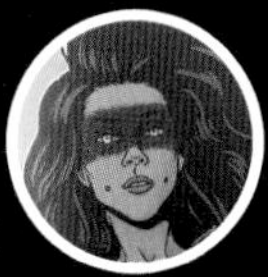

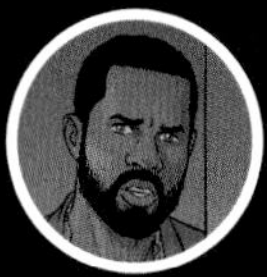

Baal. Storm god. Ex-lover of Inanna. Is now the legal guardian of Minerva.

Dionysus. Hivemind dancefloor god. Doesn't sleep and it's starting to cause problems.

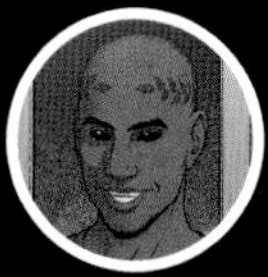

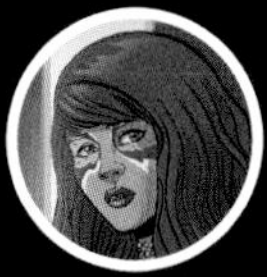

Amaterasu. Sun god with sunny disposition. Intense love of Japan from her dead father.

The Norns. Cynical journo Cassandra and crew turned from naysayers to soothsayers.

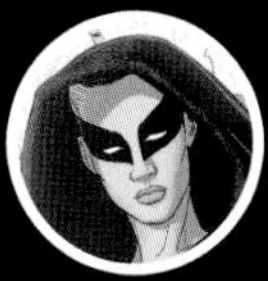

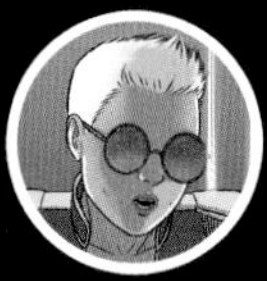

Minerva. Wisdom god with owl. Had worst birthday ever when mom and pop went pop.

Inanna. Queen of heaven. Ex-lover of Baal. Murdered by Ananke.

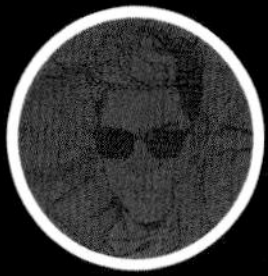

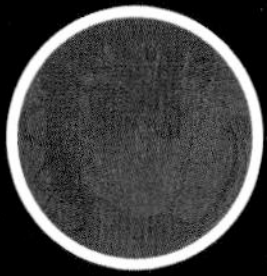

Tara. Secretly killed by Ananke in assisted suicide to frame Baphomet. No one buys it now.

23

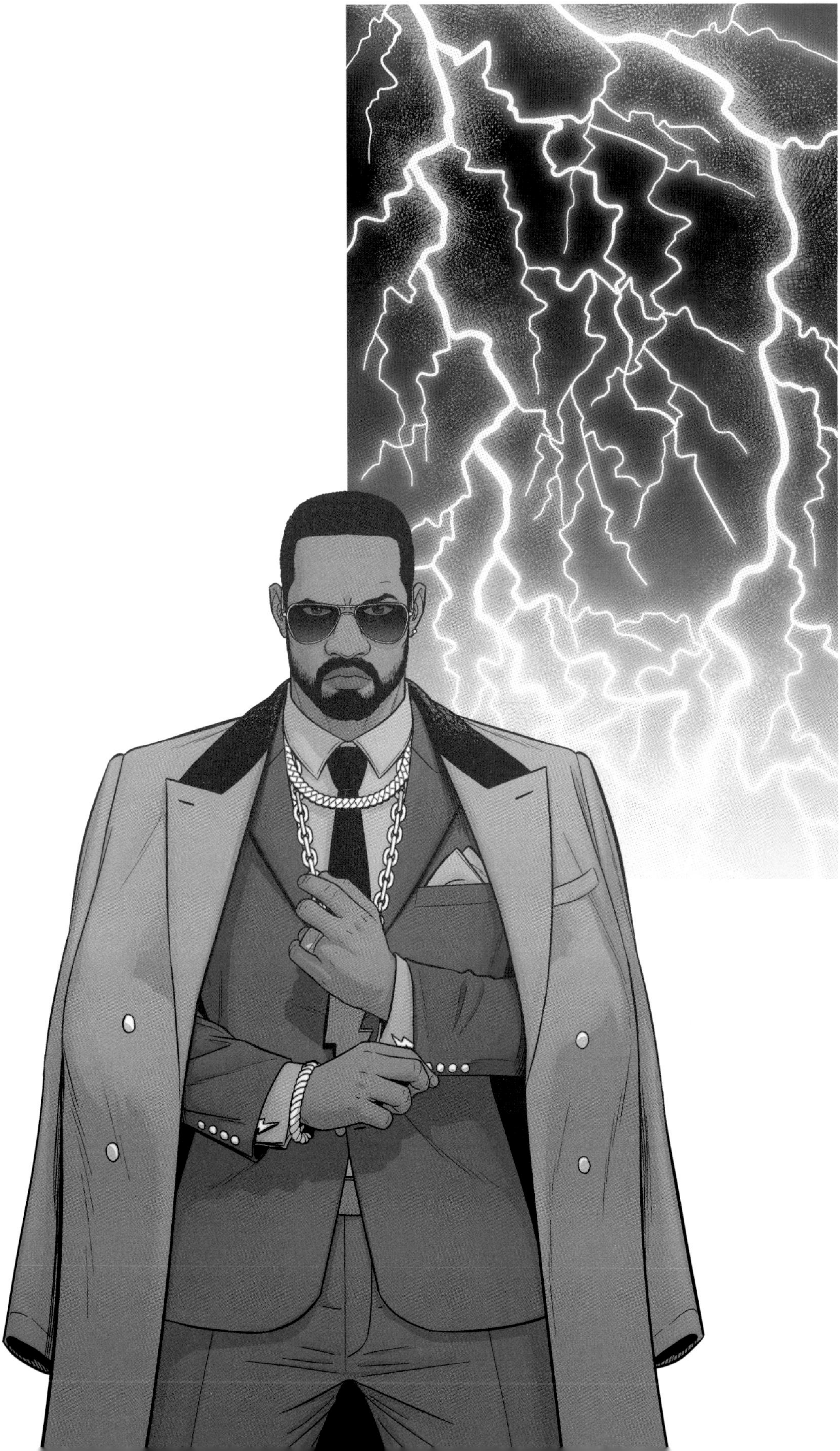

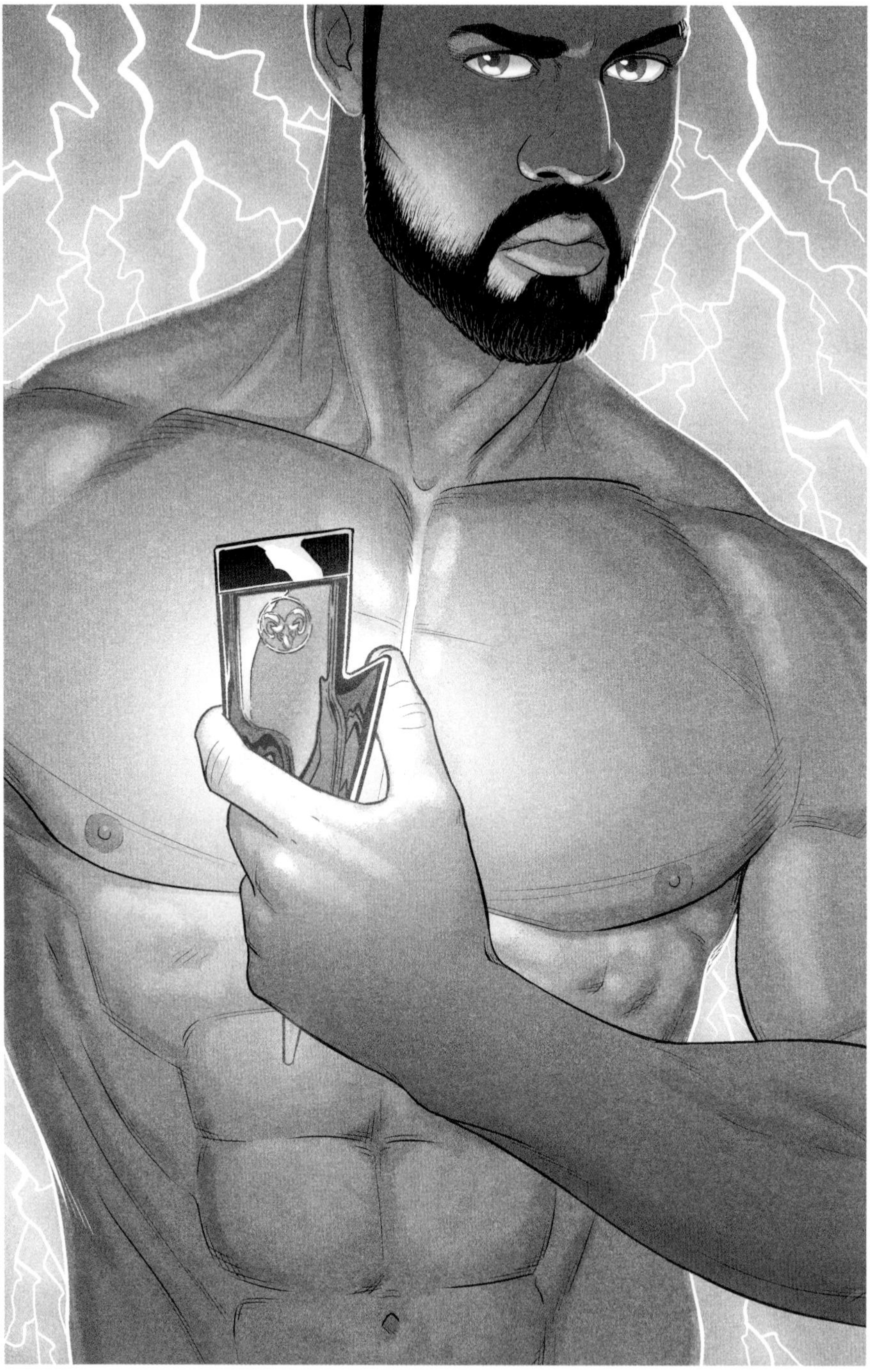

Capture lightning in a bottle

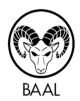

BAAL

CONTENTS

Hi,

I didn't think we could do it. How could *Pantheon Monthly* follow last month's issue? Ananke, revealed to be behind a murderous conspiracy that has claimed the lives of Inanna, Lucifer and Tara. Her plans to kill Minerva... and then Minerva's heroic rescue by the Pantheon. We're all fans of the gods or none of us would be here... but did any of you really think it'd turn out like *this*?

How can you follow that? And then a certain walking embodiment of gothic majesty gets in contact, and suddenly we've got ourselves an exclusive. She's never talked. She's never even allowed herself to be caught on film. This issue, you get both... and you won't believe what she has to say. I don't even know why you're reading this introduction. Turn the page! Get the hell out of here.

Okay. Still here? Well, if you *insist*.

Let's talk about theme. Last issue was about the collapse of the gods' old order. We all had no idea what was next. This issue is about what the gods are building out of the rubble. Baal, Amaterasu and Woden, in their own ways, were most used by Ananke. Their responses are as varied as their types, but you get a portrait of anger, resentment, shame and the gods at their most human. Plus, their plans for the future. If there's wreckage, they're working on it.

To round out the issue, we have an interview with the thin white duke of hell herself, finally released from the legal limbo it's languished in for nearly a year (for alluding to the then private relationship between Inanna and Baal, and Lucifer's part in its end). Audacious, funny, brilliant: if you'd forgotten how much you miss her, this is a reminder that it's not only the *good* who die young — it's the good at being bad.

Ananke is dead. Long live...

Well, long live *no one*.

Kieron Gillen, Editor
Pantheon Monthly, November 2014

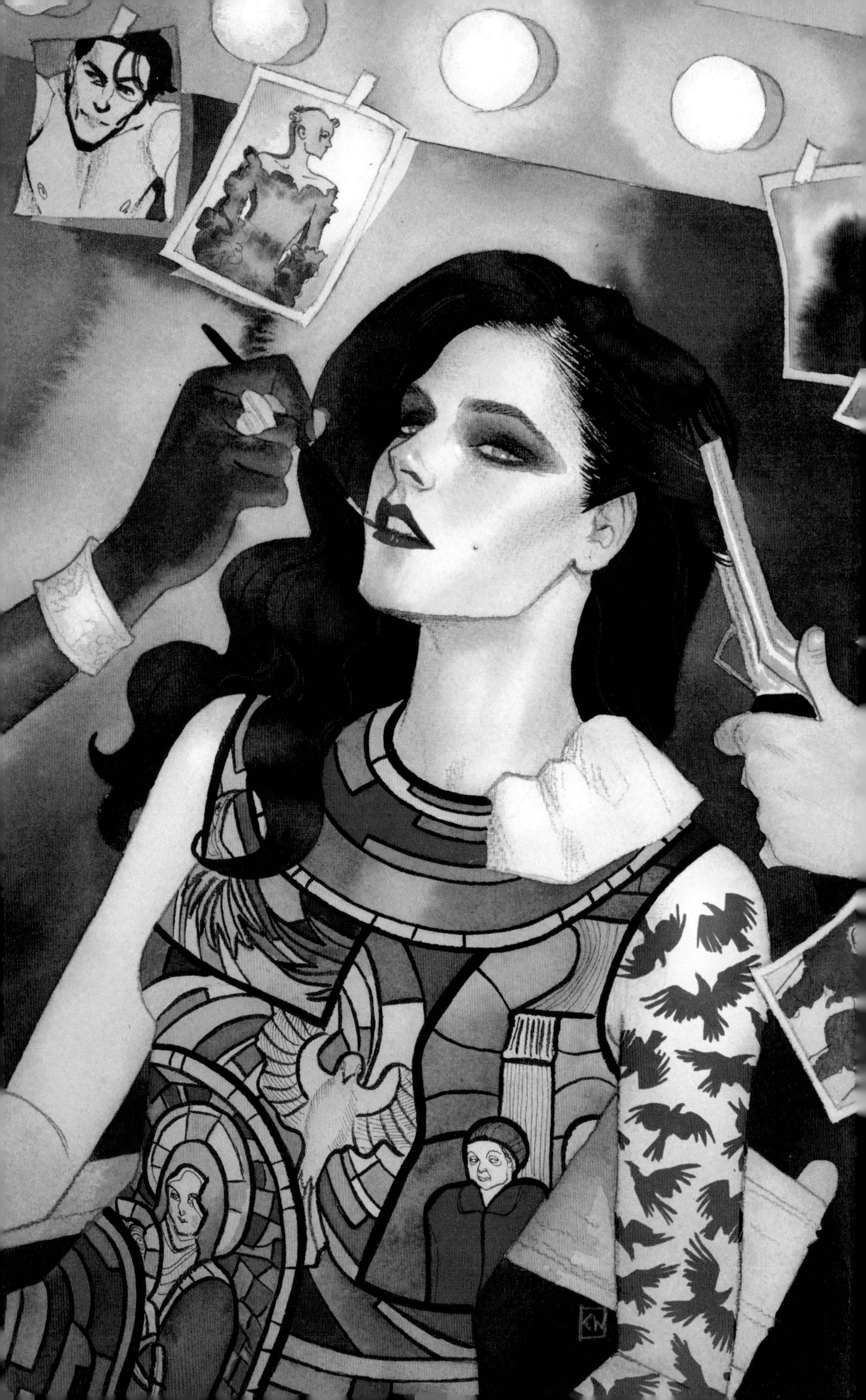

KILLING CITIES *in a* NIGHT

Leigh Alexander meets
THE MORRIGAN
in her first ever interview

Only recently did I learn that the Underground was more than a feeling, a fashion: it's a real place. I have to follow The Morrigan's instructions to get there, following endless staircases and black-clad arrows down to the Northern line. I want the last train — the train after the last train, if such a thing exists. It might not. Strangely, no one else is around — I'm alone with the echo of my footsteps and the threads of the stale air that lives down here.

There is no train on the platform and at first I think I might have gotten it wrong — but no. Already I feel bleak, the twinges of a familiar, primeval discomfort setting in. It is cold and my breath just hangs there, unmoving. It's the sense of acting against my better judgement, somehow, like the cold efficiency with which one pursues a relapse or a bad lover. It's the same reason I don't often make the effort to actually see her secret performances beneath the city: the whole time, I feel like I'm going to fall.

It's why her fans love her, I think: she creates spaces where it all feels inevitable, and therefore okay. Or definitely, assuredly *not* okay, so you can stop pretending. You can stop struggling. Or you can only struggle. Either way it's a relief.

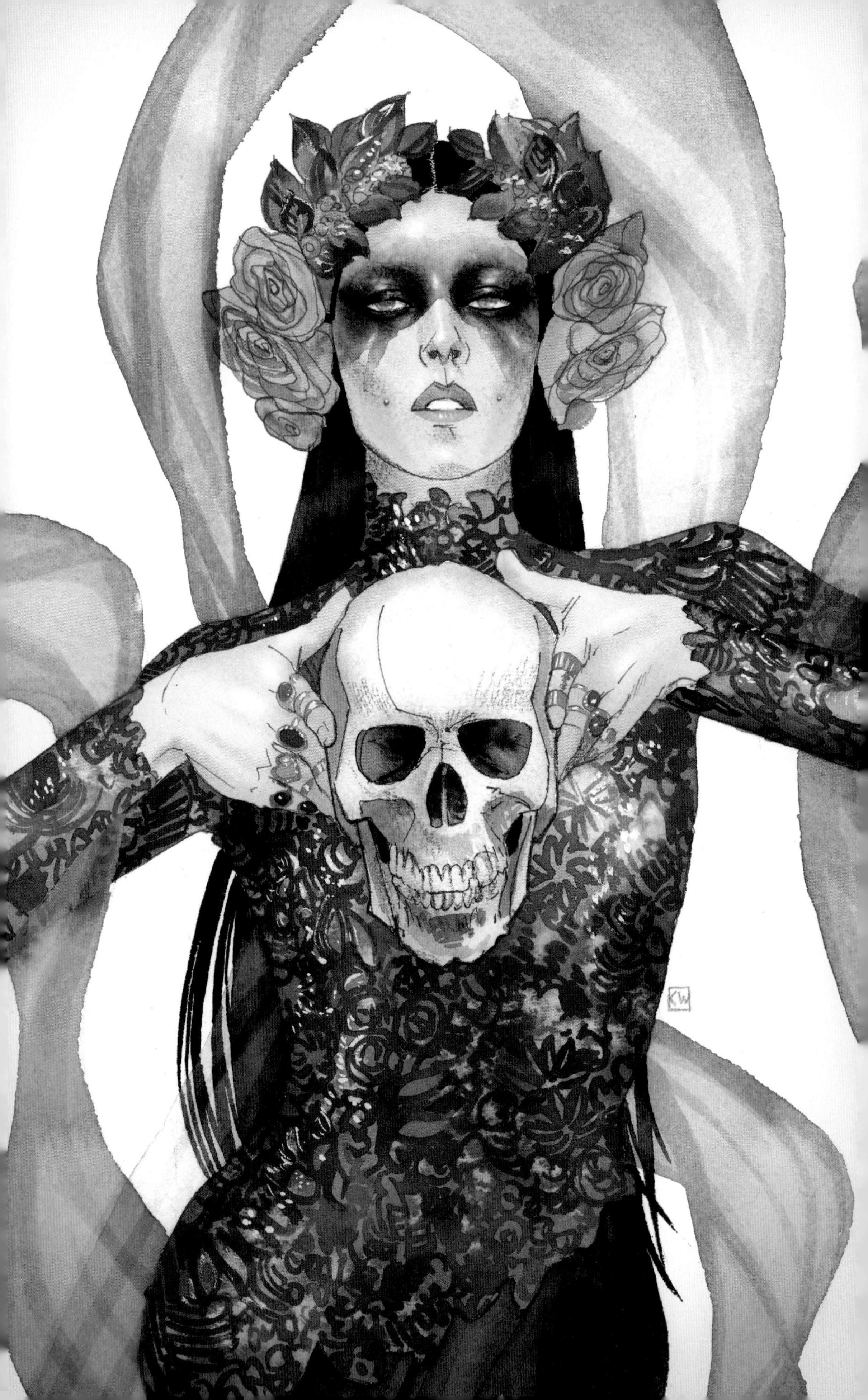

Suddenly the train is here. It's empty, the ordinary made absurd. I mind the gap; I sit down. The shriek and howl of the tracks and the tunnel are unusual, sepulchral, and the bright red letters scroll across the display: this train terminates at Morden.

I look again: THIS TRAIN TERMINATES AT MORRIGAN.

And then there she is, standing so close to me as we hurtle through the dark. She is scentless and immutable. I have forgotten to tell myself not to be frightened of her, but I probably don't have a choice. The enigmatic queen has never given an interview, so to open herself up to one now is a shock, and I believe she is ready to say something. She just says hello. She says hello to me.

She is surprisingly slight up close, pale and handmade. You could lose yourself attempting to follow the supernatural seams of her garment. People always say this about powerful women, but I expected her to be bigger, impervious somehow. I get the feeling that she is allowing me to see a loose thread. Inviting me to pull it, maybe. If I look at her just so, I can see the girls I went to school with, the shrine maidens of the smoking bathroom with whom I used to shoplift 99-cent black lipstick. But it feels like a blasphemous thought. She is no girl, but a god.

Of course, this is only one of The Morrigan's forms, although it is my favourite. While others in the Pantheon generally have one appearance, she has three: did she choose this circumstance?

"I am often unsure. Part of me thinks that no one truly chooses anything, and any who think otherwise are deluded," she says. "We are motes dancing in the wind, slaves to the breeze's fancies. This is not something I chose. It is simply something I am. It feels like a growth of the girl I once was and her many-chambered heart. I was never satisfied in a single role."

We might have been in drama club together, I think. But again, the blasphemous thought brings an unfamiliar taste into my mouth, a profound and sudden sadness. I wonder why she, this unmoving statuette, is reaching out, now. Why she's reaching out to me. Maybe it's just part of being near her — maybe it is her aura, her glamour, that makes my heart feel like it will soon strain to breaking.

Does she remember what she was like before becoming a god? I want to know. Before she became ancient, she would have been younger than I am now.

"Yes, I remember the prologue. The wounds and pains of the mortal have not deserted me. I was always fond of Elephant and Castle. Like the Elephant, I never forget," she says.

> # "Power has its charms."

She would have written terrible puns on elaborately folded paper. She would have drawn crosses on my notebook and vandalized my locker in silver. I would have made her a tape of only the sad Fleetwood Mac songs. No boys would have come near us. Now she is every raven on the Tower of London, birds raised on the blood of beheaded brides and love betrayed. But she speaks carefully, as if some part of the past were waiting, somehow, at her shoulder to take her back.

"It would perhaps be easier if one were able to forget," she tells me. "When Badb comes forth and her red rage lashes out at all, it is oft because of the long shadows of the past. We never escape ourselves. Not even as gods do we escape ourselves. In truth, my former life is closer than previous Morrigans. They are ghostly, as if viewed across a chasm.

"At the same time, I do not feel like the girl I once was. I grew from her. I feel like a wild forest grown from a single seed... Power has its charms."

Sometimes she smiles, but it's fleeting, like a glimpse of a firefly at night. Wood smoke. She says that being part of a grand chain of Morrigans is like "holding a seance with yourself" — she is, maybe, occupied with the cosmic weight of what she is. It is easy to imagine that if we keep talking I will disappear down this tunnel and never return.

This is her first interview. I ask her why speak now, all of a sudden? "It is nearly over. I am a riddle, corseted by mystery, choked by enigma. I have chosen to be as such. It is my design. Soon this comely flesh will be stripped to bare bones, and it seems fair to those lost in the game to have a few things more solid than a reputation to obsess over. A dead man's hand of Wada-framed icons, a few thesaurus-winged words, a girl not solely spectral but solid. You may argue what the truth means, but you cannot deny my truth..."

There have been so many ghost stories, she says, that she wants something else: "A story of two women on a train that shouldn't exist and the words the goddess shared with the scribe. When this Morrigan has been long a triple-corpse, these words will be on the page. Make of them what you will, pretend you understand me..."

But then, suddenly, she wants to talk about a man. Namely Baphomet, whom she says is always with her, although she lives well apart from the other gods. The inner politics of the Pantheon are mysterious, but she says that not long ago she had a physical altercation with Baal, that she was imprisoned, and that Minerva would have died without her intervention. According to Morrigan, her imprisonment occurred because she believed she was "responsible" for Baphomet, who was then

"I am not akin to most women. I could kill cities in a night, if I wished."

believed to have killed Inanna. She relays all of this with the chill, fatal air of a waning moon.

"I sat in a cage awaiting all to understand their mistake at placing me there. And then, when truth dawned, I showed it is not only the creatures of the dark we should fear," she says. "That experience does not make me long to return to the surface. That experience makes me wish to stay in my own domain, where there is no trouble but of our own making. This little kingdom, I will defend with every breath in these three-fold lungs. Any who would threaten it will be returned to the worms.

"Baphomet and I have a story none will ever truly understand, and only we have read it all," she says. The sad Fleetwood Mac songs. The Tower ravens with their bellies full of queens' blood.

Again I can't help but remember the flavour of stale, stolen smoke and the girls I roosted with and how always, eventually, it was some boy that cowed them. It is the air in Morrigan's carriage, it is the act of being near her — an infinite melancholy spirals alongside us. She has invited me to the centre of it. A place where whatever these men bring to her, she feels "responsible" for.

"The worst thing is that I am unsure in retrospect whether I would have done anything differently," she says of the conflict. "I let Baal turn his fists Morrigan-red when he took me to Ananke. Suffice to say I drew my fair share of Baal-blood on the night of Ananke's death… I suspect I felt too much sympathy for Baal. I have my own passions."

Here, she seems to be struggling with something. I do not know what it is.

"I am not akin to most women. I could kill cities in a night, if I wished."

What I do know is that she is telling me she does not have long: "Even without the curse of two years, Death could find its way into me and tear all from my ribcage. We are lost, as a Pantheon," she says. "Ananke is gone. She guided our kind for millennia. Some of us hope it means that the curse was of her making, and that now we are free. Baphomet feels that, and perhaps others. But I do not care. With whatever time we have left, be it a year or ten or seventy, I simply wish to live as well as I can."

She wants me to write one of her final portraits, to record the things that are dear to her, to write a story of her Underground, this hallowed place: "My life is

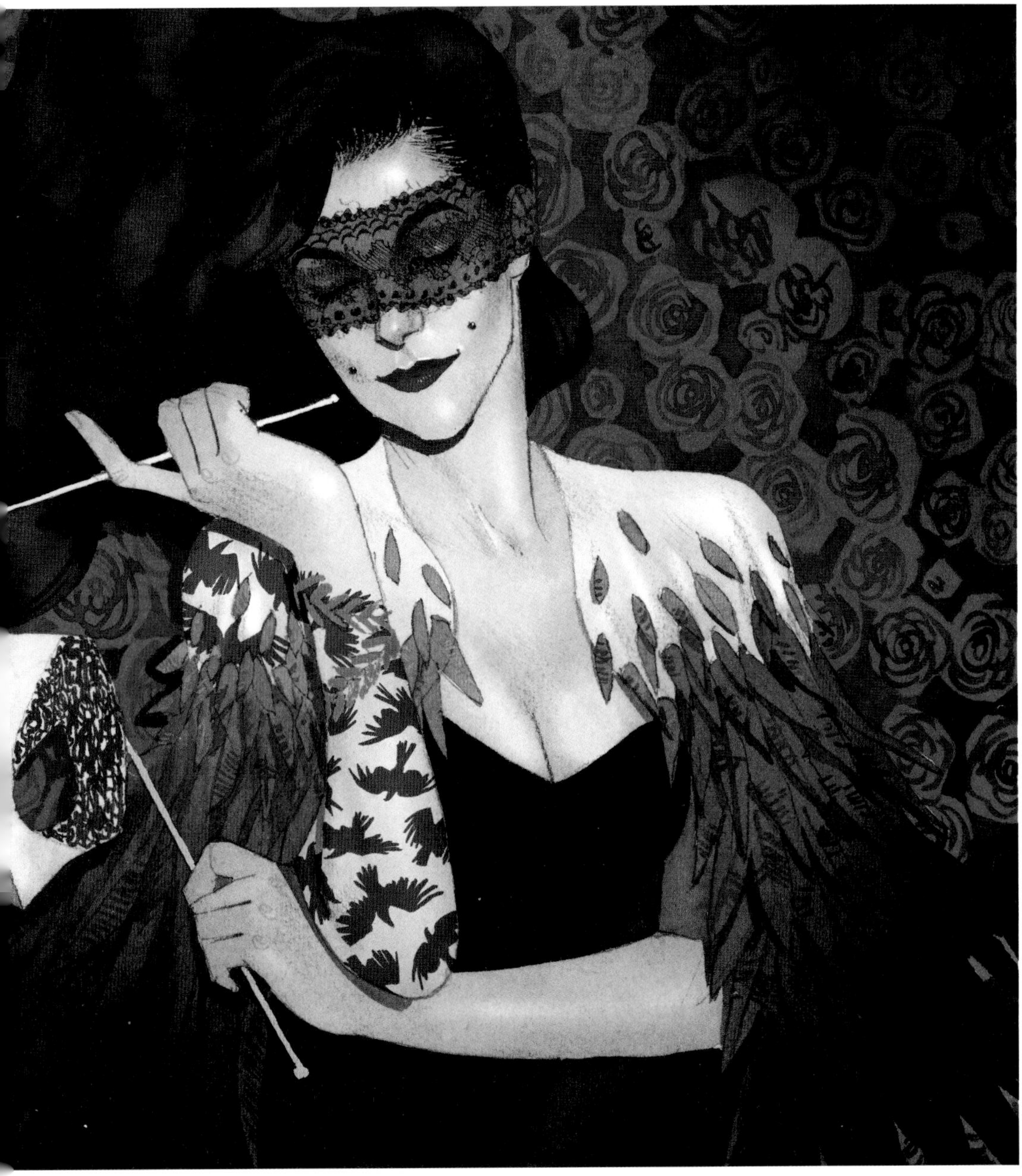

fullest in the Underground we stand in. My worshippers come. We build something beautiful and macabre and lingering. I return to my privacy," she tells me.

"I do not shadow-lurk for fancy's sake. I am a queen here, as I prefer it," Morrigan continues. "And as long as I am in this life, I will be here in the darkness."

I leave our meeting sad and afraid. It will, of course, dissipate once the cold snap of winter night and the city noise get back into my lungs. I can, if I need to, dispel the memory of this feeling with a pool of warm light, a nearby pub. But I can't hurry to shake her. I don't want to. The world may soon lose a great gift, but then — we knew we would.

It is not her darkness that haunts me. It's her responsibility, the things she feels responsible for, the things she is willing to carry in the name of keeping this space sacred. The howl that comes up from the depths of the train tunnels, the shivering of metal bones and tracks — they must be hers, centuries of hers, the echoes of generations of moon-women, druid wives and bathroom smoking covens. I can't sleep that night for remembering my own sad scratchings in that guestbook, the hearts I ground into the page with endless black ink. It doesn't pass for days. ■

A WHOLE NEW BAAL GAME

Dorian Lynskey talks to BAAL *about his plans for his future and ours...*

The moment you enter the Pantheon's new headquarters, housed over three floors in the Shard looming over London Bridge, you're aware you're being sold a message, and the message is this: everything is under control. Picture windows offer a majestic view of the river and the London sprawl. The décor might be described as corporate imperial: heavy on white and gold but minimal and anonymous. The floors above are home to Baal, Persephone and Minerva, but this room — the only room that an outsider will see — is strictly business.

Baal enters, sleek and commanding, flashes one of his million-dollar smiles and says, "Let's do this." He was always the Pantheon's most energetic spokesperson and now he's their de facto leader, too. His suit is very stylish, very expensive and very purple — probably a McQueen — and the neckline frames his signature piece of jewellery: a gold lightning bolt. The man was born to swagger but over time I can detect a tinge of humility that feels new, insofar as you could ever call Baal humble.

"I guess on a bigmouth scale of one to ten, I'm a ten," he says, unfurling that grin again. "I want to say something. Most of the gods aren't like that. They're introverts. And I know more than most, so my opinion is better." His charm is considerable but provisional. You shouldn't take it for granted. He makes a joke about smashing the table in front of us if he dislikes a line of questioning: a joke that doubles as a warning. The table is circular, glass, with what looks like a real gold thunderbolt design embedded in it. It looks like it costs more than my annual salary. Not only could he smash it, but he would.

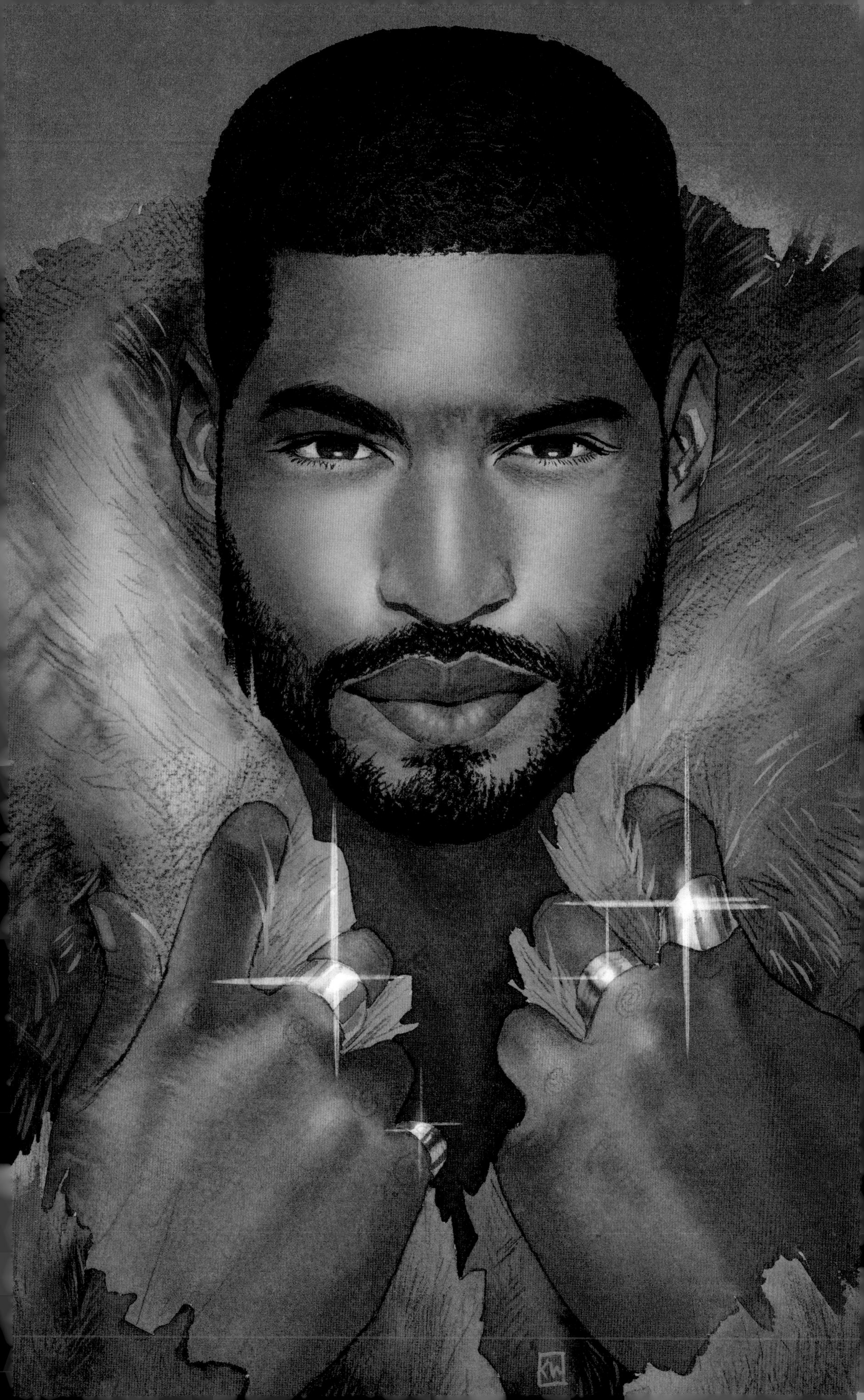

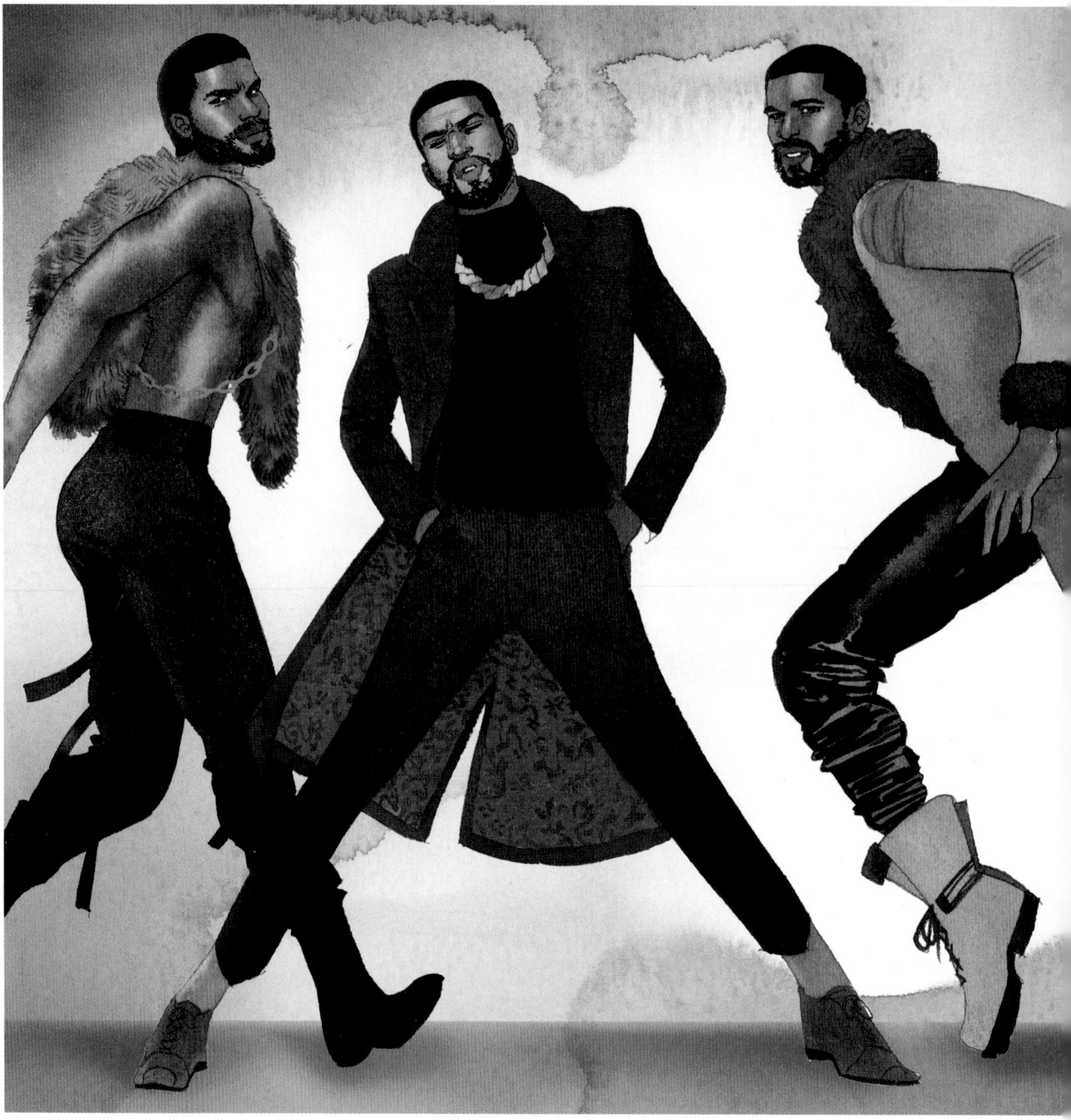

Baal has been in damage limitation mode in recent months since Ananke was exposed as a multiple murderer and manipulator who was, in turn, killed by Persephone to save Minerva. The gods knew she had a plan, but not that the plan was insane. Now they've abandoned Valhalla and they're on their own, which is as unnerving a prospect for the rest of us as it is for them. Baal's first job after Ananke's death was to meet with Government and "soothe a lot of brows". Today he needs to reassure the public, too.

"Ananke always said to keep our powers under wraps," he says. "'Don't let people come out,' she said. 'It'll only get in the way of the work. It'll scare them and fascinate them and they won't leave you alone.' She was right. Now it's out in the open, people are more scared and fascinated than ever. They can't tear their eyes away." He takes a certain theatrical pride in this. "We're the greatest show on Earth, and they'll be talking about us for the rest of their lives."

The thing to remember about Baal is that he was the first of the Pantheon to return and he stood by Ananke's side before any of the other gods arrived. His seniority gives him a sense of responsibility that he takes very seriously, as well he should. The Pantheon are an erratic bunch. If he doesn't step up, who else will? "I've been doing the god thing the longest," he says thoughtfully. "I was the only one who was alone, dealing with this. It's a job. I always saw it like that, but even more so now. Someone needs to make sure everyone is okay. Someone needs to put people back in line when they're not."

He pauses and his gaze drifts towards the river. "I worry what'll happen after I'm gone. I came first so

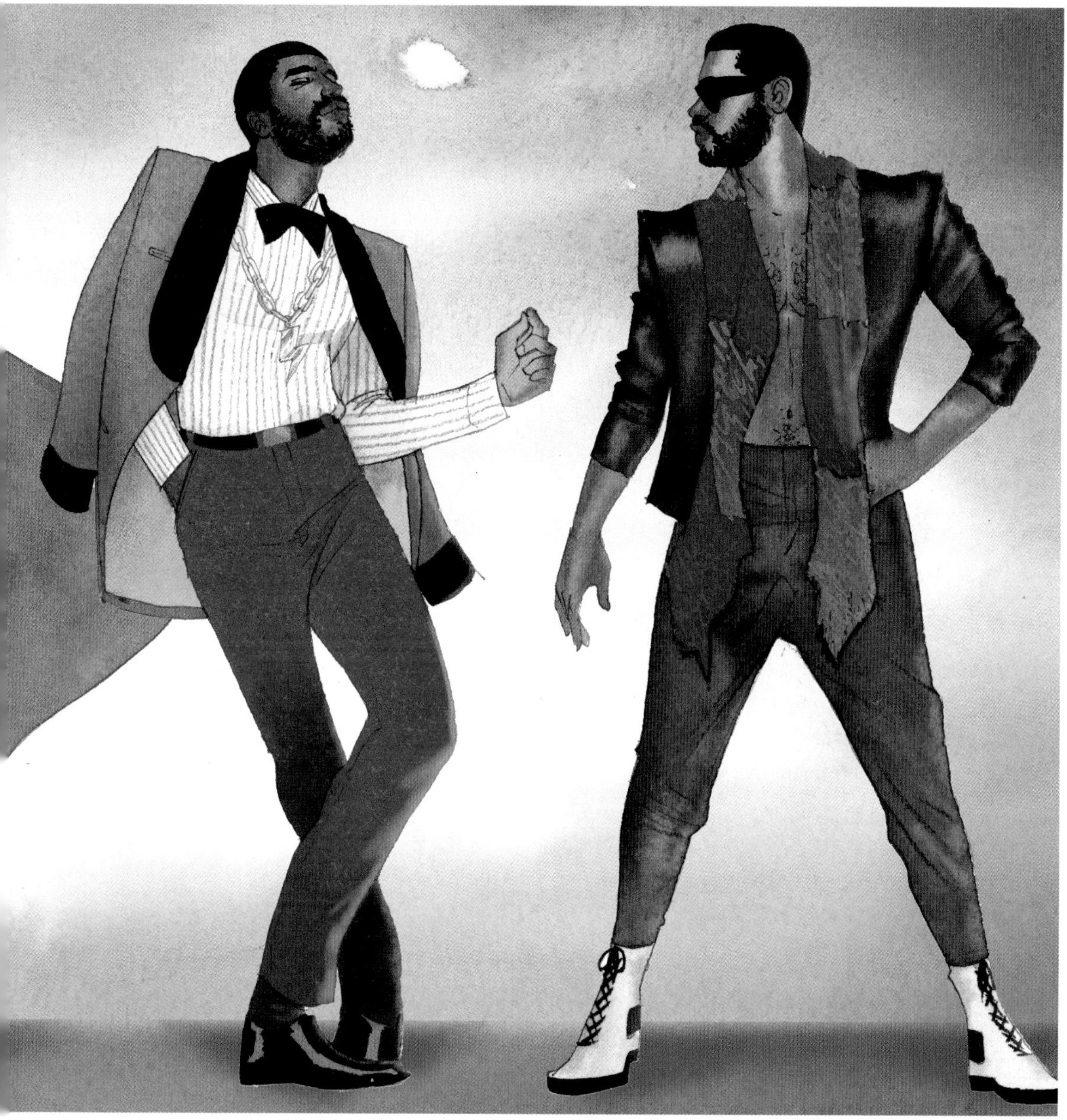

I'll be gone first. Not sure if anyone could do what I do." Another pause. "Maybe the Norns, but they'd get it all wrong, so I'd better make sure it's all cleaned up before I go."

I wonder if that same sense of duty, that instinct to hold things together and suppress disunity, is what made him trust Ananke for far too long, an error that almost cost Minerva her life. When I ask this question his smile abruptly falls, like a curtain dropping, and his voice lowers. "Yeah, that's the thing," he says. "I'm not exactly a guy who scares easily, but thinking I was alone in a room with a murderer that often?" He looks spooked, which is a new look for Baal. "All that time with Ananke at the start meant I went along with her later and for longer than I should. I look back at what happened towards the end and wish I was someone like Chronos so I could do time travel. But you can't go back, and you can't help what you are."

So you don't do regret?

"You make mistakes and you never make them again," he says. "That's me. I don't look back."

He would say that, wouldn't he? But there's a flicker of guilt in his voice that stops me from fully believing him, and that flicker makes me warm to him. After all, if he had realised the truth about Ananke earlier, then his lover Inanna would still be alive. Baal's ultra-confidence is schtick — hugely entertaining, but schtick nonetheless — so it's endearing to see the facade crack a little.

Lately, Baal has been making amends for his poor judgement. Most importantly, he has become a father figure for the recently orphaned Minerva. "She's doing better than you'd expect," he says. "I'd expect her to be curled up in a ball. No one should ever have to go through what she went through.

"Part of me would love to throw politicians through walls, but that's just an ego trip. I could make it rain but that's not solving why people are hungry."

We're doing what we can. There's professionals helping her. But if you see your mum and dad turned to mist right in front of you, you can't expect to be a happy bunny."

There's also the question of Baal's assault on The Morrigan, which I'm reluctant to ask about head-on. That table still looks awfully smashable. Has he, I say carefully, had to mend some bridges with certain gods?

"There's a lot of feelings in the group," he says heavily. "We came together when we realised what was really happening, but there's a lot of bad blood. I made mistakes. I owe some people apologies. That's all part of the new order for me. We all fucked up in different ways and if I'm going to keep a clean house now? I got to own up to mine, too."

Some people?

"The better half of the goth kids," he says. The Morrigan. "She was trying to do the best she could and I came at her angry. I want her to know I haven't forgotten that. It got fucked up as all hell and it's my job to make sure it never gets that bad again. I owe it to them all."

The elephant in the room is what happens next. In a way the whole Pantheon, not just Minerva and Persephone, have been orphaned. When the person who brought them to life and told them what to do turned out to be a murdering lunatic, their entire purpose was called into question. How do they come up with a new plan for the time they have left?

"That's the question, innit?" says Baal. "I'm making them pull together. We're still wrestling. You may be surprised, but there's a lot of strong personalities in this lot. What we've got to do is find what's actually true and what we have to do. Ananke was 10,000 years old and off her fucking head, but there's a reason for all of this. That's what we're here for. And now, for the first time since man had fire, we're going to have to do it without her help. We've come so far.

Now we just have to finish it." He grins. "No pressure."

So what exactly *do* they intend to do?

"There's avenues. A work in progress."

That sounds very enigmatic.

"You can excuse a god a little mystery," he says with a teasing smile. "It's a good look." He turns solemn and leans forward. "This is the big deal. Look at the world and there's all kinds of shit. Part of me would love to throw politicians through walls but that's just an ego trip. I could make it rain but that's not solving why people are hungry. You change things in a big way. It's all systems. If we don't do our thing, you're all going to be in a stone age in 30 years."

So it's your basic, old-fashioned saving-the-world deal?

"Yeah," he says, cocksure once more. "We give you the world and all of you work out what to do with it. That's what gods do."

This, then, is Baal's spin for the day: there will be a plan. We mortals might not know what it is, it may not even be decided yet, but there will be one. Do I believe it? I'm not sure. But I believe that Baal believes it. After so much blood and chaos, he *needs* to believe it.

Baal gets up from his chair, gives me a presidential handshake and strides across the room but, just before he reaches the door, he turns around. "Oh yeah, I forgot. Persephone wanted me to mention this. We're seeing each other. There's your exclusive."

Before I can respond, he disappears in a crackling blaze of lightning, making the whole room glow moon-white and leaving nothing behind but a pungent whiff of ozone. It's such a terrific coup de théâtre that I feel like applauding the void where Baal used to be. For a moment back there I saw a quieter, more self-doubting Baal, but he couldn't resist leaving me with a final display of unearthly power, a flamboyant reminder of what he was insisting all along: everything is under control. ■

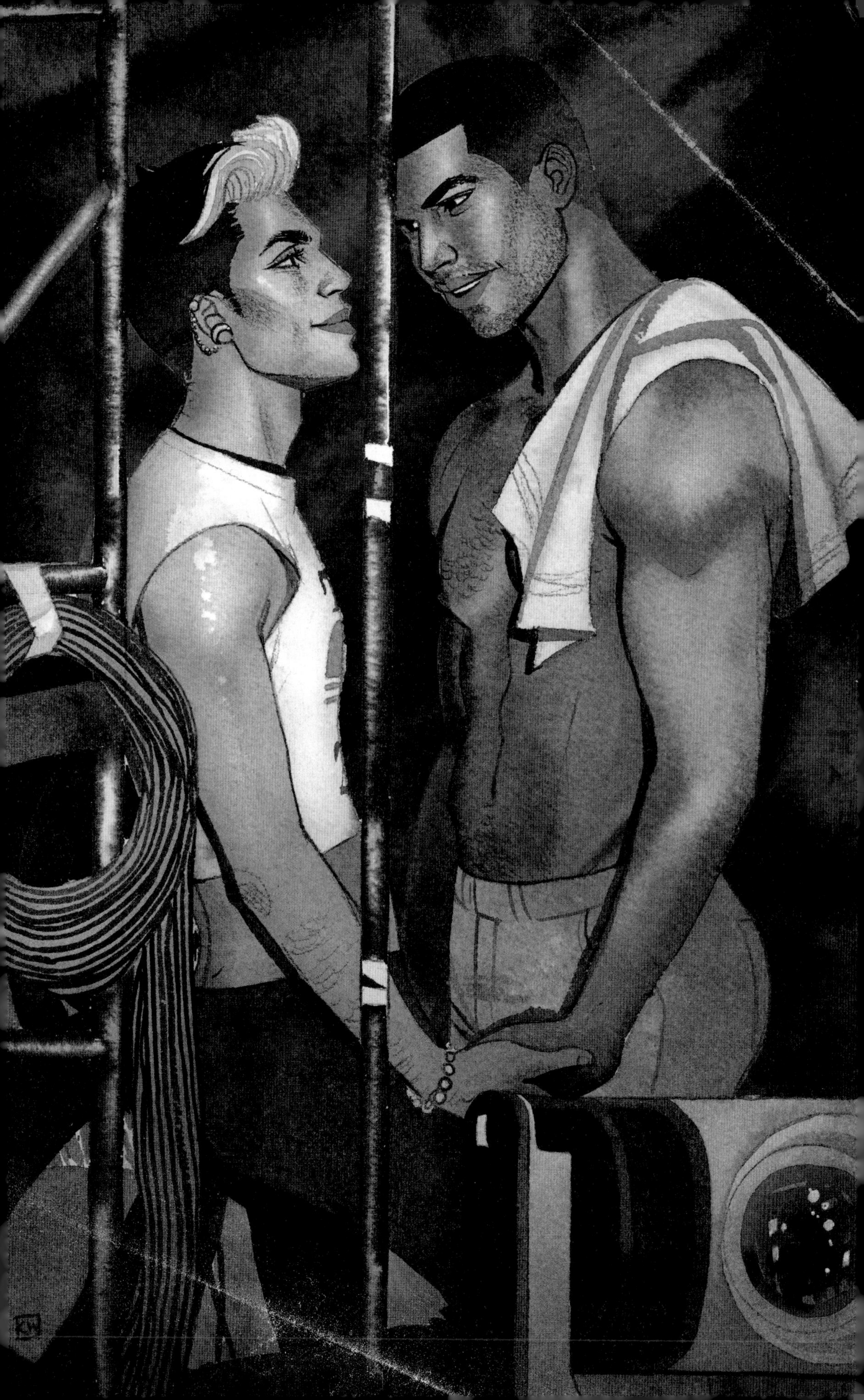

SYMPATHY
for the
NICE
GUY

Laurie Penny spends a morning chatting feminism with WODEN. *What could go wrong?*

Everyone's least favourite member of the Pantheon invited me to meet him at a private bar at the top of the Shard, London's answer to the Tower of Orthanc and its most phallic edifice, which must be why confused men keep trying to climb it. The symbolism is both obvious and boring, and I really don't want to give Woden the satisfaction.

Being repulsive is Woden's job, and also his hobby. Sexist, racist, and vilified by his press and public — for acting, however unwittingly, as Ananke's henchman and weapons' engineer over a year of murderous machinations which have left three gods dead and two orphaned — Woden is different in one key way. He himself does not perform. He allows other people to perform. This was not the assignment I was hoping for when I was told I was on the Pantheon beat. "Kieron," I said to my editor, "the country is collapsing and my girlfriend just left me to live in the country with a man named Cherry with full face tattoos. Send me to interview someone nice. Amaterasu. Dionysus. Or the hot one with the good hair. The one I fancy. Lucifer?"

"Lucifer's been dead for nearly a year," he said.

"In that case it'll be an easy interview."

"I'm not paying you for a fucking seance," he replied. "You love hanging out with people you hate. Bring a copy of *Delusions of Gender* and a can of mace. Have fun."

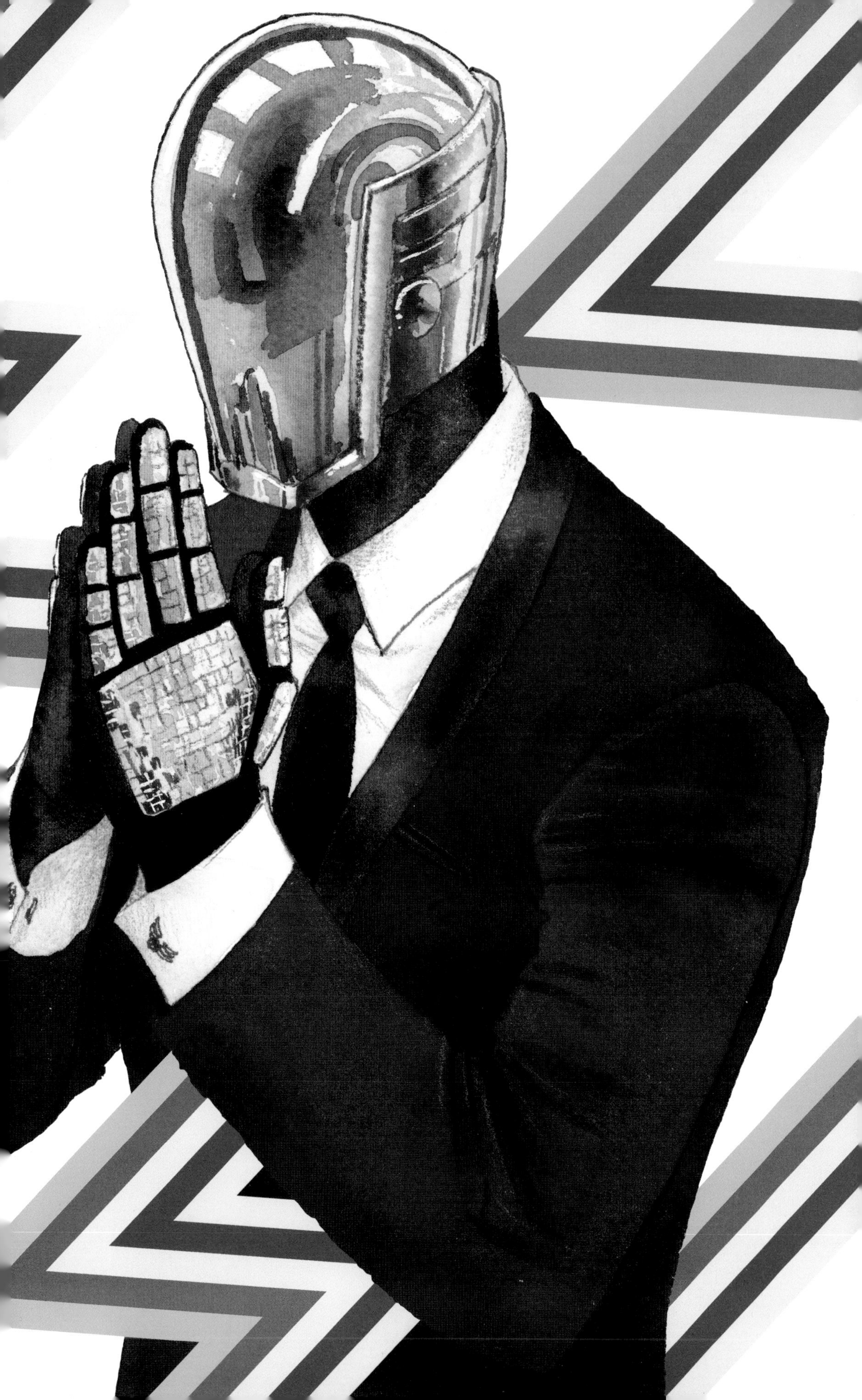

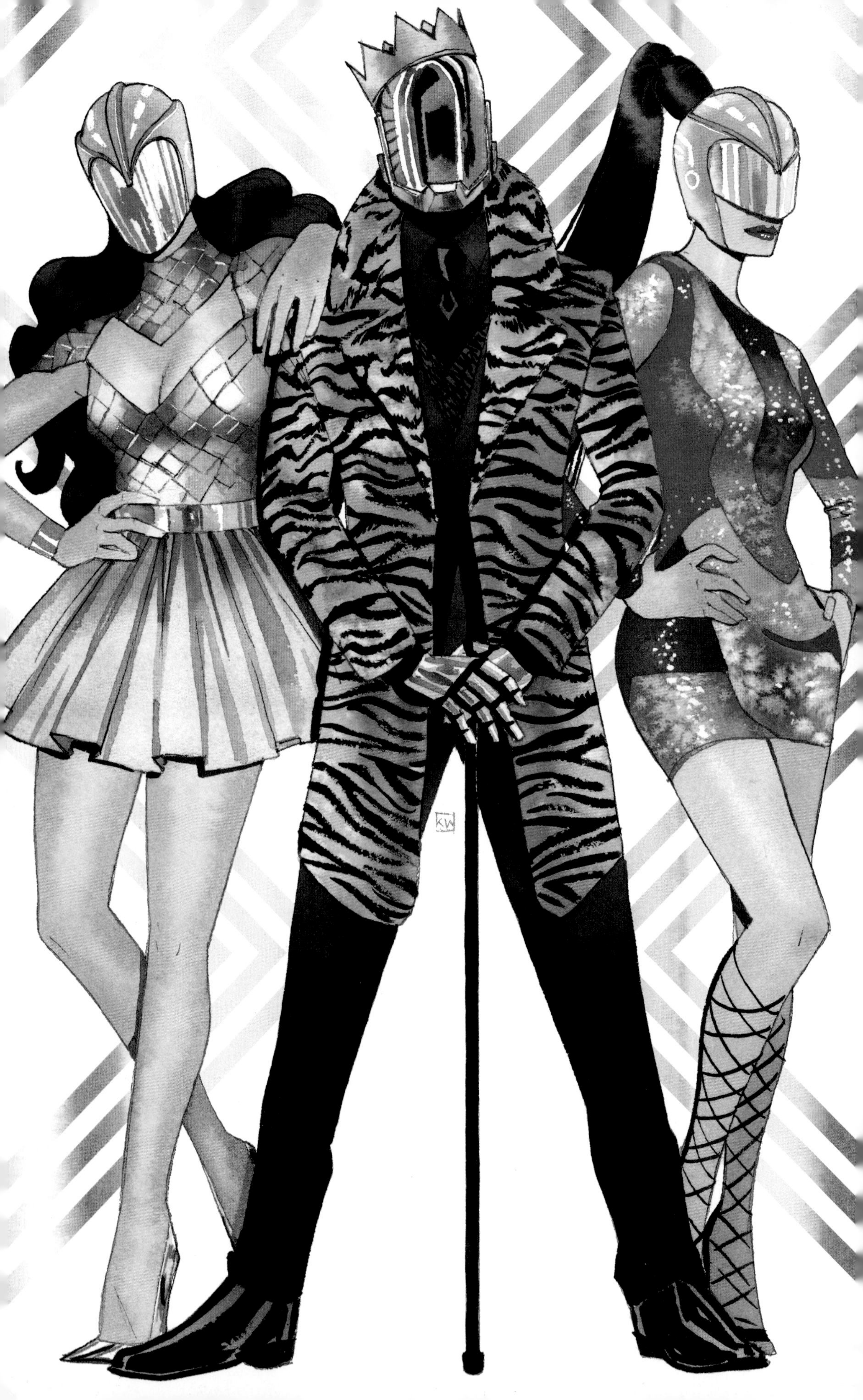

So here I am at the Shard, at ten in the morning, when any self-respecting hack should be sleeping off a hangover. I pass through the security gates and am ushered by a harried-looking PA into a swanky spaceship bridge of a bar. Below us, London is spread out like a map of itself in greyscale. Miles away to the south, Valhalla glows thinly through the morning mist.

Three bright circles appear on the floor, and Woden appears, flanked by two Valkyries. Göndul and Eir, I think, though with the helmets it's hard to tell. Woden has dressed for the occasion in his usual paranoid-android ensemble. He's shorter than you'd imagine. He stands there for a second, as if he's considering me carefully, and then walks up to the table.

"Did they bring you a drink?"

The PA freezes. I'd kill for a coffee, but I don't want to be waited on by a harassed Booth Babe with a mad boss who has built-in lasers. Instead, I introduce myself to the Valkyrie on my left.

She glances at Woden for a second. He nods, and she shakes my hand. Woden laughs. It's like a Wario sound effect. I wonder what his mum thinks of all this?

"You know, I'd like to claim I don't have a mum," he says, "And say that I burst from the head of Zeus, like divine spots popping... but my mum doesn't call me anything. I have a lack of... strong parental influences."

Woden is just forthcoming enough about his pre-Pantheon days to invite a measure of pity, which is the point. "I was at university when Ananke came calling. You know the kid who moved away from home and decided to not be themselves any more? Complete Image Change? That was me. Then Ananke entered my life, and I realised... I'm never coming back from university. My mum hasn't known anything about me since I was about six. My dad did the parenting. He was... not a good father. All he had going for him was that he was there, mostly."

I've a vision of a hundred deadbeat dads looking at the dates and wondering if their kid is the prick in the mask. Woden has tolerated this line of questioning long enough.

"Just write down 'Issues With Parents And Acting Out' and be done with it," he says. "Boo-hoo-fucking-hoo." Göndul and Eir hover around us, their feet making no sound. Woden's misogynist aesthetic is well-honed and wholly unoriginal. He takes women and turns them into videogame cheesecake. He takes women and turns them into something less than human, something comprehensible and controllable, with clear win conditions.

"Are you being paid a living wage to do this?" I ask Göndul.

"Answer freely," says Woden.

"Yes," says Göndul, quietly. "Money isn't what it's about though."

"Baal insists everyone gets paid," says Woden.

"Woden is very good to all of us," says Göndul. "He's given us huge opportunities and... and..." She trails off. Neon helmets don't show blushes.

"They're scared of me," says Woden, relaxing in his chair. "It isn't ideal. I treated Brunhilde like shit, and that was front of house. But I have one major plus on most bad bosses. I will be dead soon."

And here the self-pity. It all comes out in a slosh of self-justifying red-pill logic that you really don't need me to describe. The biggest issue of all is Woden's specific limitation: unlike the other gods, he can only make magic for other people, which must be a bummer for a misanthrope.

"I can do bits and pieces for myself, but it's nothing compared to what I can give the Valkyries. I can put them on stage and make them do what the rest of the Pantheon do... and that high? It's the same for the performer as the crowd. You've been at the gigs. You know what that's like."

I haven't, but I've heard it described. It sounds like a robot toddler having a tantrum in a bin.

"Ananke said I couldn't do... that. But I made a machine and tried it anyway. I figured I was good enough. But I was arrogant, and now... well, I prefer to wear a mask. You wouldn't believe how tiring getting stared at is."

He pulls what he seems to believe is a pose in his seat. I wonder if the mask makes it hard to see past his own reflection, whatever it is. He runs his hand over his helmet's forehead. It's an oddly human gesture, for once.

"You know who else did that? Doctor Doom. I am literally Doctor Doom."

"You are not literally Doctor Doom," I say. "Your use of 'literally' here is way off base."

"I literally don't care. What was the Pratchett line? Turning people into things is the only sin. I want to make it easier for people to turn me into a thing. I want to dehumanize myself. I've built this little myth around myself, and I play up to it. But I'm not scary. I'm scared."

But what about the rest of us? Woden's a frightened, furious manchild who's not as smart as he wants to be. I've met those before, and so have you. What happens when they become powerful?

What happens is someone has to handle them. After the death of Ananke and the revelations about her year-long deicidal killing spree, the Pantheon is regrouping under the stewardship of Baal, reforming like bread dough bashed back into shape. If you believe the hype, they haven't got much time left. Whatever they do next, they'll do it together — and that means no dickhead left behind. Not when they've got Woden's kind of arsenal.

"People should be scared of scared people," says Woden. "They'll fuck you up. Hey — do you want to see something?"

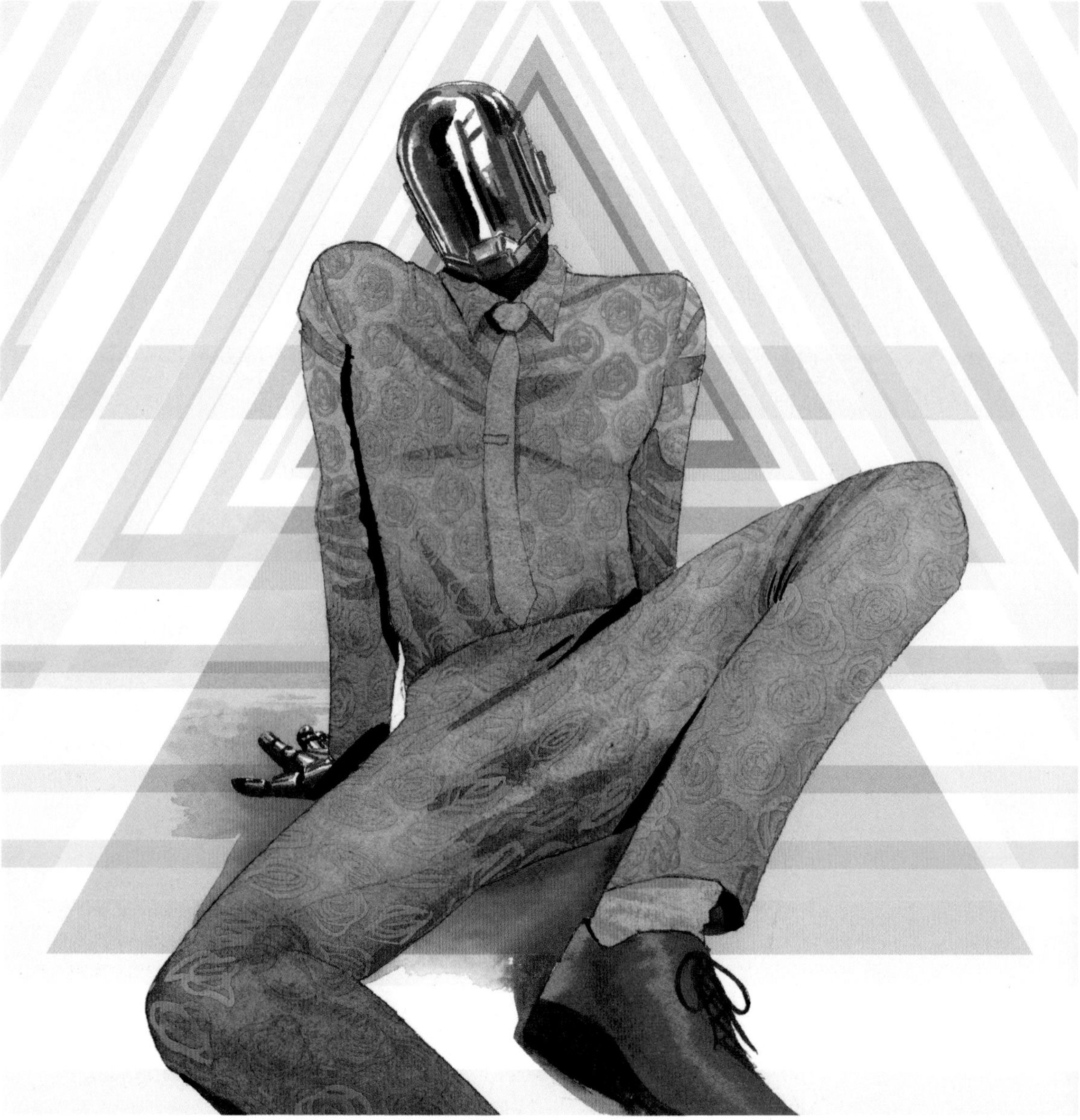

Of course I do. I'm in here at ten o'clock on a Monday morning. I want to see everything.

A light from somewhere out of the world covers the two of us, as if this were a film and we were about to dance. Instead, the world dances drunkenly around us, my stomach lurches, and we are — somewhere else. Somewhere dark, and spacious, and livid with technology.

"This is my lab," Woden says. "This is where I do most of my work. It's in Valhalla."

I'm not sure whether or not to believe him. The space is illuminated with beating striplights. Think of the holodeck in *Star Trek*. Or the world's most impressive game of *Dance, Dance: Revolution*. Or a Burning Man version of the Batcave.

"Impressive," I say. "Where's Alfred? Or... no, hang on. You're Alfred."

"Welcome to my lair," says Woden, and I imagine him pulling faces behind the mask. "This is where I spend... about 60% of my time. The other gods sleep in, relax, play *Minecraft* or whatever else. I work. I make machines. I don't get to be a performer. I get to help other people be great. I'm still the good little worker."

He stalks around the place. "Every single thing I make is unique, and each new one as hard work as the first," he says. "It takes hours. I work harder than *any* of them, and get less back. That suit I burned in front of Brunhilde? Days of work. Days. It wasn't just casually cruel — it was carefully put together and planned. That's fucking awful, even for me."

So why do it?

"Because there's no reason not to."

"You're a huge nerd," I say, and it isn't a question.

"Oh god, yes."

I ask what his fandom is, just to get a rise out of

"I know why 90% of the shit I do is wrong. My problem is just... why not? I can't think of a good reason any more. Or at least no reason good enough to stick."

him, but he ignores me. He's got his villain speech all planned and is getting into the groove.

"I am not kinder because there is no reward for kindness," he says. "I've read a lot. I know the arguments, but it all just crumbles at the fact we live in a world that could make us nothing any second. Gods come back every 90 years, but you mortals are just dead. There is no reward. So take everything you can."

"That's pretty," I say. "I remember writing something similar in my diary when I was 14 and first reading Nietzsche."

There's a machine in the corner which Woden keeps checking on, like an anxious baker waiting for a cake to rise. Even to my untrained eye, it looks half-completed. It pulses quietly.

"I know why 90% of the shit I do is wrong," he says suddenly. "My problem is just... why not? I can't think of a good reason any more. Or at least no reason good enough to stick.

"What happened with Ananke says everything. She had us all fighting each other, killing each other. I should have known better. I think I'm smart, but I was played and played hard. I'm far from perfect... but to be a part of that makes me scream. She had me make the machine she was going to use to butcher Minerva piece by piece so I didn't know what it was. Thank fuck for Persephone."

"You're scared of her," I say. "You're scared of most women, but her most of all."

"Possibly," he says. "My desire to have this Pantheon of my own consisting solely of carefully selected beautiful women? That's about control. That's about fear. That's about fear of power. And Persephone is powerful in a way that I just don't understand. I'm petrified of her. Everyone should be."

Here's the part that still confuses me. "You're a master builder," I say. "How could you possibly not know what she was asking you to make?"

Woden says nothing for a long time before giving me an answer. "It's a god thing. You wouldn't understand."

I'm suddenly aware that I'm alone heaven knows where with a heavily armed sociopath, and I may just have gone too far.

If I get out of here, I'm going to be having words with my editor.

Woden seems to sense my alarm. He presses a button in his wrist, "Hey, Eir, get us back."

That light again... and then we're back in the Shard. Looking out at Valhalla. Which is where we were, if you believe him. I'm not sure I do.

"What was that machine?" I ask, quietly. "The one you were looking at."

"A new project," he says. "I'm inspired by my peers. I've always liked seeing if I can mimic the other gods' performances. I'm good at Baal and Sakhmet — I've had the most time studying them. But Persephone?"

He turns his helmet, looking out across London, or perhaps at his own reflection. "I don't get her at all. I'd like to." There's a noise like an engine exhaling. I think it's a sigh.

"Thank you," I say. "I have one last question."

"Hit me."

"Do you have any friends?"

A long, long pause.

"What do you think?"

Woden turns to leave, followed by the Valkyries, who summon the portal.

"Oh, one more thing."

"Yes?"

"You asked about my fandoms," he says. "*Game of Thrones*. Huge fan. I'm going to die before it ever ends. I mean, it's deeply problematic..."

Woden steps through the portal.

"But who isn't?" ■

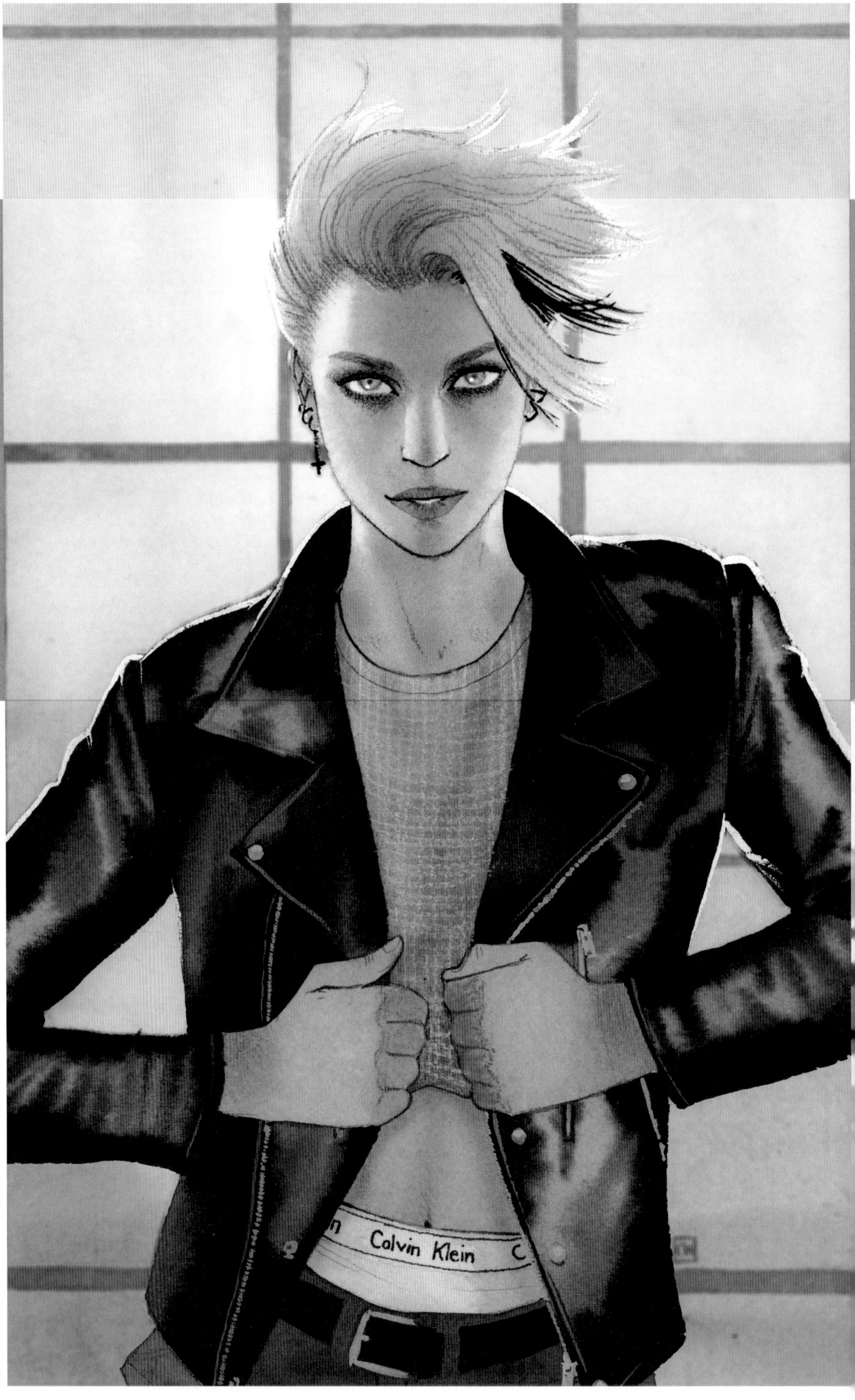
Calvin Klein

I SAW YOU KISSING
SATAN CLAUS

Recorded just days before her final Christmas, for the first time we are able to publish Mary HK Choi's legally suppressed interview with LUCIFER...

It's almost Christmas in London's Soho neighbourhood and I'm meeting Lucifer née Eleanor Rigby, 18, at The Groucho Club. It's an apt backdrop for a drink with a god of the Pantheon — a member's only establishment — and though it's not yet noon, Lucifer's seated at the back of the bar swilling a Bloody Mary. "This morning's been somewhat purgatorial," she tells me behind sunglasses.

In the same way that true black is extra-terrestrial, Rigby is clad in her customary bespoke suiting: a white so incandescent it doesn't exist in nature. It's conspicuous — cheekily celestial. And even in a venue frequented by those who like to be seen (but not gawped at) the lulls in conversation betray a palpable collective interest. People don't know who she is, though they do suspect she's someone. Someone with a staggering dry-cleaning bill.

Rigby, for all her fans — the fervent tribe that follow her and her fellow gods to their immersive, fever-dream, performance-art concerts — is only teetering at the brink of fame. She's not yet a household name, though she will be. The correct imprimaturs are in place: the Young, the Cool and social media. Slight, gamine, with a phosphorescent pallor and a dramatic platinum coif that lends credibility to her "light-bringing" devil schtick, the celebrity trajectory for Lucifer is as predestined as the lore behind it.

"Inanna's a puppy. I wish I wasn't the sort of person who occasionally kicks puppies. ...The surfeit of happiness was utterly unbearable."

The Pantheon's official PR line reads as follows: "Just because you're immortal doesn't mean you're going to live forever." Rigby in tandem with her divine cronies will be adored for two years. Then they die. Fans prone to more literal interpretations are convinced that an actual shucking of the mortal coil will occur: "It's a suicide pact," writes 666atanail on the Fantheon forum. "They'll have a massive gay orgy and on the stroke of midnight they'll drink hemlock." And though the general consensus amongst the press is that it's like the Puerto Rican boy band Menudo, and they'll simply age out and return to whatever humdrum pop-culture Elba from whence they came (Chelmsford, in Rigby's case), the commitment to the storyline is convincing. Rigby appears world-weary, pensive, with an unmistakable undercurrent of angst.

"Being the devil is knowing you've lost," she says ordering another drink. Rigby's a slippery interview. And it's cryptic transmissions like these that you can expect to most queries. She takes unnaturally long pauses before she speaks, assessing your questions along with your appearance and parrying with jejune missives that have little to do with what's asked.

"You are on that side of the curtain," she says putting her hands up, forming a wall between the two of us. "I am on this side. There are things in my life you will never know. I wouldn't feel too bad — it's awful back here. The rider is terrible."

* * *

A second location is called for. The Groucho's declared too staid and predictable (the club is after all named after the famous quote for which Marx shaded the Friar's Club: "I don't care to belong to a club that would have me as a member") and we slip out, losing her PR flack a few seats over.

We're reminded that it's only afternoon as we thread through the shopping tourists and make our way into a narrow alley. Rigby knocks on an unmarked door and we huddle into a dimly lit cocktail bar where she orders an Old Fashioned and submits to the one line of questioning she enjoys, the topic for which she most frequently makes the tabloids.

"So, my love life," she says, plucking the cherry from her glass. "I'll describe it as lively, but not much actual love." Lucifer admits that she's slept with the languid, sloe-eyed Sakhmet, confirming the veracity of the recent paparazzi pics. "She's beautiful, intense and knows exactly what she wants," she says. "I would feel sorry for anyone who gets in the way of that."

But it seems Lucifer's carnal agendas are just as persuasive. The alluring feline deity isn't the only god she's known on *biblical* terms. Rigby's affairs include Inanna, another member of the Pantheon, bucking — then doubling down on — the conventional wisdom of how terrible an idea it is to bump uglies with a member of the same band. "Well, we have a shared interest in orgasms and the accumulation thereof," she says of Inanna. "So it does make some degree of sense. But he's *so* nice. I had to make it bad somehow."

The bad, according to Rigby, is that Inanna had been committed to someone else. The fallout was deleterious. "Inanna's a puppy," she says. "I wish I wasn't the sort of person who occasionally kicks puppies. It was cruel and petty and I was feeling cruel and petty. The surfeit of happiness was utterly unbearable." There's a doleful cast to her voice but she's quick to compose herself. "The devil having contrition would be most unlike me, wouldn't it?" she says, sly grin recovered. "Playing the serpent is on brand."

The brand, especially when acknowledged repeatedly, gets to be tiresome. Not to mention the evasion. After months of chasing Lucifer for an interview after her publicist sent us these images, there were weeks where she'd only agree to questions answered over email. But then a sit-down was agreed to and an invitation to a Brixton performance followed. The show was categorically brilliant.

Still, for Lucifer's undeniable charisma and talent there's something about the experience that reads expensive — at its best, convincingly miraculous. The quality and the hypnotic light show glitters with the multi-million-dollar sheen of a major label marketing machine, with oft lysergic effects on the audience. Frankly, it's disingenuous to the back-breaking work of countless unnamed engineers to insist that the performance owes its marvel to the divine.

But when you enquire about the story behind the story, the speculation that the Pantheon is as manufactured as One Direction by an oily Svengali, the spiritual offspring of a Lou Pearlman or Simon Cowell, Rigby is maddeningly coy. "Who's your Brian Epstein, Ms. Rigby?" you'll ask, alluding to the Beatles' manager. "Our Epstein is quite the person," she says. Raising fingers to lips, she volunteers nothing else.

When Lucifer touches your arm flirtatiously you know she's about to change the subject, but racing through London for another bar, this time at the front of the Southbank Center, you can't help but admit that celebrity couldn't have anointed a more engaging subject. Lucifer, if nothing else, is fun to hang out with. "It's Christmas, you're American and Consumerism is our religion," she says. "We're going to the mall!"

> ## "I doubt many people forget me."

This is the exact moment when you experience something adjacent to pity. Lucifer is perfect right now — vibrant and happy. And while there is a humane aspect to the fatalistic branding, the finite relevance that is the reality of the celebrity industrial complex in the age of social media, it's still super sad.

When she's skipping to the mall, shuddering at how her parents (unrepentant Beatles fans) conceived her on the night of a Blur gig, giddily performing sleights of hand like lighting her cigarette with a dramatic snap of her fingers (a nifty feat likely attributable to a jury-rigged zippo trick), she is very much a kid. A kid swaggering to impress you and the thousands of people for whom everything is performance.

"I doubt many people forget me," she says when I ask about the end. And when we meet a friend of hers, a stunning, flame-tressed girl complete with Coachella costuming and face paint, everyone around us raises their phones unquestioningly and begins filming... even before she says she's a newly minted god. Certain people just are famous. As costly as it is. I tell Lucifer to be good to herself, to which she predictably replies: "I don't need to be. I have adoring fans for that." ■

CLOUDBUSTING

Ezekiel Kweku talks with
AMATERASU
in San Francisco

"They will be loved. They will be hated," goes the Pantheon prophecy, and members of the Pantheon have echoed it over the past several months. But Amaterasu doesn't want to be hated. I'm not even sure she wants to be loved. What she wants is to be believed. She doesn't just want an acknowledgment that she is something more than human — even the most skeptical among us can't deny her that any more — she wants you to believe *in* her. If there is a central truth about this girl, a key that unlocks her, this is it.

I meet the girl born as Emily Greenaway (and formerly known as Hazel Oak Ash Thorn Greenaway) in Réveille Coffee Co. in North Beach. It's a typically overcast San Francisco morning, but her red hair still shimmers somehow in the fog-filtered light. She sits across from me, dressed in all white and carefully poised, as if I am going to paint her icon and mount it in a cathedral's alcove. It would be hard to take seriously if she hadn't just materialized, through the window, out of a shaft of sunlight. And if she didn't look like an immortal. But since she had and she does, it is awe rather than amusement I have to stave off as we start talking.

Amaterasu tries to choose her words with care as we talk, selecting each for weight and simplicity, as if her every phrase is destined to become an aphorism, pored over and parsed by cynics and disciples alike. "Before, there was only confusion and fear," she says, of her pre-godhood life. But all that is over now. "My course is true, direct and beautiful."

She doesn't want you to see in her a deconstructed divinity, she wants to appear as whole and uncomplicated as an undivided beam of light. But there are prisms everywhere, and Ammy sometimes refracts into Emily in vulnerable moments. One such moment comes when I ask her about Ananke, the Pantheon's

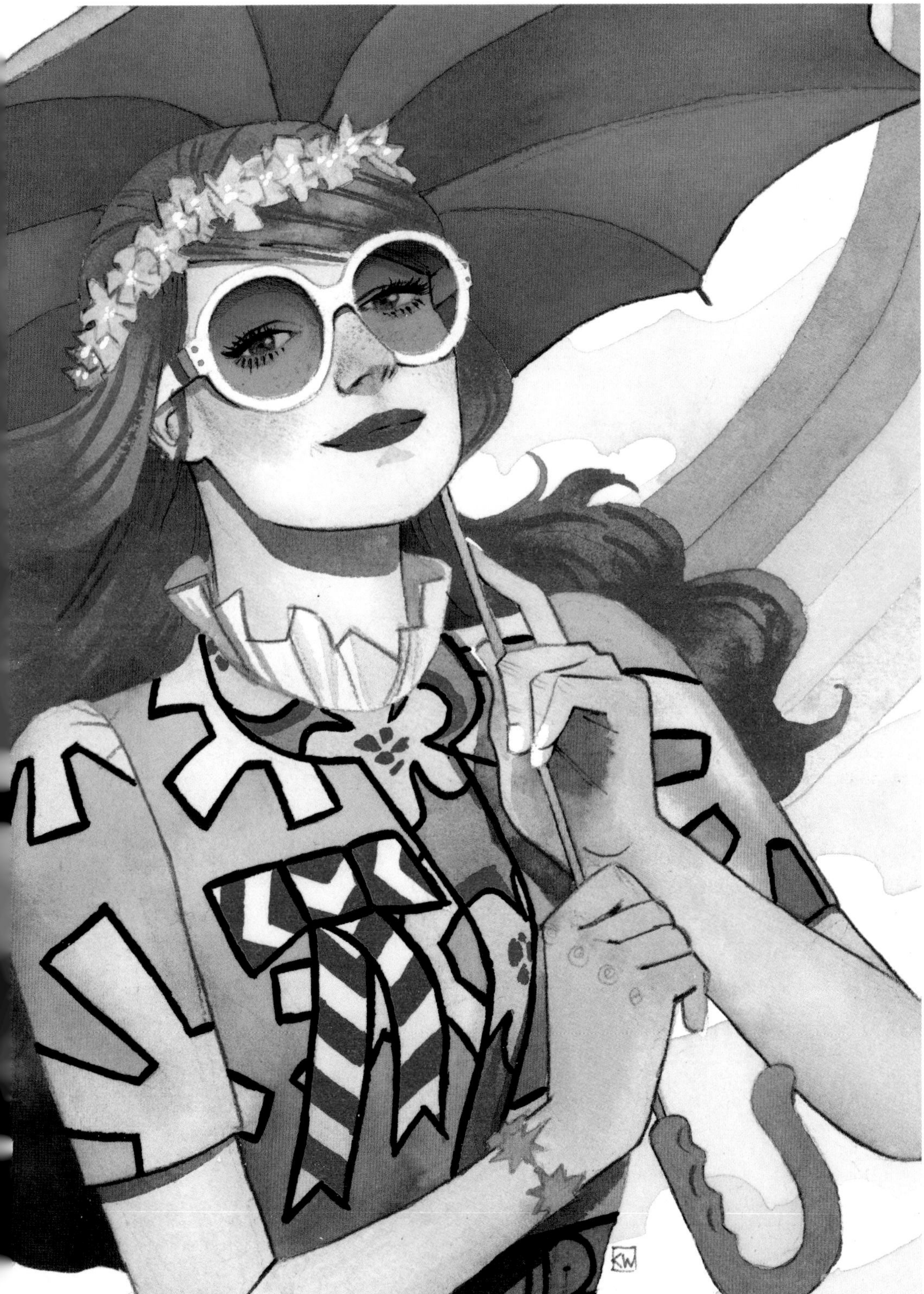

manager, discovered to have been a murderer a few months ago. "I think she went mad. She has been alone for a long time. She did such... awful things. Terrible things. What she did to Minerva's poor parents..."

A cloud passes over her face as she speaks, and she suddenly looks and sounds like the 17-year-old girl she is. Far too young to be so familiar with so much pain and loss. I remember again that she will be dead in a year, and feel a twinge of sadness. She pauses, then makes a small gesture with her left hand, as if to banish the past. "But her plan is not our purpose. We are here to bring light, and keep the night away," she says. She looks preternaturally serene, godlike once more. For some reason, this makes me even sadder.

I ask her about the late Eleanor Rigby, who had been her closest friend. They had met in the early days of the community of Pantheon fans that sprung up online. Then Rigby became Lucifer, and the first person Amaterasu went to after her own transfiguration (which happened, incidentally, whilst watching the sunset on December 21st, the

"I can't lose my faith now."

winter solstice — also Amaterasu's birthday). Now Lucifer is gone — Ananke's first known victim. "I miss her. She was my friend. Of course I miss her... but eternity is a long time, and immortality is forever. I can't lose my faith now. And this feeling," she says, lightly pressing her hand to her chest, "It is still burning. I feel holy and possessed."

It is this bone-deep conviction that gives her performances their legendary power — she makes the world she believes in real by sheer force of will. The perpetual crescendo of her shows, like a sunrise that somehow lasts for hours — it is driven by the urgency of someone who is trying to save us all, and buoyed by the joy of someone who is sure that they will. You could call this hubris. You could also call it faith.

Amaterasu wants to be the kind of god that Emily Greenaway believes in. Her connection to Shinto was formed long before she took on the role of its sun god. It even predates her Pantheon fandom. It began in her father's library, when she was a little girl. "I was always interested in myth and legend and fantasy, and he had all these old books. I loved

> "We are still here and we are still working and our story is not yet done. This is only one chapter of many. We will save everyone."

reading them." A trip to Japan with her father when she was eight, filled with visits to holy places, solidified her bond to the faith. But that bond didn't prevent her from spending most of her teenage years feeling lost. "I've tried so many things," she says, including the druid phase that inspired her to change her name to Hazel. But godhood came with an epiphany. "This is what he was preparing me for," she says quietly. In a way, being Amaterasu keeps the memory of her late father alive. She still visits Japan, secretly making her way to the shrines to pray.

This god still needs parents to rely on. "I think that's what Baal and Urðr are," she smiles. "The Pantheon's mother and father." They've taken those roles out of necessity. Their former matriarch was a monster. Amaterasu and Minerva were the only witnesses to Ananke's murder of Minerva's parents. Amaterasu is still haunted by it, and her memories seem garbled by trauma. "I wanted to help and tried but… she was just too powerful," she says, speaking haltingly. "It was lucky it was dawn. If it wasn't, I'd have been splattered too. She sent me flying through the wall."

The first person she went to in that, her most desperate moment, was Urðr — the professional sceptic and reluctant god. "She is good at cutting through lies," Amaterasu explains. And there's a tension here, if not an outright contradiction — Amaterasu believes in her purpose to the core of her being, but the person she trusts the most doesn't believe in the mission of the gods. Urðr doesn't even believe in Amaterasu, which started a fight that, infamously, ended with Amaterasu bursting into a giant false sun over Hiroshima. "I was so into showing her what I was I just… acted badly," Amaterasu says, and it's obvious that this highly public and grossly insensitive loss of self-control still bothers her.

In a way, her fierce need to be believed in is just an amplified version of a teenager's need to be validated. For Amaterasu, a denial that the gods are worth believing in is a personal attack, an attempted destruction of her identity. "We are still here and we are still working and our story is not yet done. This is only one chapter of many," she says, her eyes flashing with intensity. "We will save everyone."

The Pantheon would like us to believe that everything is fine, but the fact that they are now being led by a mercurial fist and an atheist sybil doesn't inspire much confidence. Neither does the fact that for months, they were being shepherded by an unstable serial murderer — without any of them realizing it. Worse, none of this seems to have inspired much internal reflection in their ranks. Their attitude seems to be that Ananke was nothing more than a tragic aberration. Their task is the same as it was before.

"I can't help but believe this is all happening for a reason. It's going to be okay. I don't know what it means, but I know it," she tells me. I hope she's right, and when I tell her so, she thanks me and smiles. And somehow I know this is not Amaterasu's smile, or even Hazel's smile. It is Emily's smile.

When she leaves, her departure reminds me less of a sunset than it does a extinguished wick — Amaterasu is there, then she is not. The only trace of her left is a dim, pulsing afterimage. And a small gap in the clouds. ■

DEATH IN VALHALLA

The undisputed facts about the infamous night...

1. A recording of Ananke during the period, recovered by Woden from the memory of Minerva's Owly, features Ananke saying: "Three dead, but the fourth is always hardest", as well as saying Minerva is "ready for the knife", and is a "fatted calf". The first statement is taken as her being involved with all the deaths of the Pantheon so far, supporting Persephone's claims that Ananke killed Inanna — and her parents.

2. This now-famous footage was gathered on the day of the 24th itself, whose revelation led to overwhelming public sympathy and outright horror. A small documentary team filming the events were overlooked by Ananke during the rampage, and managed to immortalise the cold-blooded murder of Minerva's parents. An upload of this footage accompanied the Pantheon's first public statement of events.

3. After the death, Amaterasu was unable to prevent Minerva being knocked unconscious and taken to the basement. Surviving Ananke's rage, she managed to gather the Norns and help bring the events to a conclusion. The surviving Pantheon members gathered together and confronted Ananke, in the process of performing a bizarre blood sacrifice in the shadow of a machine whose purpose has yet to be ascertained.

4. In the aftermath, the Pantheon contacted the authorities and offered their complete cooperation, while simultaneously releasing a statement describing the above. After intensive questioning they were released, and their names cleared. The exceptions to all of the above are Baphomet and The Morrigan, the former still wanted for the assault of a police officer from earlier in the year. Neither has made a public appearance since. ∎

KEVIN WADA's *photography has graced the covers of magazines for all the major publishers. This is the first time his lavish work has illustrated an entire magazine. We are not worthy.*

LEIGH ALEXANDER *writes on culture and tech for* The Guardian *and* Vice. *Her non-fiction includes* Breathing Machine *while her fiction includes* Monitor.

DORIAN LYNSKEY *has written on music for* The Guardian, GQ *and* Q. *He is the author of* 33 Revolutions Per Minute: A History of Protest Songs.

LAURIE PENNY *writes on politics, culture and feminism for outlets including* New Statesman *and* The Guardian. *Her most recent book is* Unspeakable Things: Sex, Lies and Revolution.

MARY HK CHOI *writes for* GQ, The New York Times *and* Wired. *She is the host of* Hey, Cool Job! *a podcast about jobs, and is the culture correspondent at* HBO's Vice News Tonight.

EZEKIEL KWEKU *writes on economics, race, sports, politics and culture. He writes about politics and the politics-adjacent for* MTV News. *He hasn't written any books. Yet.*

KIERON GILLEN *is the editor of* Pantheon Monthly, *and journalist of 20 years' standing. He is also the writer of* Phonogram: Rue Britannia, *a graphic novel. He hopes one day to do more comic work.*

JAMIE McKELVIE *has worked in advertising for over a decade. He is also the artist of* Phonogram: Rue Britannia. *He hopes one day to do more comic work, but ideally not with Kieron.*

MATTHEW WILSON *has worked in advertising for a decade. He occasionally dreams of being forced to colour all the comics in the world, and wakes in a cold sweat. Thank god it was only a dream.*

SERGIO SERRANO *is a designer, who is still thinking about adding to this, and clearly running out of time. Tick-tock, tick-tock.*

CHRISSY WILLIAMS *has been an editorial intern for ten years and has high hopes of getting something out of it soon.*

NO LIFE LEFT

WH... WHAT ARE WE GOING TO DO!?
MOBILE DIO-SCO

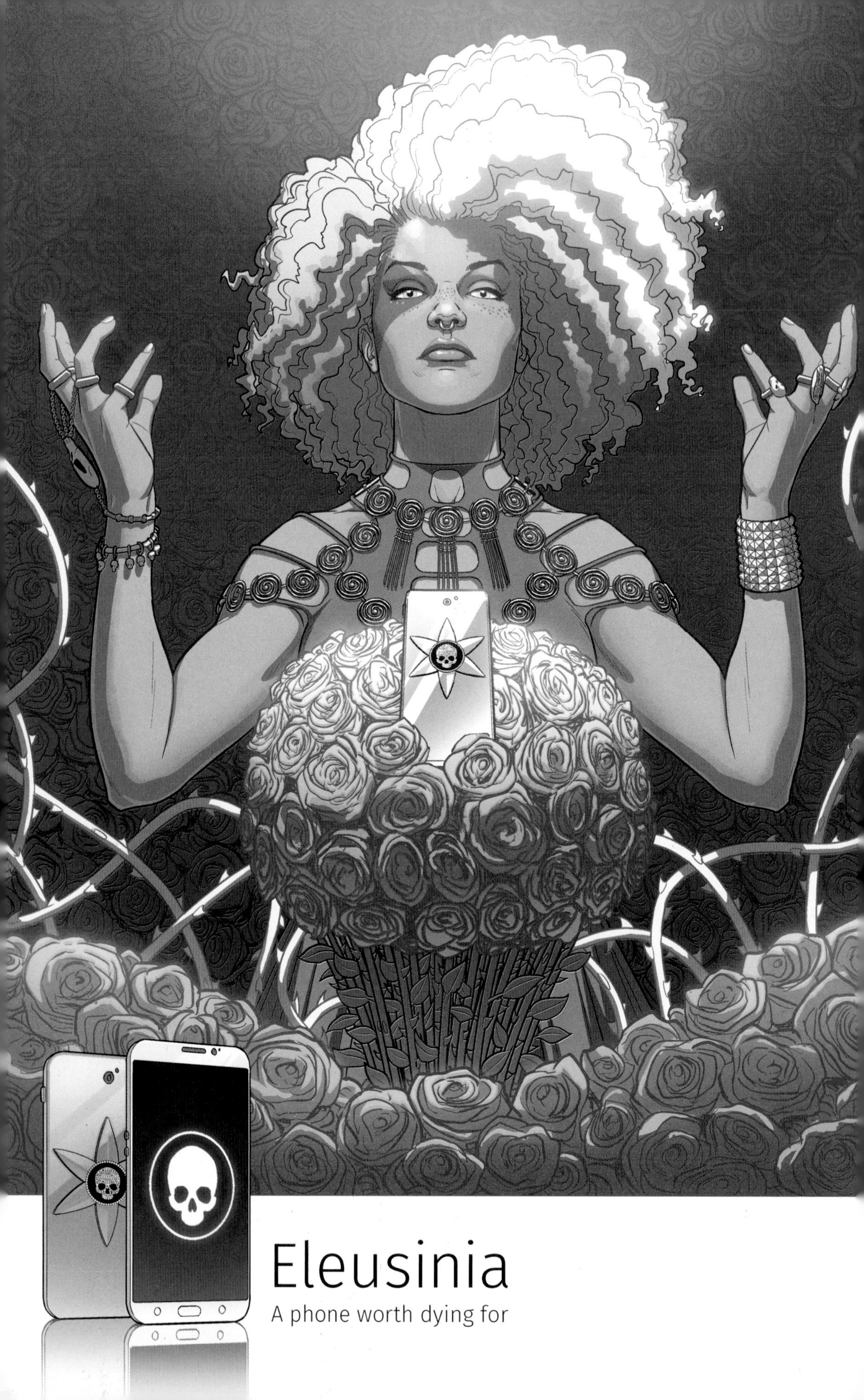
Eleusinia
A phone worth dying for

THE
WICKED

+

THE DIVINE

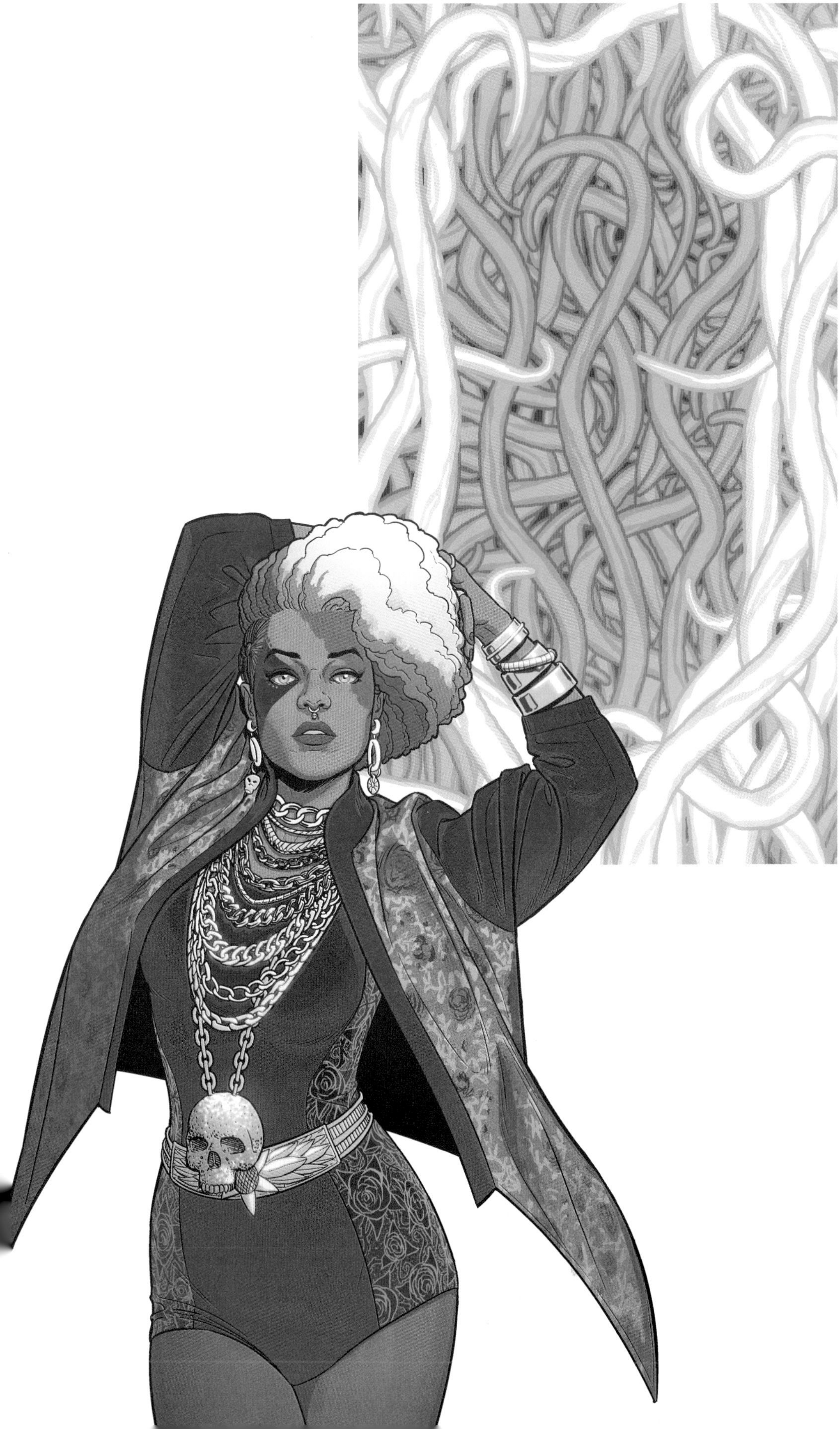

THE
WICKED
+
THE DIVINE

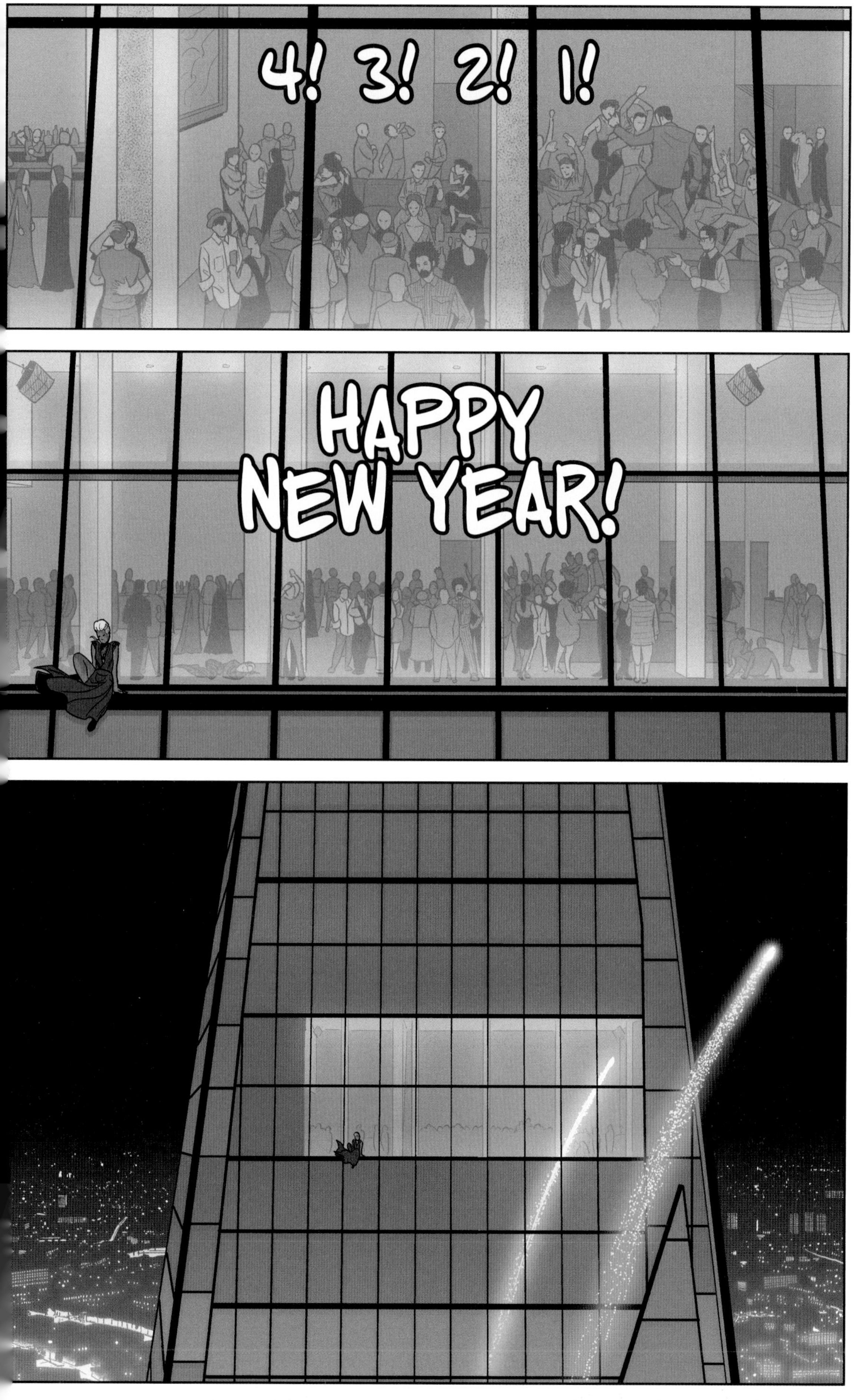
4! 3! 2! 1!
HAPPY NEW YEAR!

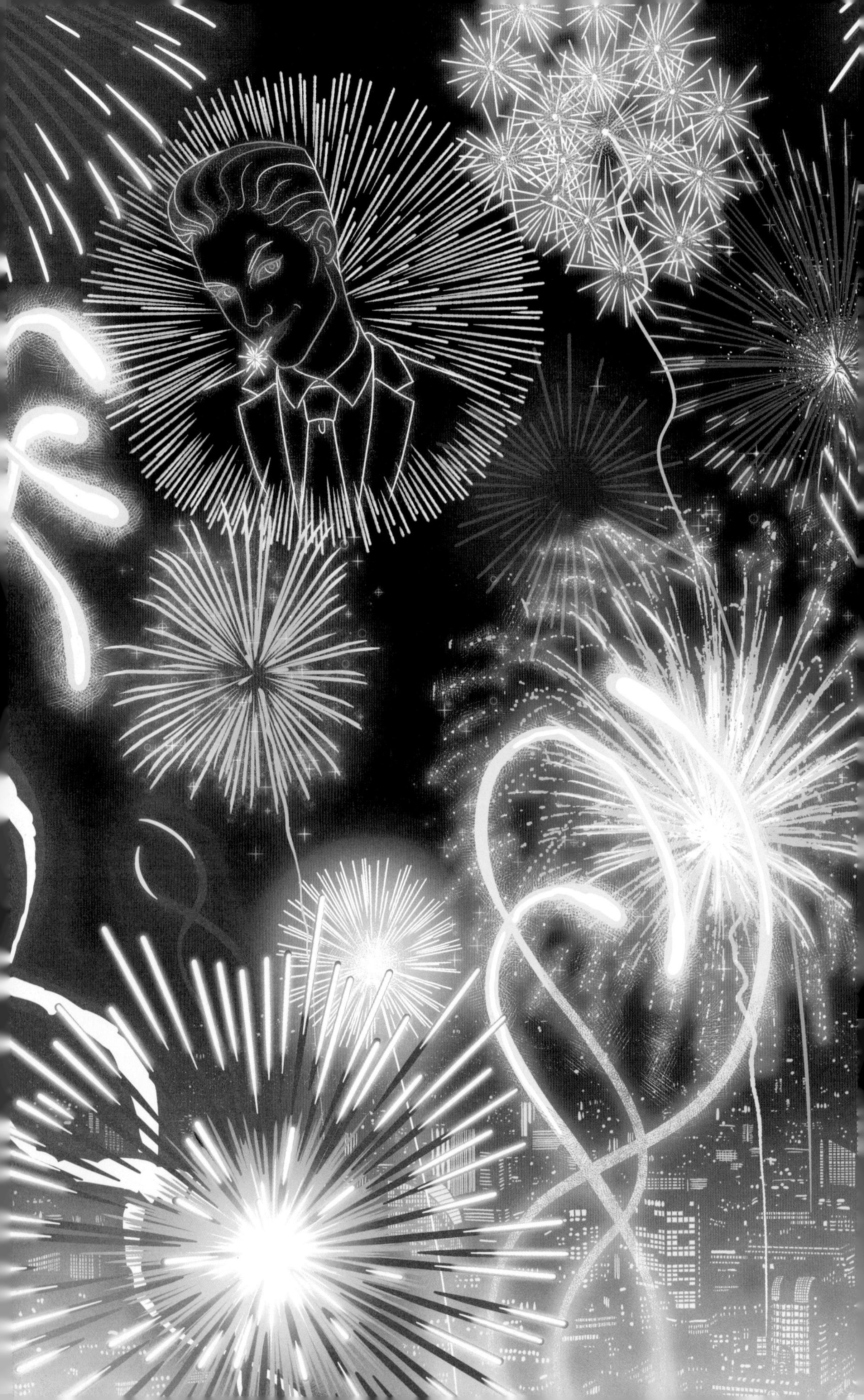

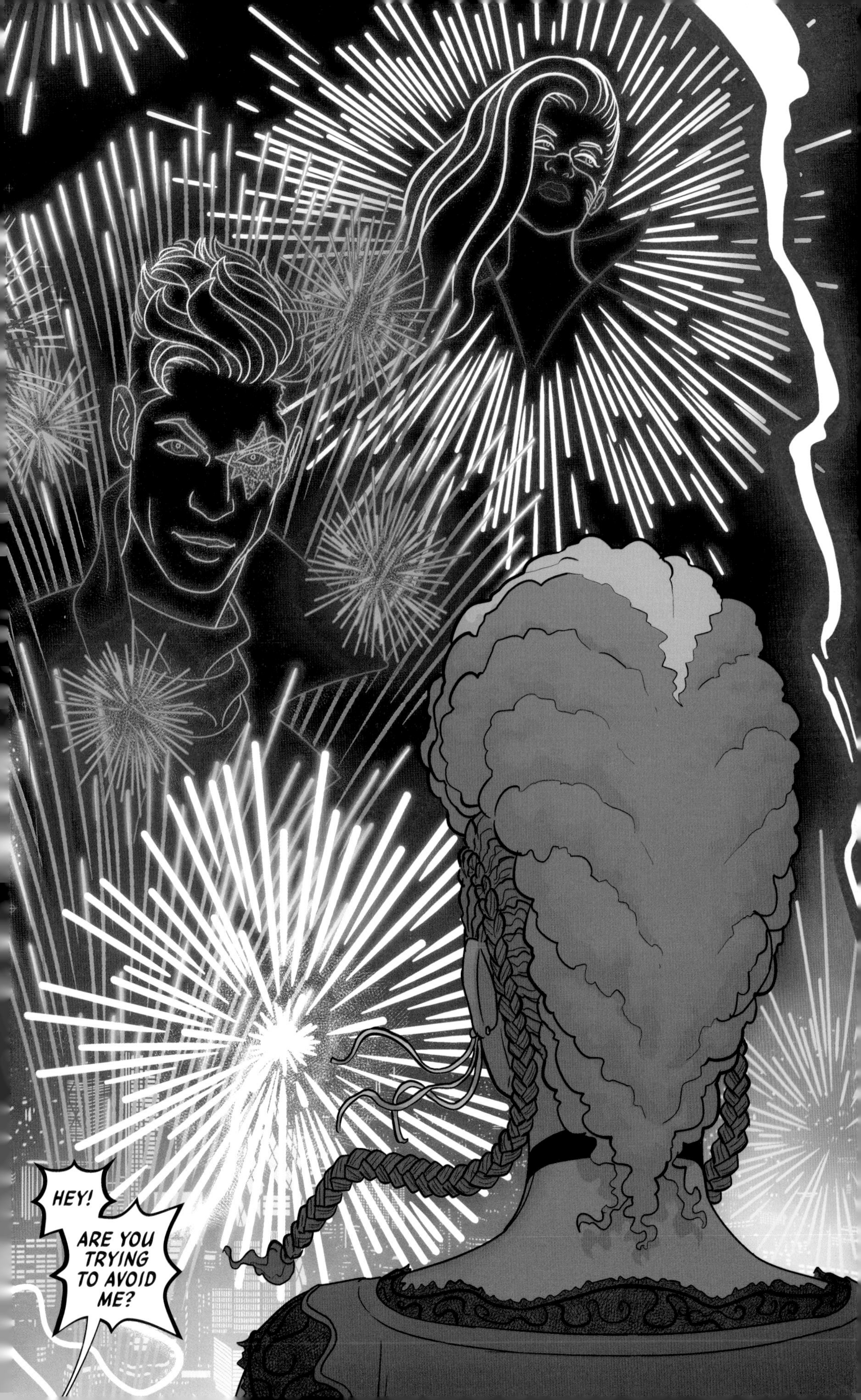
HEY!
ARE YOU TRYING TO AVOID ME?

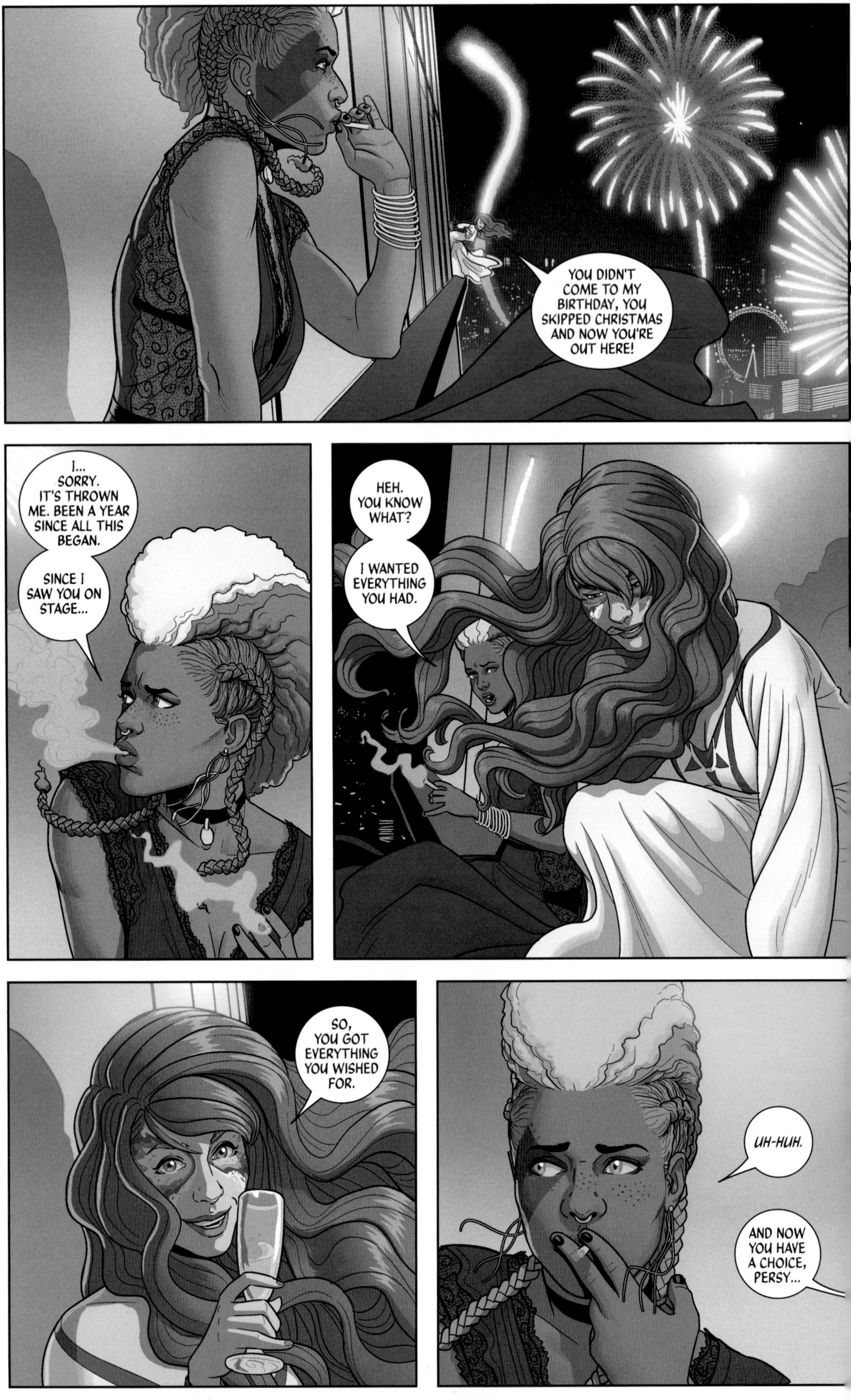
YOU DIDN'T COME TO MY BIRTHDAY, YOU SKIPPED CHRISTMAS AND NOW YOU'RE OUT HERE!
I... SORRY. IT'S THROWN ME. BEEN A YEAR SINCE ALL THIS BEGAN.
SINCE I SAW YOU ON STAGE...
HEH. YOU KNOW WHAT?
I WANTED EVERYTHING YOU HAD.
SO, YOU GOT EVERYTHING YOU WISHED FOR.
UH-HUH.
AND NOW YOU HAVE A CHOICE, PERSY...

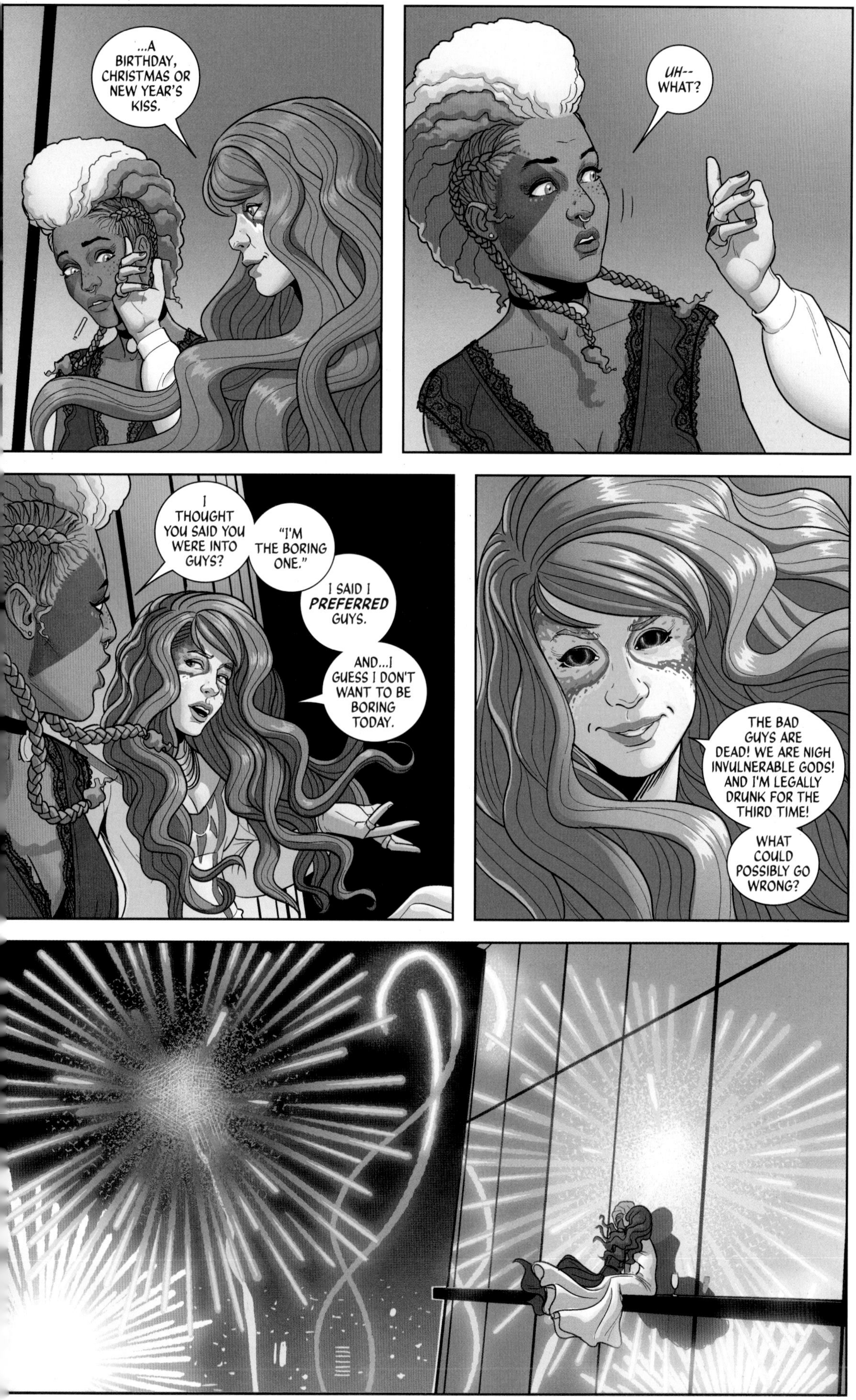
...A BIRTHDAY, CHRISTMAS OR NEW YEAR'S KISS.
!
UH-- WHAT?
I THOUGHT YOU SAID YOU WERE INTO GUYS?
"I'M THE BORING ONE."
I SAID I PREFERRED GUYS.
AND...I GUESS I DON'T WANT TO BE BORING TODAY.
THE BAD GUYS ARE DEAD! WE ARE NIGH INVULNERABLE GODS! AND I'M LEGALLY DRUNK FOR THE THIRD TIME!
WHAT COULD POSSIBLY GO WRONG?

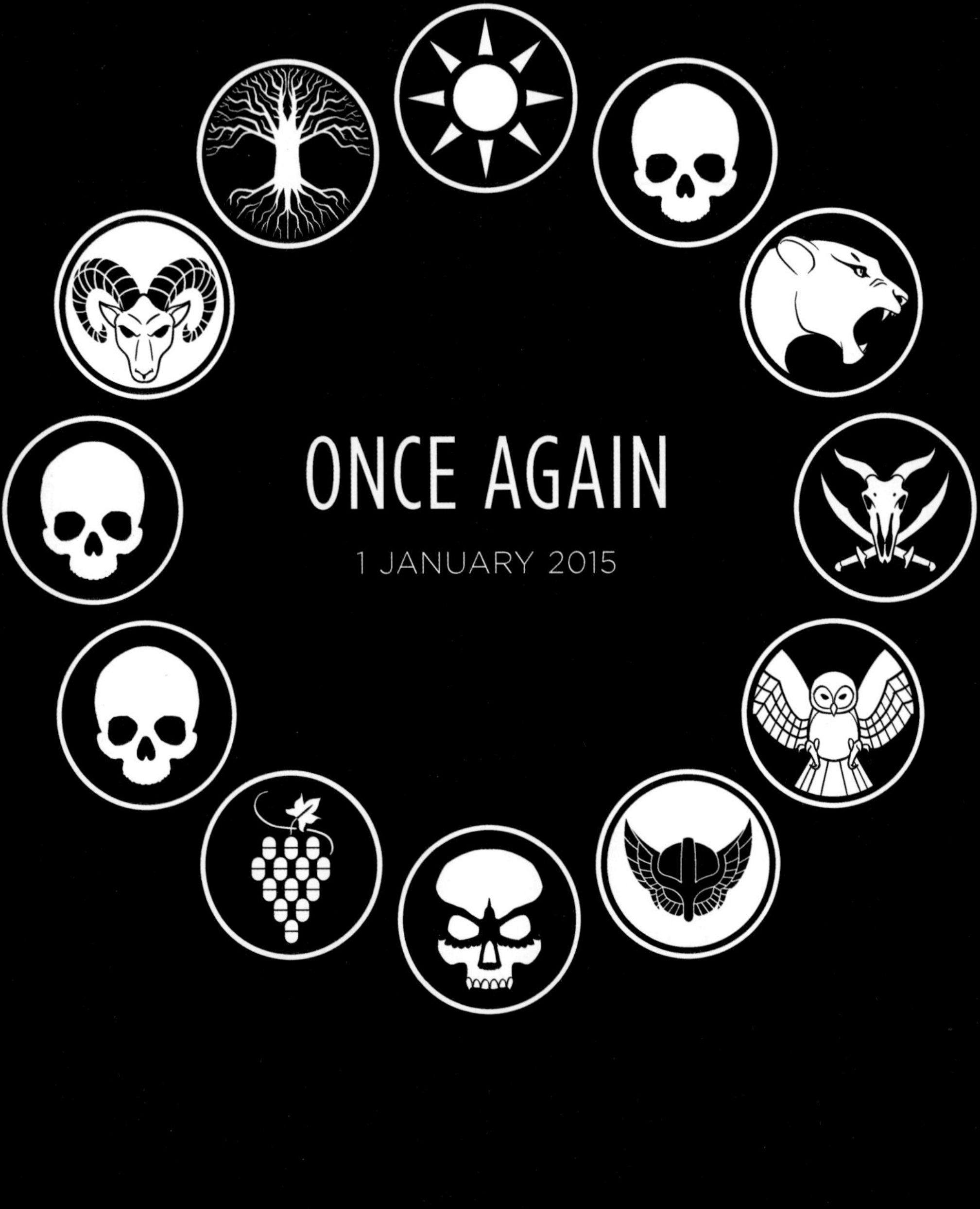

ONCE AGAIN

1 JANUARY 2015

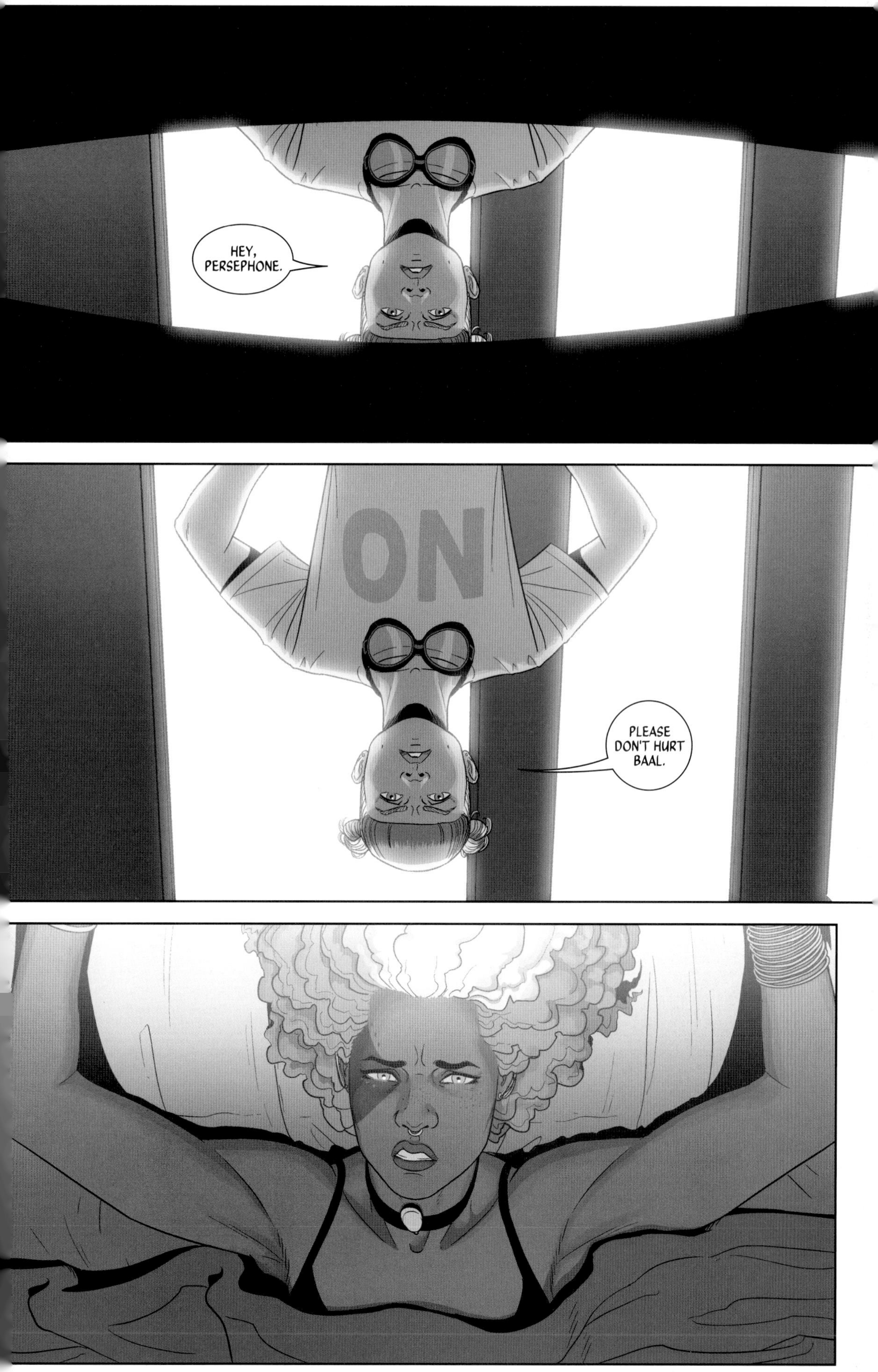
HEY, PERSEPHONE.
PLEASE DON'T HURT BAAL.

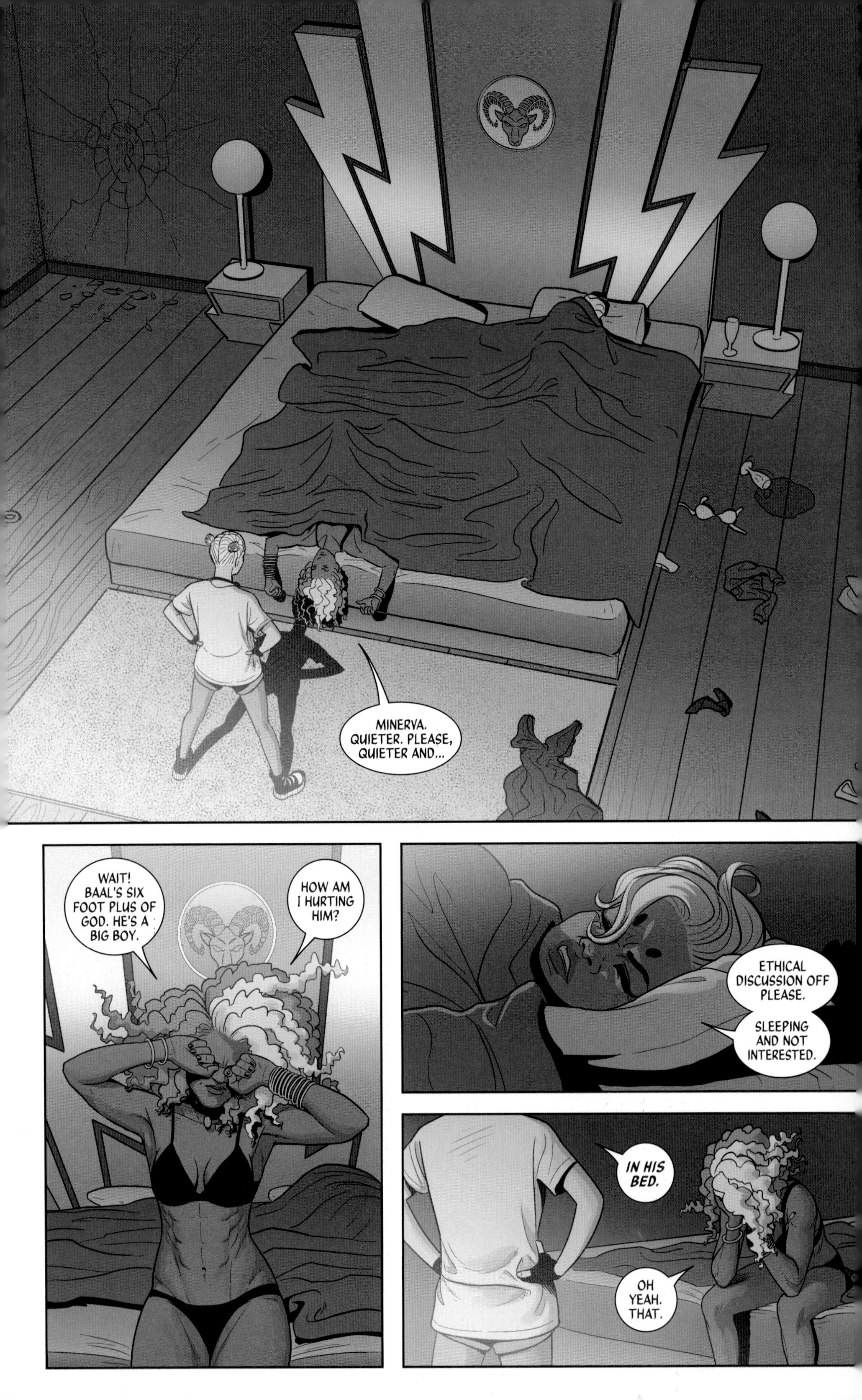
MINERVA. QUIETER. PLEASE, QUIETER AND...
WAIT! BAAL'S SIX FOOT PLUS OF GOD. HE'S A BIG BOY.
HOW AM I HURTING HIM?
ETHICAL DISCUSSION OFF PLEASE.
SLEEPING AND NOT INTERESTED.
IN HIS BED.
OH YEAH. THAT.

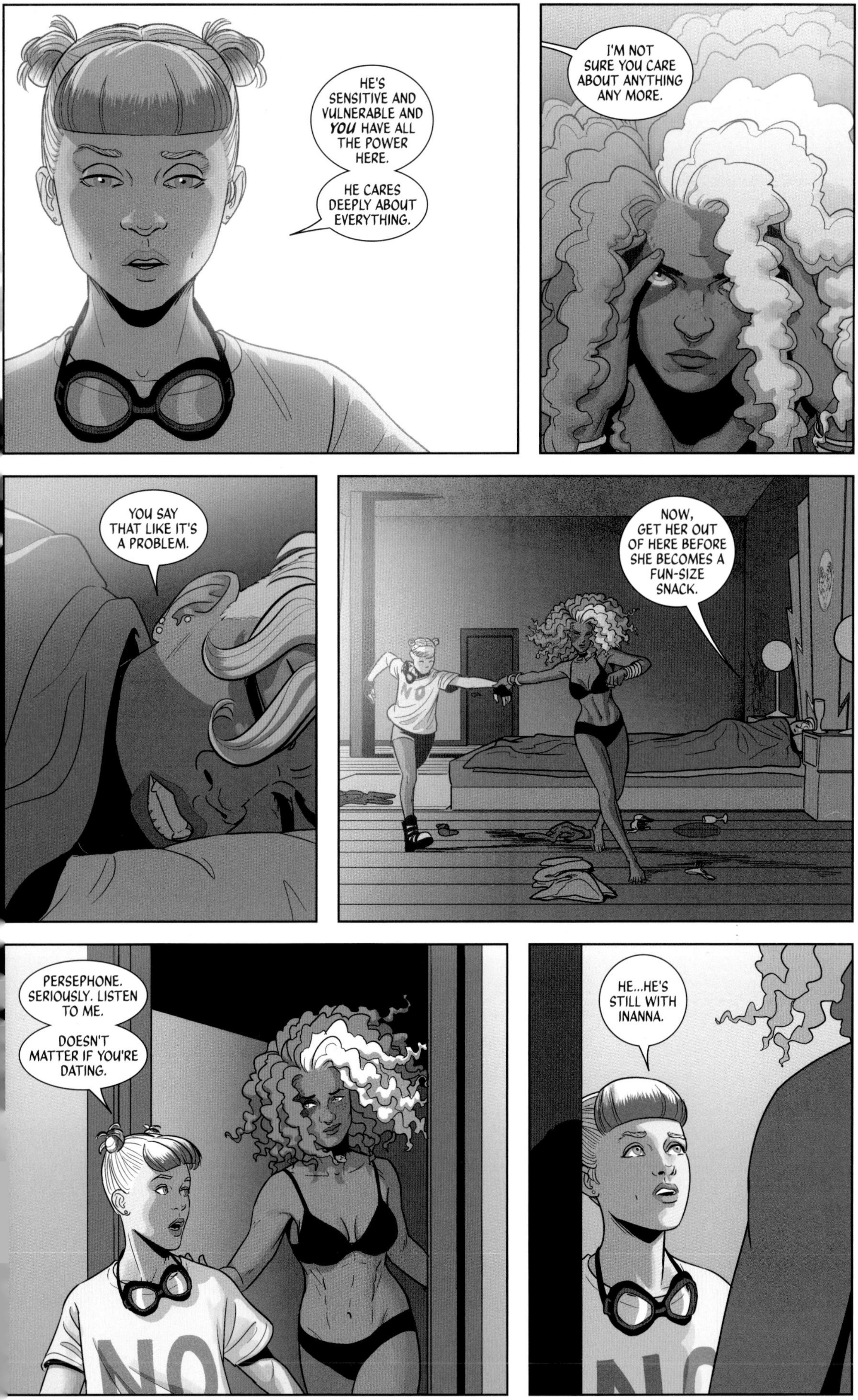
HE'S SENSITIVE AND VULNERABLE AND *YOU* HAVE ALL THE POWER HERE.
HE CARES DEEPLY ABOUT EVERYTHING.
I'M NOT SURE YOU CARE ABOUT ANYTHING ANY MORE.
YOU SAY THAT LIKE IT'S A PROBLEM.
NOW, GET HER OUT OF HERE BEFORE SHE BECOMES A FUN-SIZE SNACK.
PERSEPHONE. SERIOUSLY. LISTEN TO ME.
DOESN'T MATTER IF YOU'RE DATING.
HE...HE'S STILL WITH INANNA.

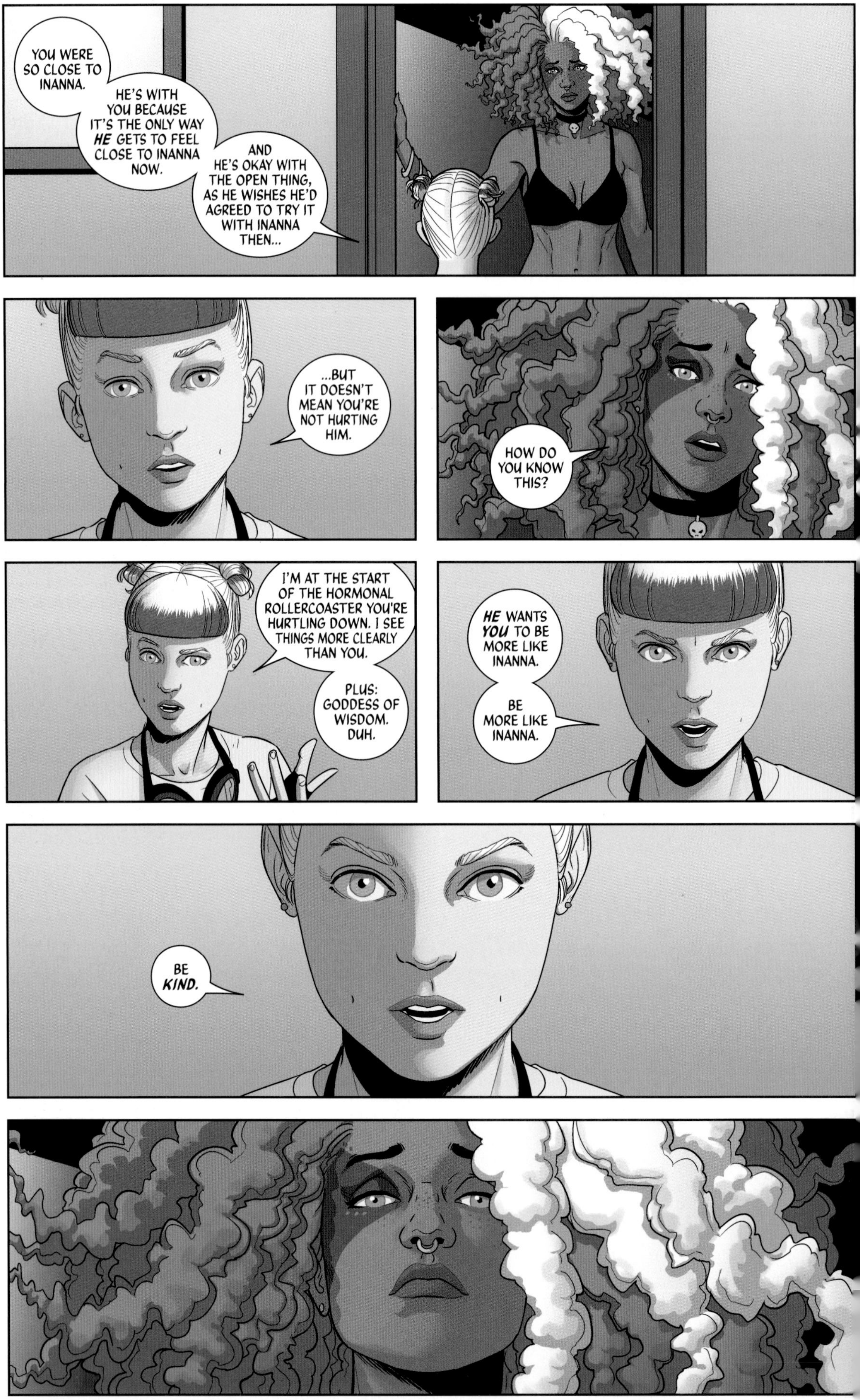
YOU WERE SO CLOSE TO INANNA.
HE'S WITH YOU BECAUSE IT'S THE ONLY WAY HE GETS TO FEEL CLOSE TO INANNA NOW.
AND HE'S OKAY WITH THE OPEN THING, AS HE WISHES HE'D AGREED TO TRY IT WITH INANNA THEN...
...BUT IT DOESN'T MEAN YOU'RE NOT HURTING HIM.
HOW DO YOU KNOW THIS?
I'M AT THE START OF THE HORMONAL ROLLERCOASTER YOU'RE HURTLING DOWN. I SEE THINGS MORE CLEARLY THAN YOU.
PLUS: GODDESS OF WISDOM. DUH.
HE WANTS YOU TO BE MORE LIKE INANNA.
BE MORE LIKE INANNA.
BE KIND.

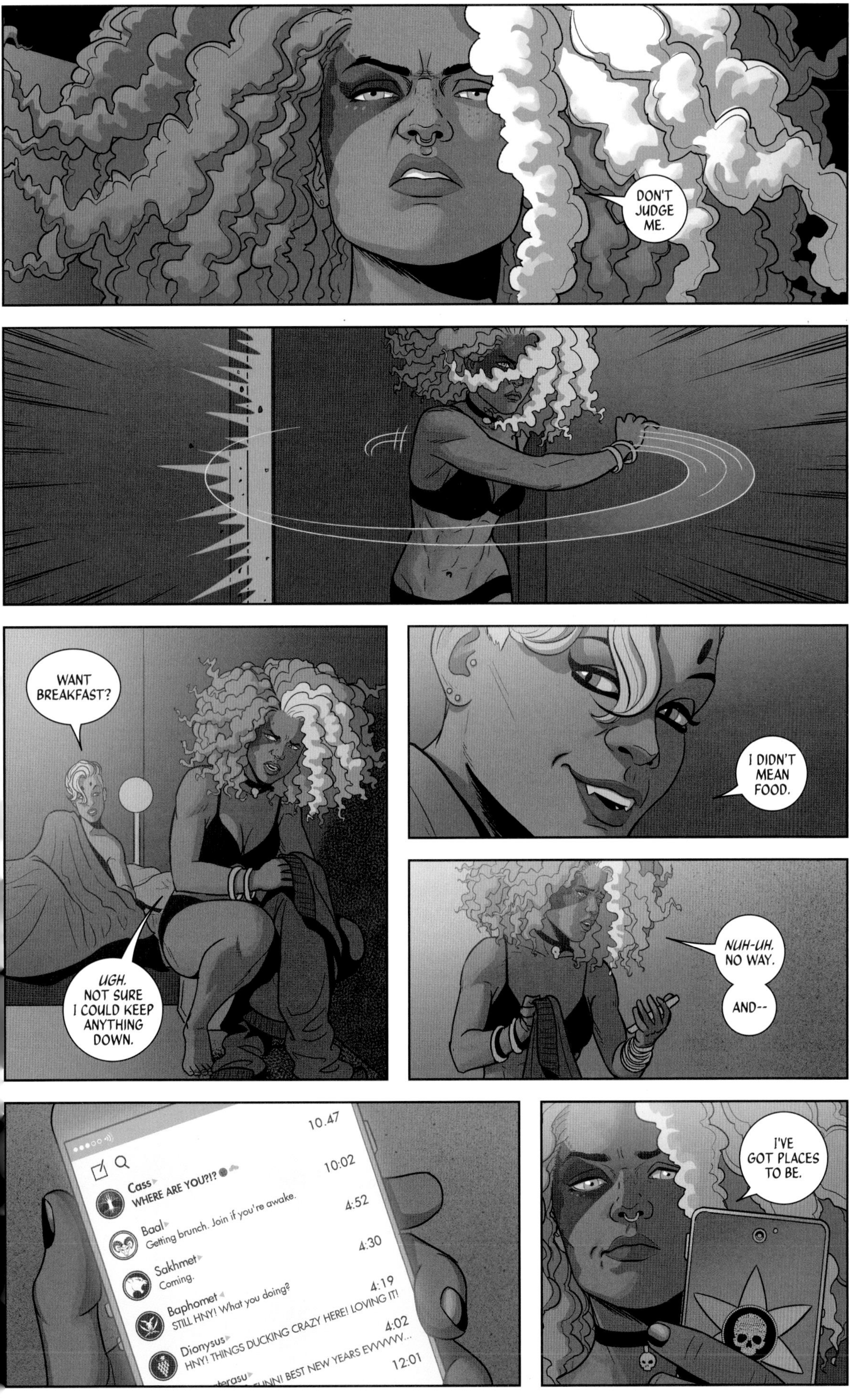
DON'T JUDGE ME.
WANT BREAKFAST?
UGH. NOT SURE I COULD KEEP ANYTHING DOWN.
I DIDN'T MEAN FOOD.
NUH-UH. NO WAY.
AND--
10.47
Cass
WHERE ARE YOU?!?
10:02
Baal
Getting brunch. Join if you're awake.
4:52
Sakhmet
Coming.
4:30
Baphomet
STILL HNY! What you doing?
4:19
Dionysus
HNY! THINGS DUCKING CRAZY HERE! LOVING IT!
4:02
BEST NEW YEARS EVVVVVV...
12:01
I'VE GOT PLACES TO BE.

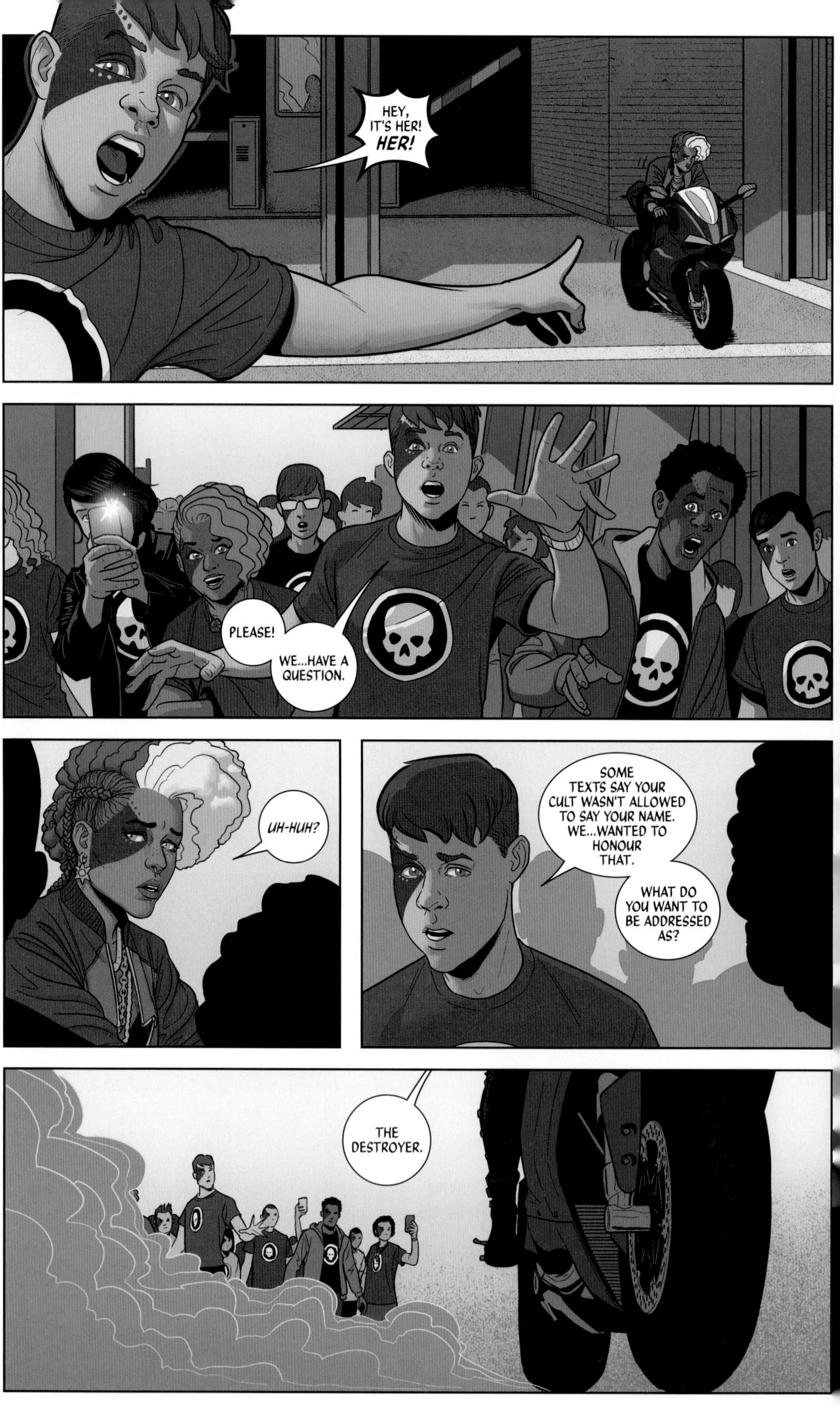
HEY, IT'S HER! HER!
PLEASE!
WE...HAVE A QUESTION.
UH-HUH?
SOME TEXTS SAY YOUR CULT WASN'T ALLOWED TO SAY YOUR NAME. WE...WANTED TO HONOUR THAT.
WHAT DO YOU WANT TO BE ADDRESSED AS?
THE DESTROYER.

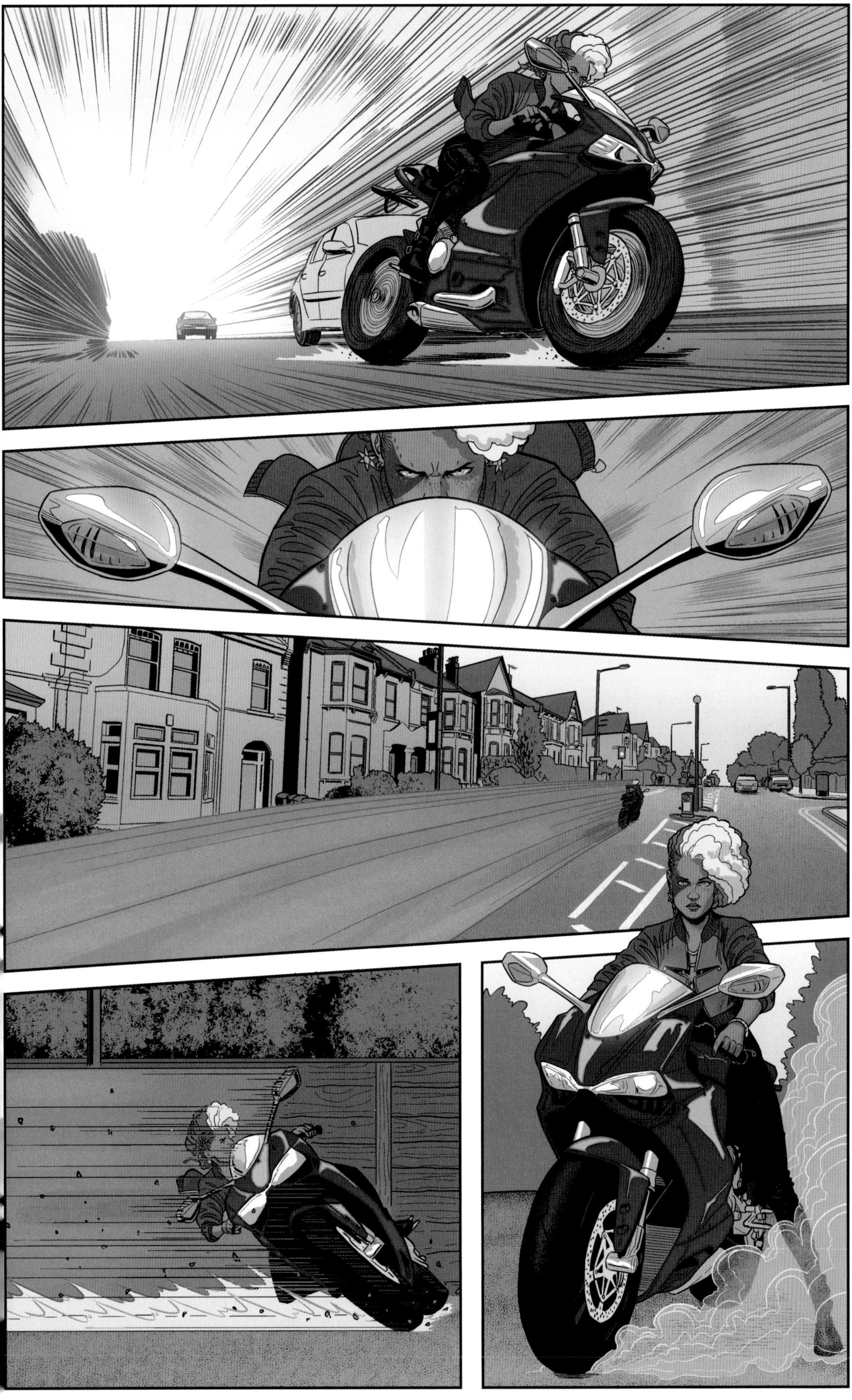

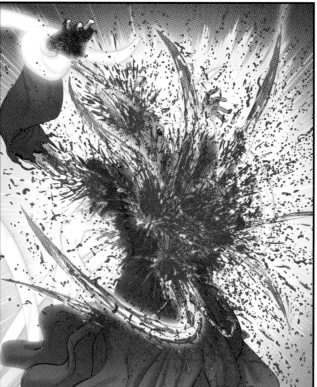

WE RETURN

1 JANUARY 2015

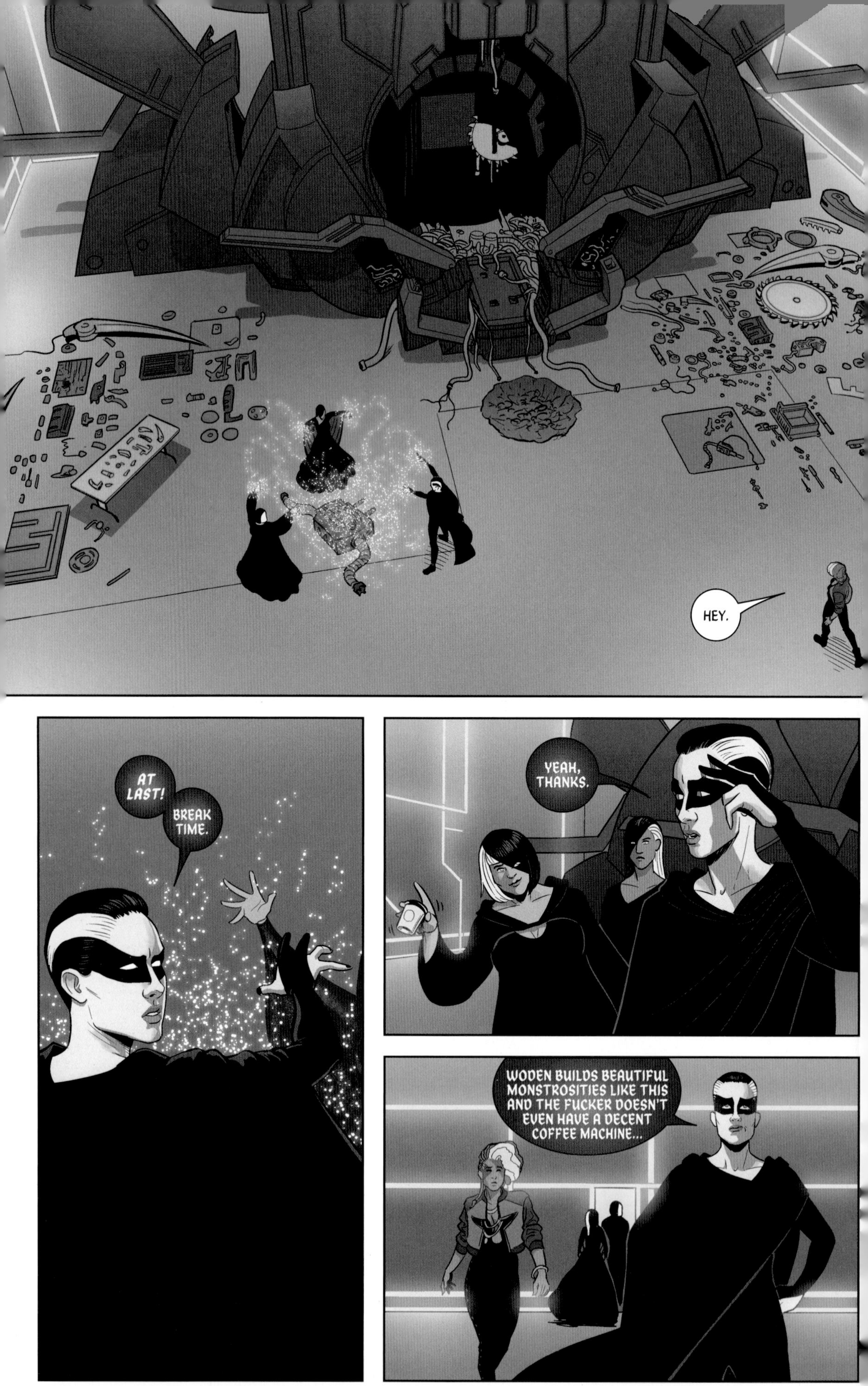
HEY.
AT LAST!
BREAK TIME.
YEAH, THANKS.
WODEN BUILDS BEAUTIFUL MONSTROSITIES LIKE THIS AND THE FUCKER DOESN'T EVEN HAVE A DECENT COFFEE MACHINE...

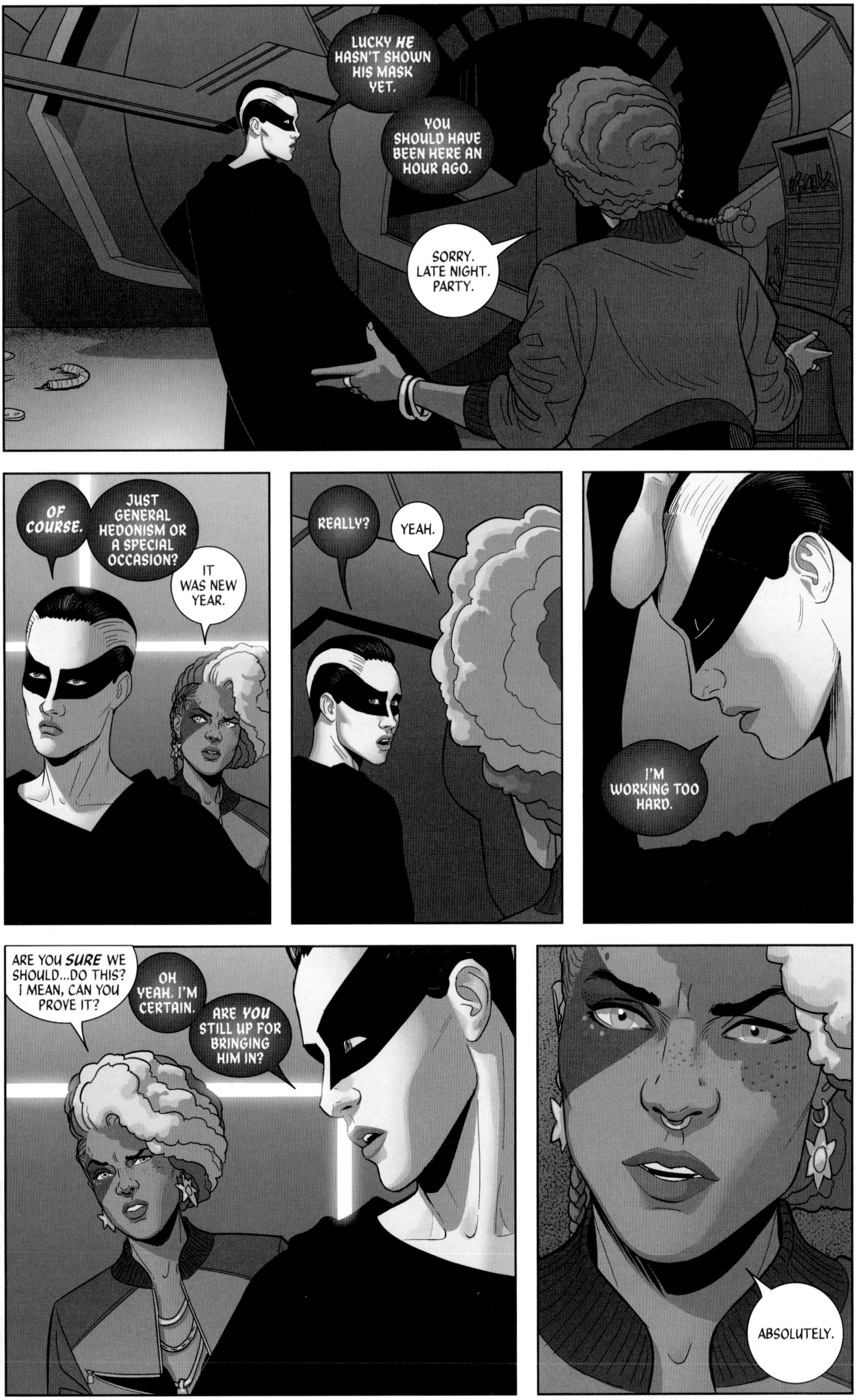
LUCKY *HE* HASN'T SHOWN HIS MASK YET.
YOU SHOULD HAVE BEEN HERE AN HOUR AGO.
SORRY. LATE NIGHT. PARTY.
OF COURSE.
JUST GENERAL HEDONISM OR A SPECIAL OCCASION?
IT WAS NEW YEAR.
REALLY?
YEAH.
I'M WORKING TOO HARD.
ARE YOU *SURE* WE SHOULD...DO THIS? I MEAN, CAN YOU PROVE IT?
OH YEAH. I'M CERTAIN.
ARE *YOU* STILL UP FOR BRINGING HIM IN?
ABSOLUTELY.

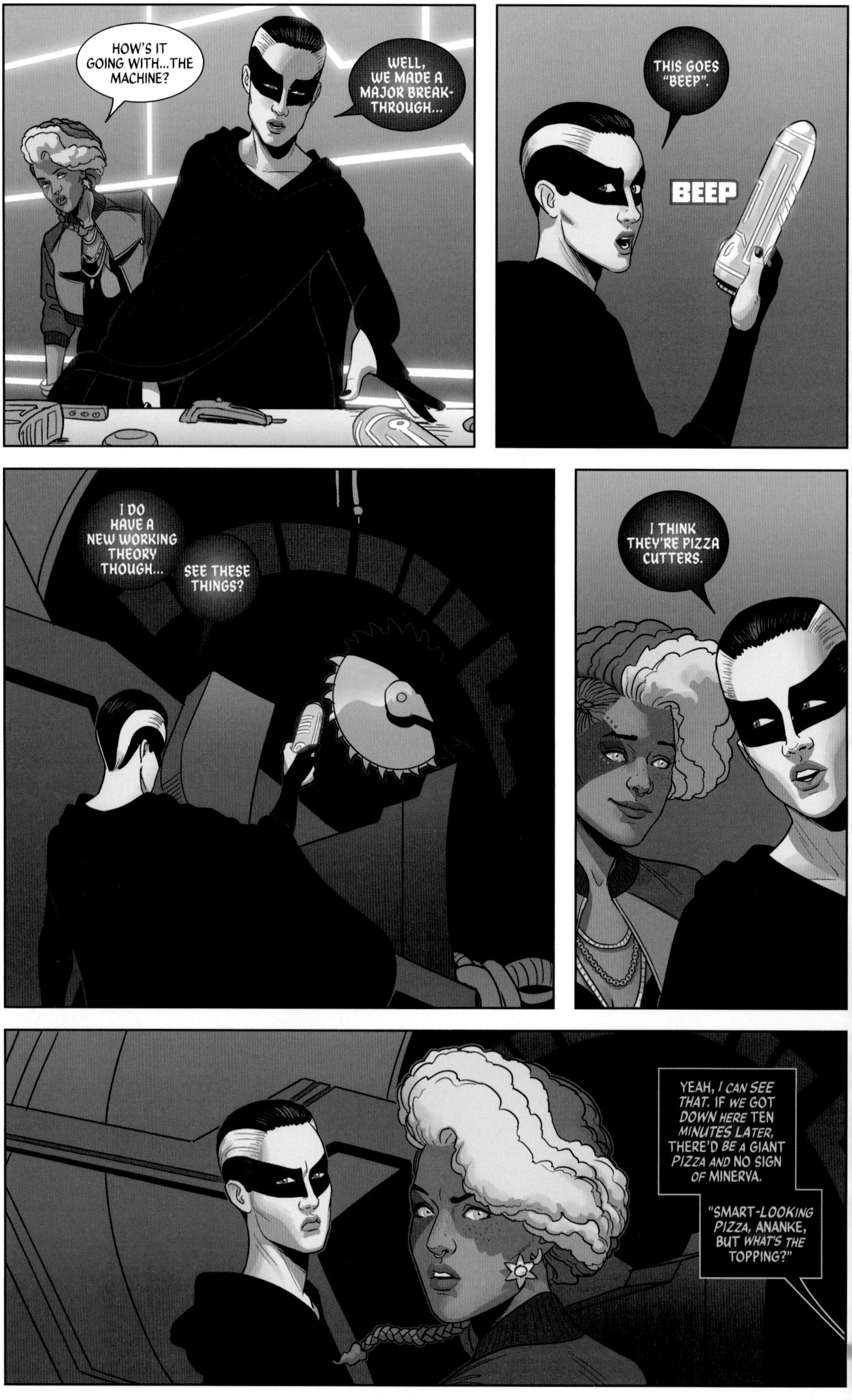

HOW'S IT GOING WITH...THE MACHINE?
WELL, WE MADE A MAJOR BREAK-THROUGH...
THIS GOES "BEEP".
BEEP
I DO HAVE A NEW WORKING THEORY THOUGH...
SEE THESE THINGS?
I THINK THEY'RE PIZZA CUTTERS.
YEAH, I CAN SEE THAT. IF WE GOT DOWN HERE TEN MINUTES LATER, THERE'D BE A GIANT PIZZA AND NO SIGN OF MINERVA.
"SMART-LOOKING PIZZA, ANANKE, BUT WHAT'S THE TOPPING?"

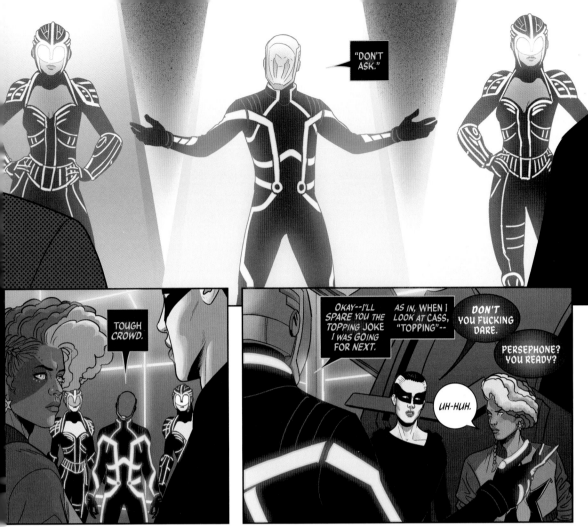

"DON'T ASK."

TOUGH CROWD.

OKAY--I'LL SPARE YOU THE TOPPING JOKE I WAS GOING FOR NEXT.

AS IN, WHEN I LOOK AT CASS, "TOPPING"--

DON'T YOU FUCKING DARE.

PERSEPHONE? YOU READY?

UH-HUH.

OKAY, WHAT'S THIS ABOUT? WHY DID YOU WANT TO SEE ME?

I HAVE MY OWN SISYPHEAN RESEARCH PROJECTS AND MEANINGLESS SEXUAL DEPRAVITY TO BE GETTING ON WITH...

YOU BUILT THIS, YEAH?

YES. I TOLD YOU THAT. AND I TOLD YOU THAT I DIDN'T KNOW WHAT IT WAS FOR.

IF I DID, I WOULD NEVER HAVE BUILT IT.

YEAH... BUT I'VE BEEN LOOKING AT IT CLOSELY.

IF THIS IS YOUR HANDIWORK...

...THEN SO IS THIS.

THE REMAINS OF THE BOMB FROM MY GIG.

IT CAME THROUGH ONE OF *YOUR* TELEPORTERS.

IF I HADN'T CUSHIONED THE BLAST, THE CROWD WOULD BE DEAD.

IT'S PROOF YOU WERE COMPLICIT WITH ANANKE IN ATTEMPTED MURDER AND LIED ABOUT IT...

...SO WHY SHOULD WE BELIEVE YOU ABOUT ANYTHING ELSE?

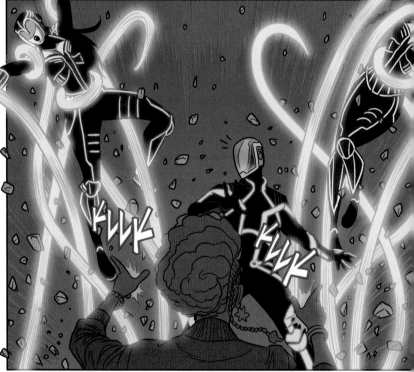

KLLK

KLLK

I...YOU...YOU *SAW* WHAT SHE *DID* TO ANYONE WHO GOT IN HER WAY.

I DID.

AND YOU SAW WHAT I DID TO HER. DON'T RESIST.

OR DO.

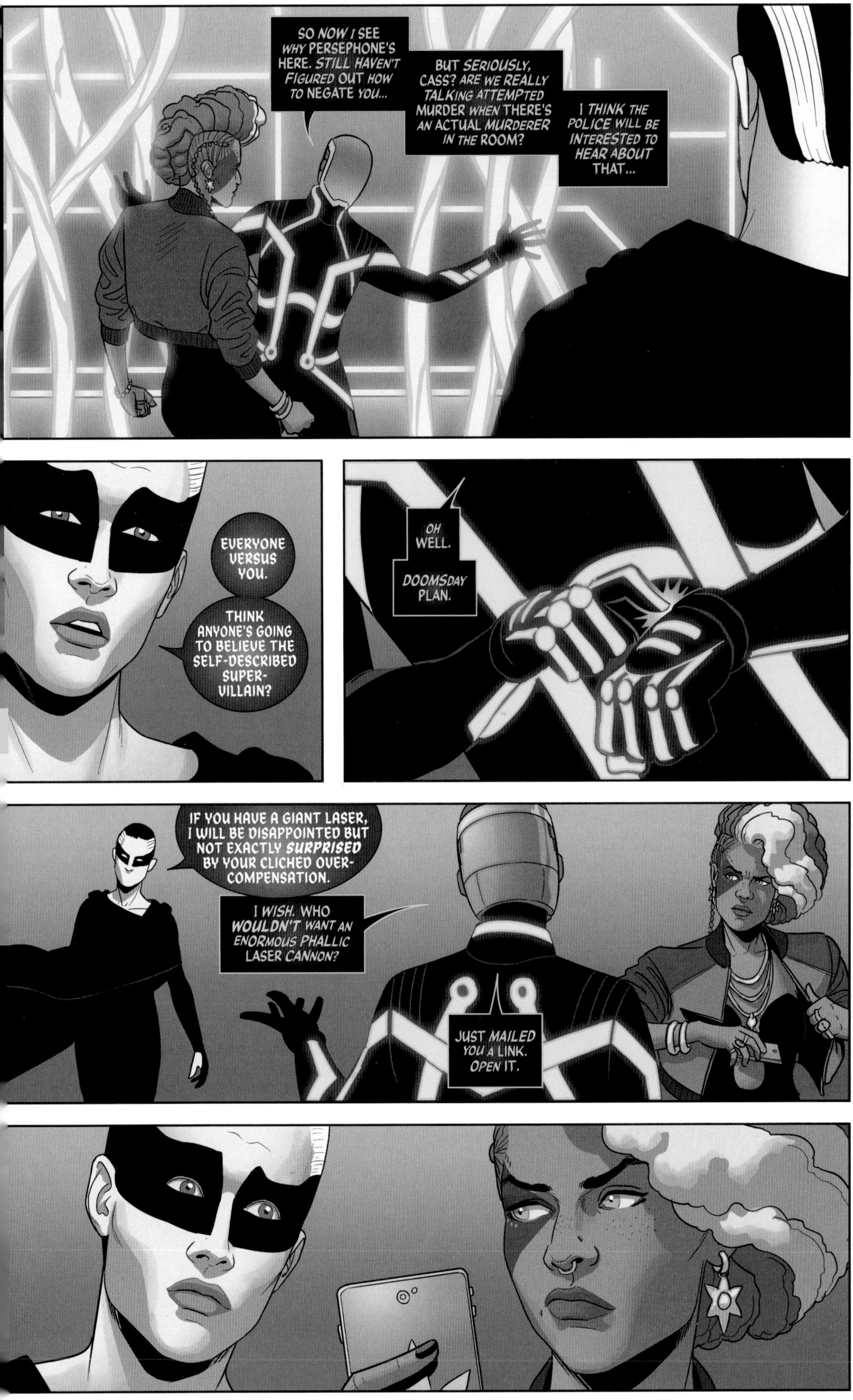
SO NOW I SEE WHY PERSEPHONE'S HERE. STILL HAVEN'T FIGURED OUT HOW TO NEGATE YOU...
BUT SERIOUSLY, CASS? ARE WE REALLY TALKING ATTEMPTED MURDER WHEN THERE'S AN ACTUAL MURDERER IN THE ROOM?
I THINK THE POLICE WILL BE INTERESTED TO HEAR ABOUT THAT...
EVERYONE VERSUS YOU.
THINK ANYONE'S GOING TO BELIEVE THE SELF-DESCRIBED SUPER-VILLAIN?
OH WELL.
DOOMSDAY PLAN.
IF YOU HAVE A GIANT LASER, I WILL BE DISAPPOINTED BUT NOT EXACTLY SURPRISED BY YOUR CLICHED OVER-COMPENSATION.
I WISH. WHO WOULDN'T WANT AN ENORMOUS PHALLIC LASER CANNON?
JUST MAILED YOU A LINK. OPEN IT.

07:03:57 24.9.2014

07:03:59 24.9.2014

07:04:03 24.9.2014

IT WAS SELF-DEFENCE.

IT'S WHAT WE'RE SAYING IT WAS.

WAS... IT?

07:04:15 24.9.2014

THERE'D BETTER NOT BE ANY CAMERAS IN THE TOILETS.

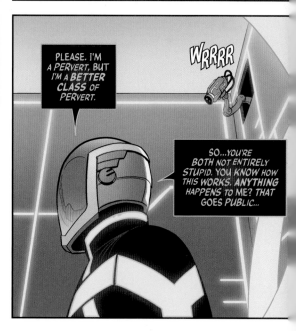

PLEASE. I'M A *PERVERT*, BUT I'M A *BETTER CLASS* OF PERVERT.

WRRRR

SO...YOU'RE BOTH NOT ENTIRELY STUPID. YOU KNOW HOW THIS WORKS. ANYTHING HAPPENS TO ME? THAT GOES *PUBLIC*...

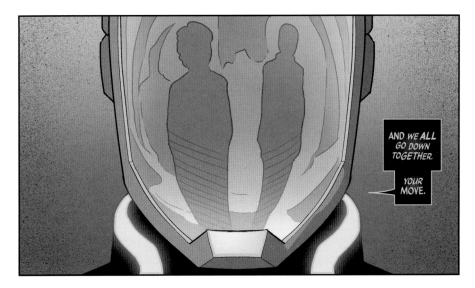

AND *WE ALL GO DOWN TOGETHER.*

YOUR MOVE.

I'M THE DESTROYER.

YOU KNOW MY MOVE.

TEMPTING FATE

1 JANUARY 2015

THE
WICKED
+
THE DIVINE

25

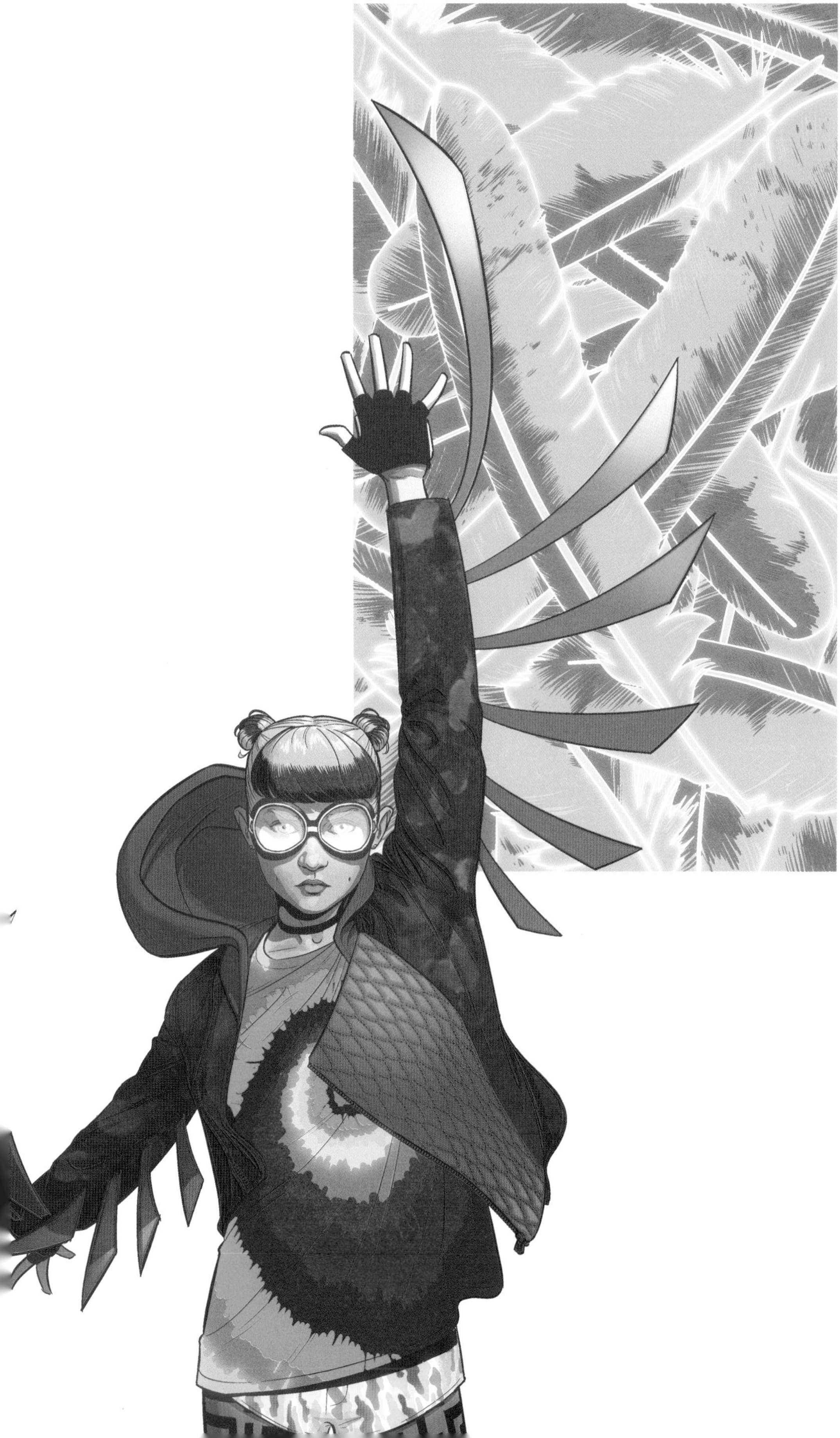

THE
WICKED
+
THE DIVINE

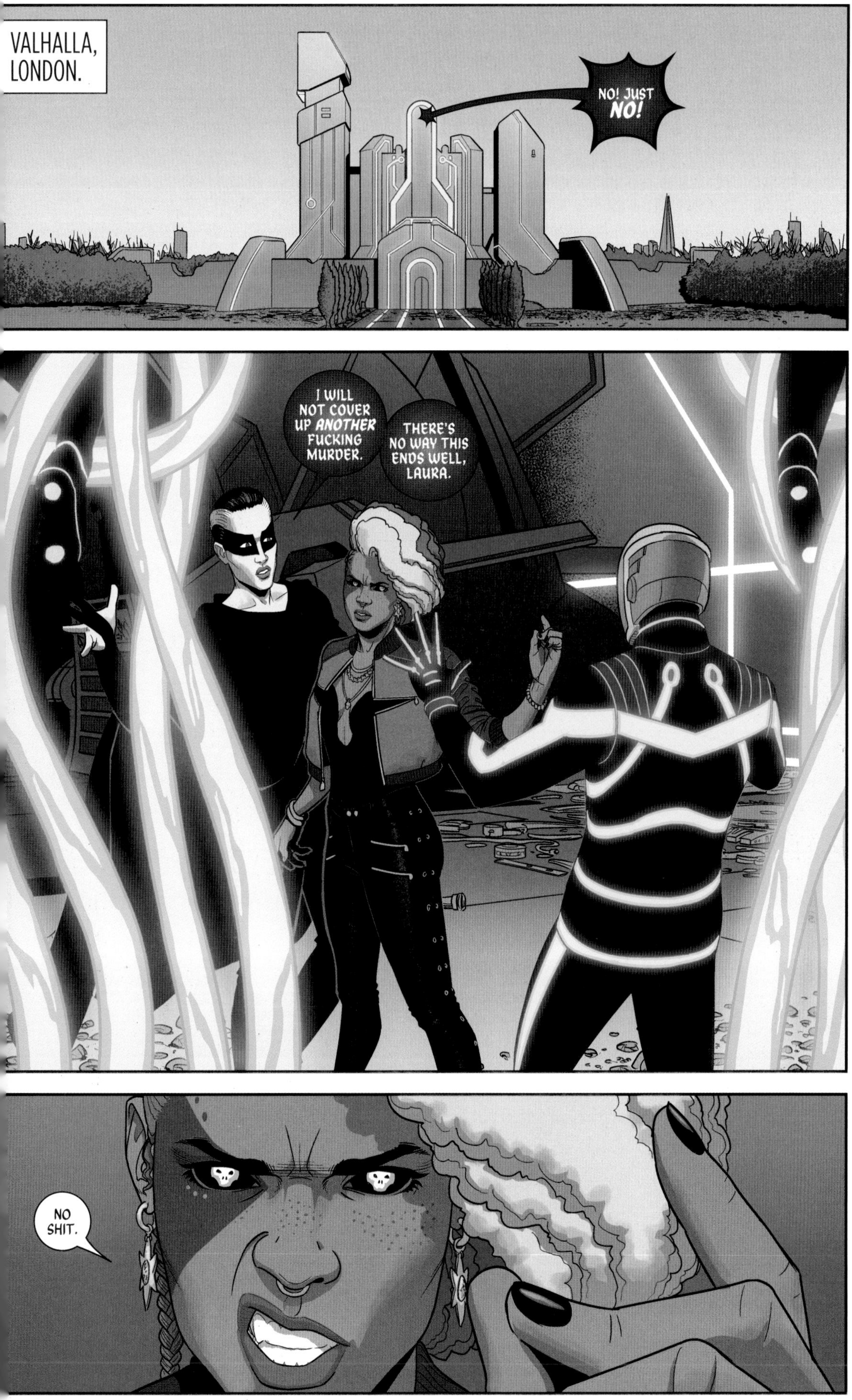

VALHALLA, LONDON.
NO! JUST NO!
I WILL NOT COVER UP ANOTHER FUCKING MURDER.
THERE'S NO WAY THIS ENDS WELL, LAURA.
NO SHIT.

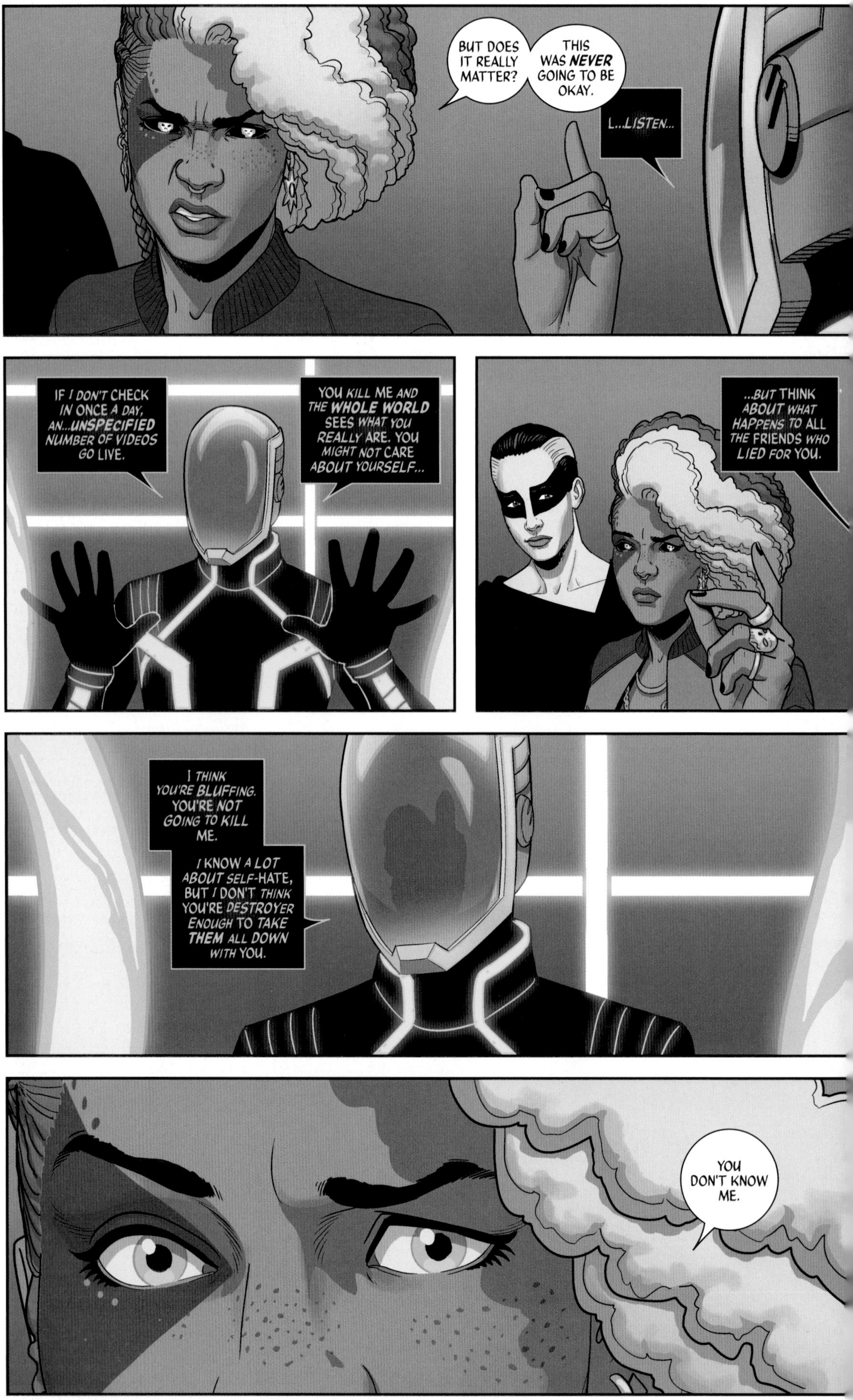
BUT DOES IT REALLY MATTER?
THIS WAS NEVER GOING TO BE OKAY.
L...LISTEN...
IF I DON'T CHECK IN ONCE A DAY, AN...UNSPECIFIED NUMBER OF VIDEOS GO LIVE.
YOU KILL ME AND THE WHOLE WORLD SEES WHAT YOU REALLY ARE. YOU MIGHT NOT CARE ABOUT YOURSELF...
...BUT THINK ABOUT WHAT HAPPENS TO ALL THE FRIENDS WHO LIED FOR YOU.
I THINK YOU'RE BLUFFING. YOU'RE NOT GOING TO KILL ME.
I KNOW A LOT ABOUT SELF-HATE, BUT I DON'T THINK YOU'RE DESTROYER ENOUGH TO TAKE THEM ALL DOWN WITH YOU.
YOU DON'T KNOW ME.

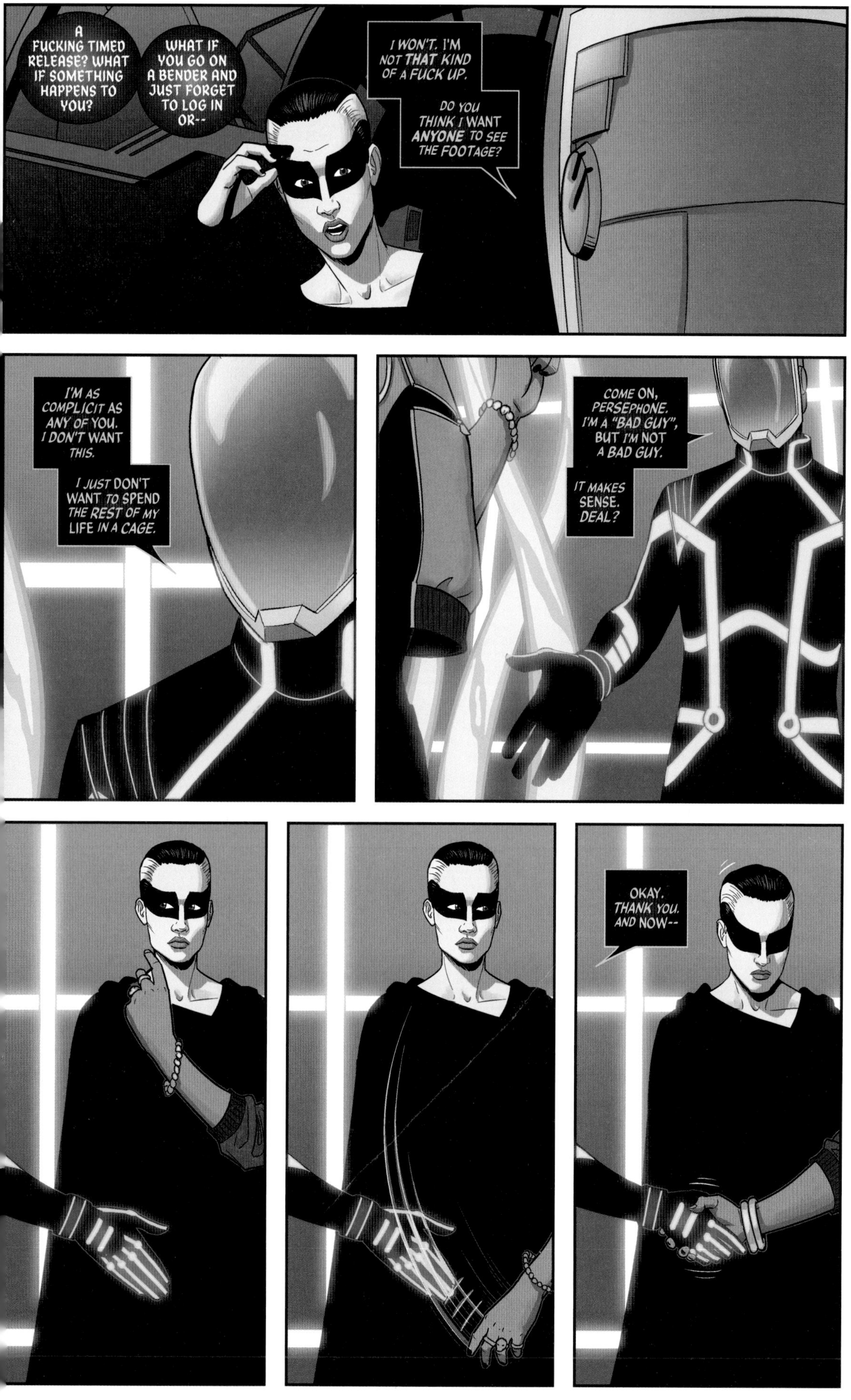
A FUCKING TIMED RELEASE? WHAT IF SOMETHING HAPPENS TO YOU?
WHAT IF YOU GO ON A BENDER AND JUST FORGET TO LOG IN OR--
I WON'T. I'M NOT THAT KIND OF A FUCK UP.
DO YOU THINK I WANT ANYONE TO SEE THE FOOTAGE?
I'M AS COMPLICIT AS ANY OF YOU. I DON'T WANT THIS.
I JUST DON'T WANT TO SPEND THE REST OF MY LIFE IN A CAGE.
COME ON, PERSEPHONE. I'M A "BAD GUY", BUT I'M NOT A BAD GUY.
IT MAKES SENSE. DEAL?
OKAY. THANK YOU. AND NOW--

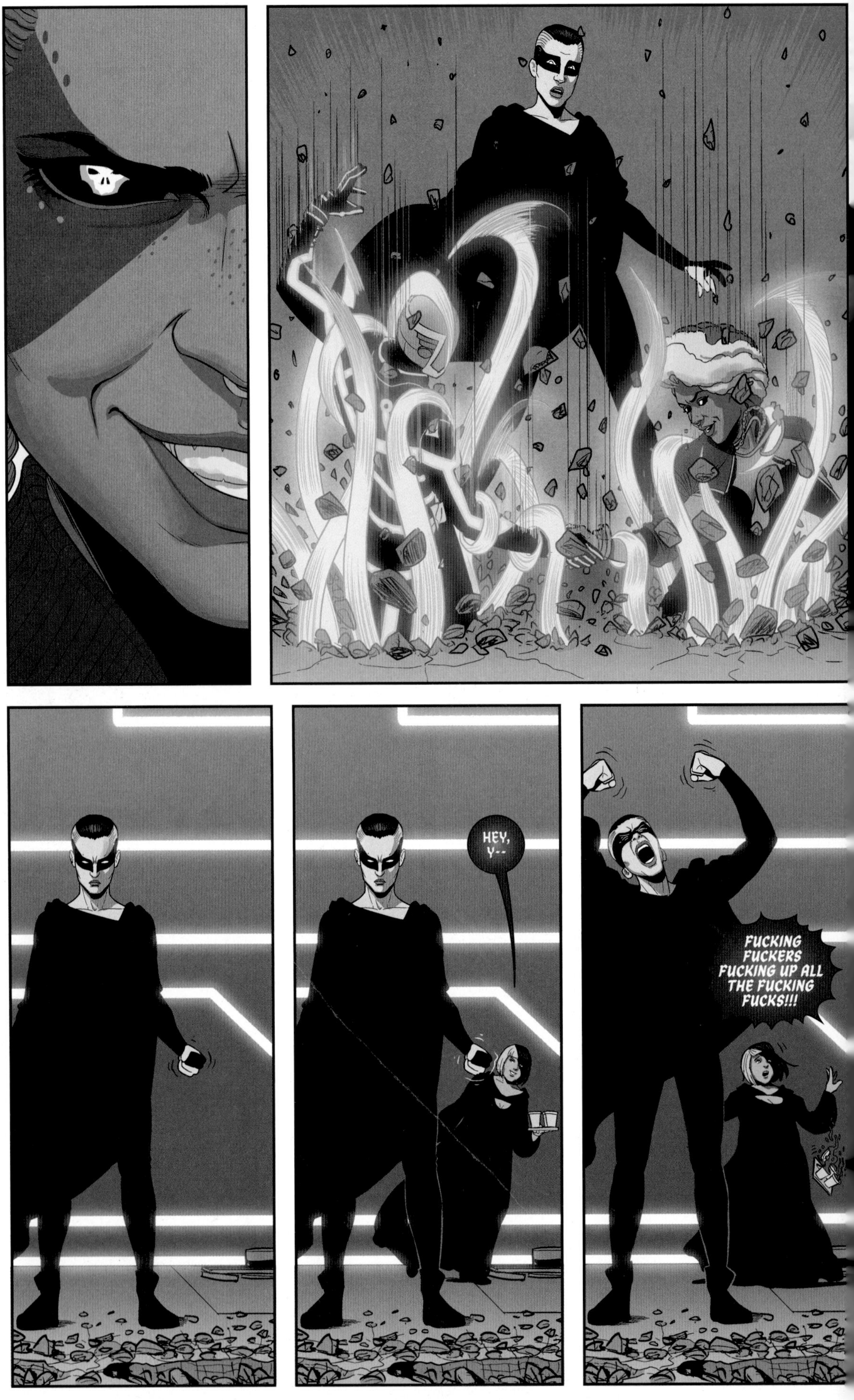
HEY, Y--
FUCKING FUCKERS FUCKING UP ALL THE FUCKING FUCKS!!!

RIDDLES IN THE DARK

1 JANUARY 2015

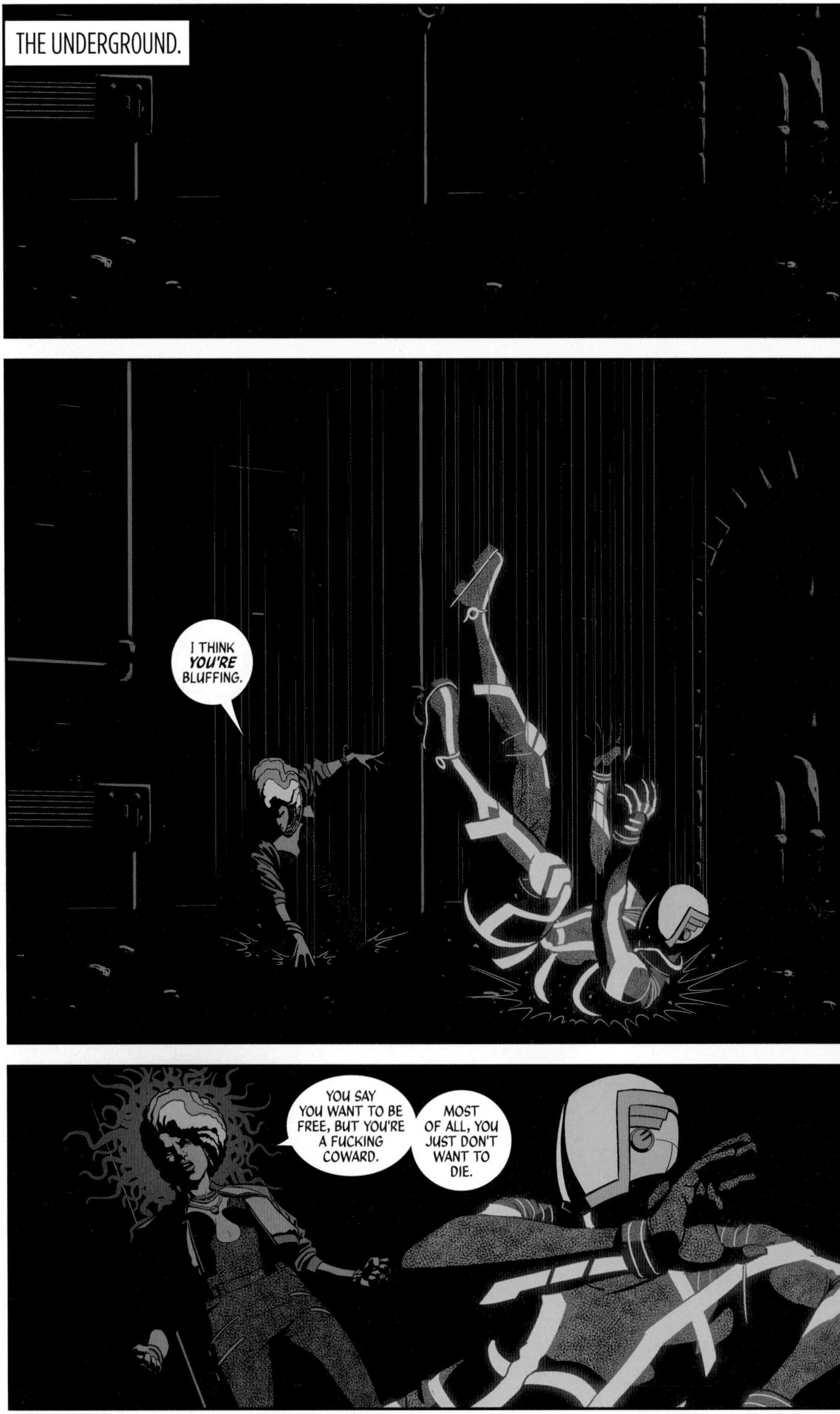
THE UNDERGROUND.
I THINK YOU'RE BLUFFING.
YOU SAY YOU WANT TO BE FREE, BUT YOU'RE A FUCKING COWARD.
MOST OF ALL, YOU JUST DON'T WANT TO DIE.

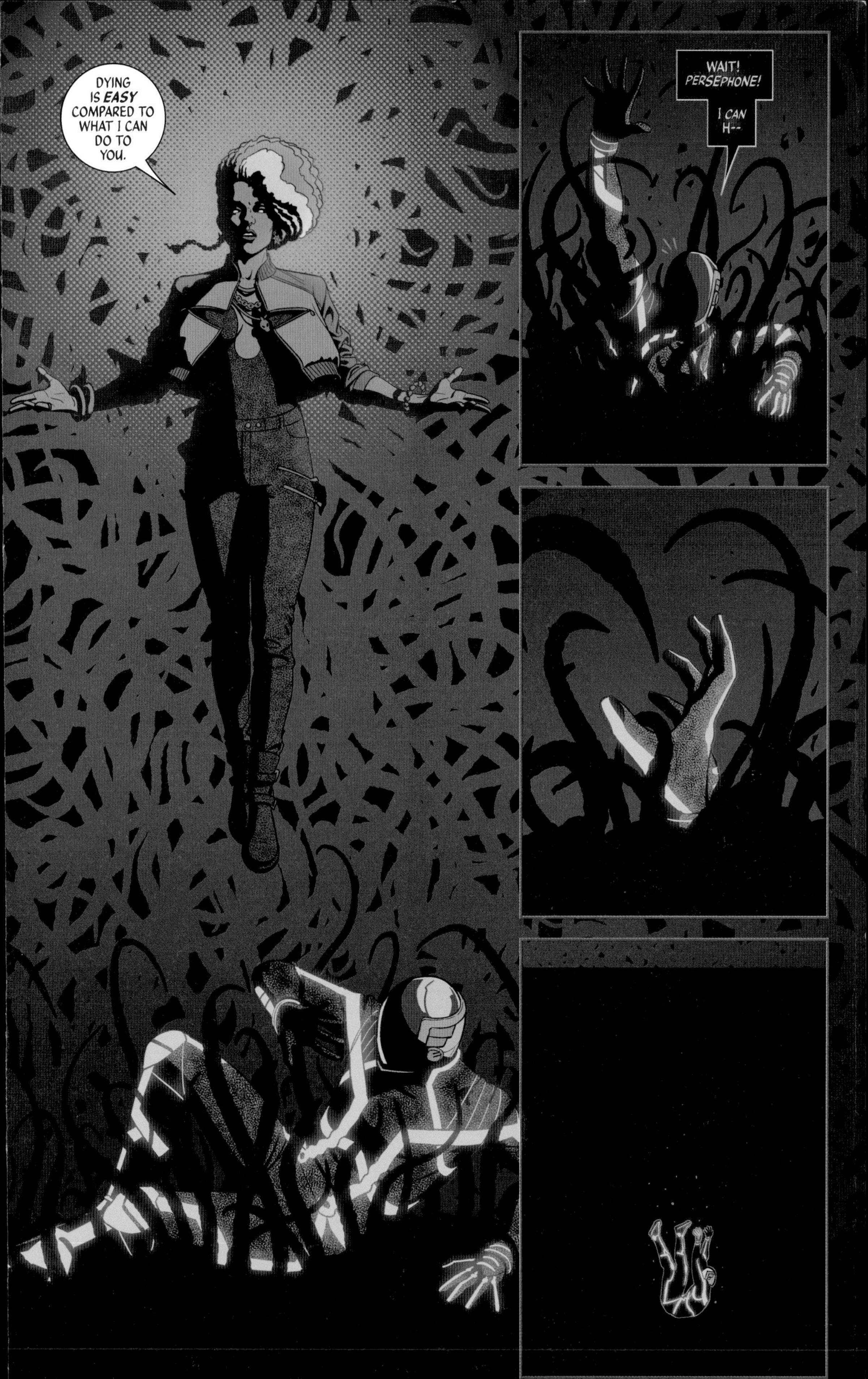
DYING IS *EASY* COMPARED TO WHAT I CAN DO TO YOU.
WAIT! *PERSEPHONE!*
I *CAN* H--

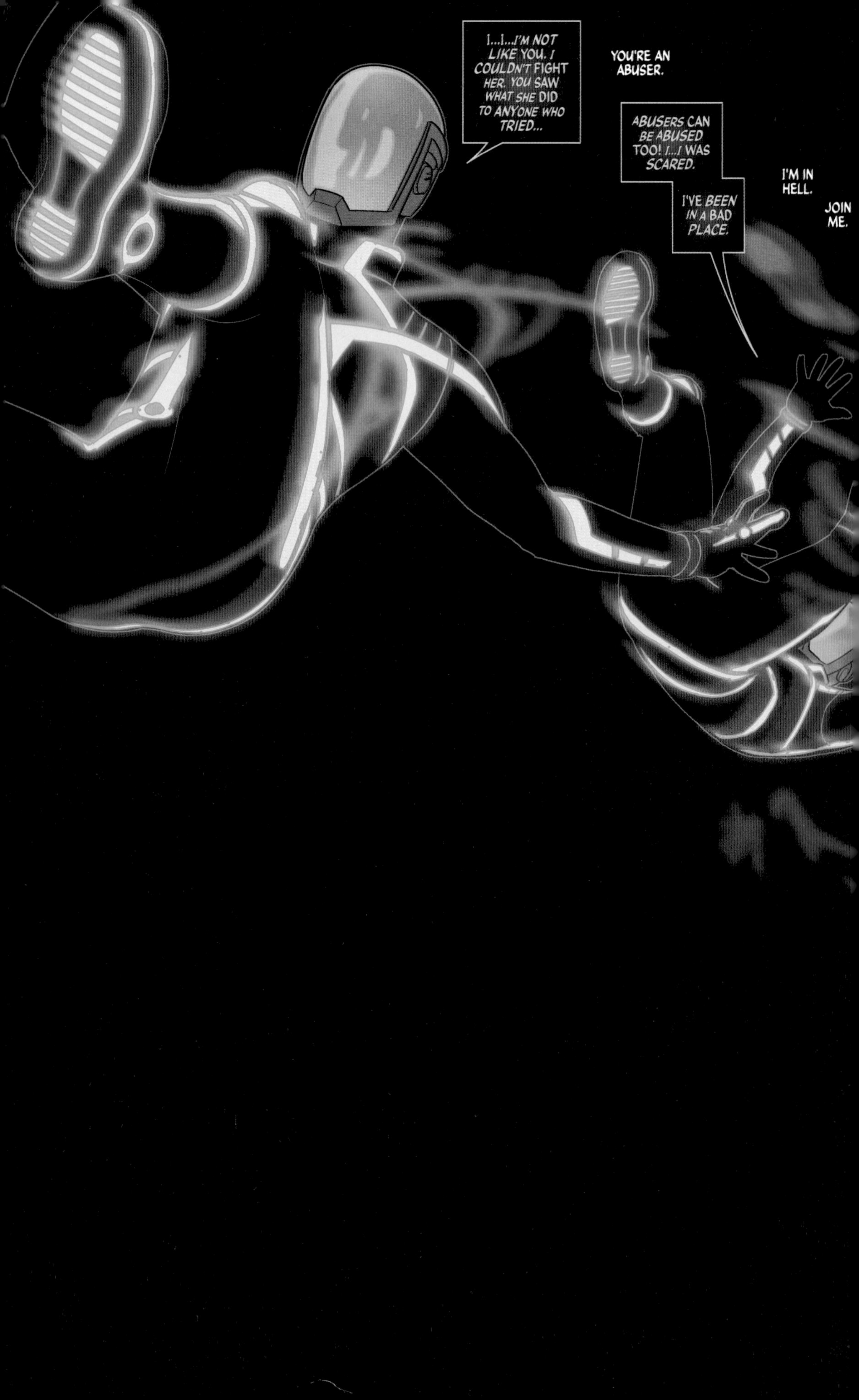
I...I...I'M NOT LIKE YOU. I COULDN'T FIGHT HER. YOU SAW WHAT SHE DID TO ANYONE WHO TRIED...
YOU'RE AN ABUSER.
ABUSERS CAN BE ABUSED TOO! I...I WAS SCARED.
I'VE BEEN IN A BAD PLACE.
I'M IN HELL.
JOIN ME.

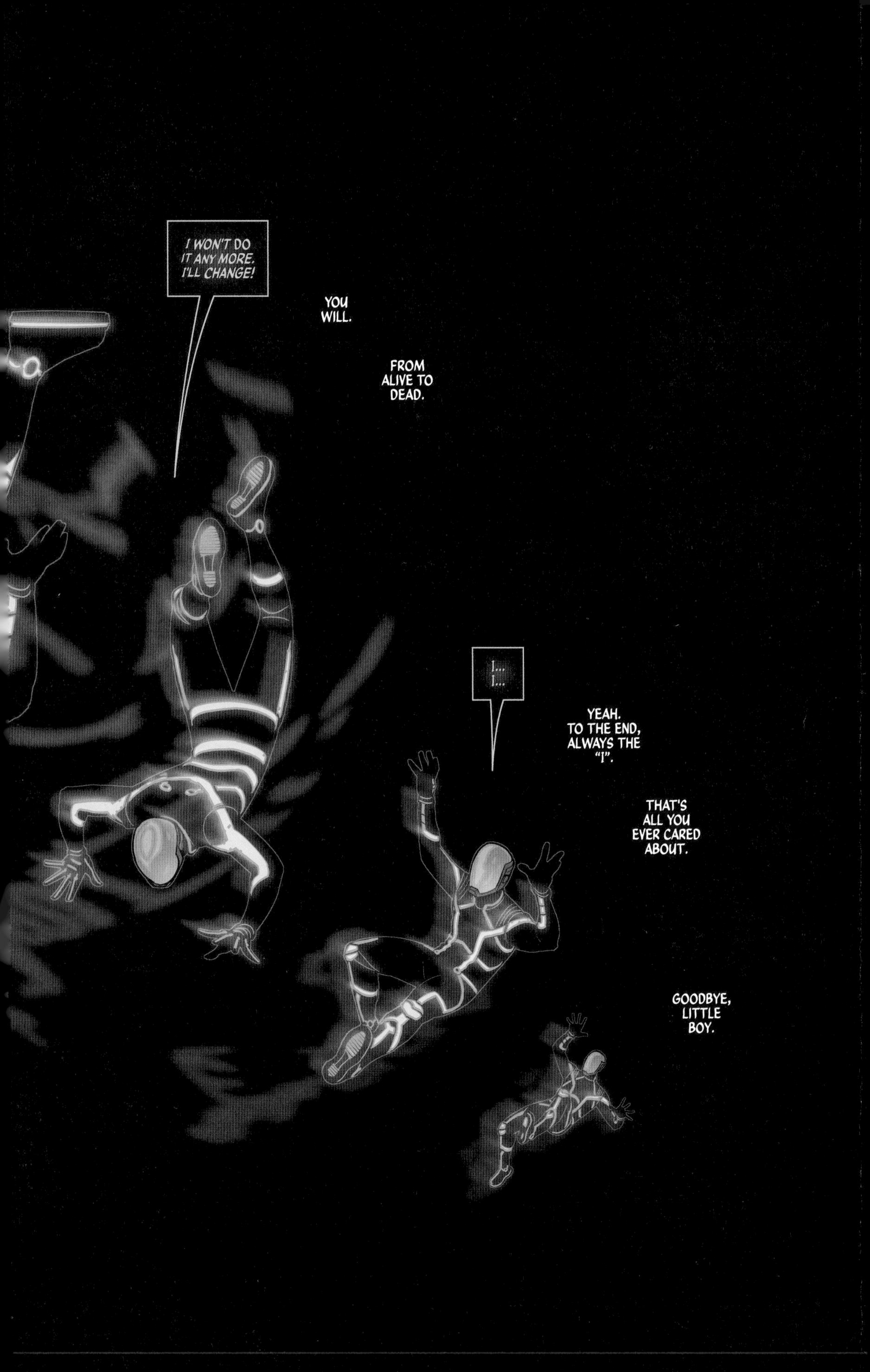
I WON'T DO IT ANY MORE. I'LL CHANGE!
YOU WILL.
FROM ALIVE TO DEAD.
I... I...
YEAH. TO THE END, ALWAYS THE "I".
THAT'S ALL YOU EVER CARED ABOUT.
GOODBYE, LITTLE BOY.

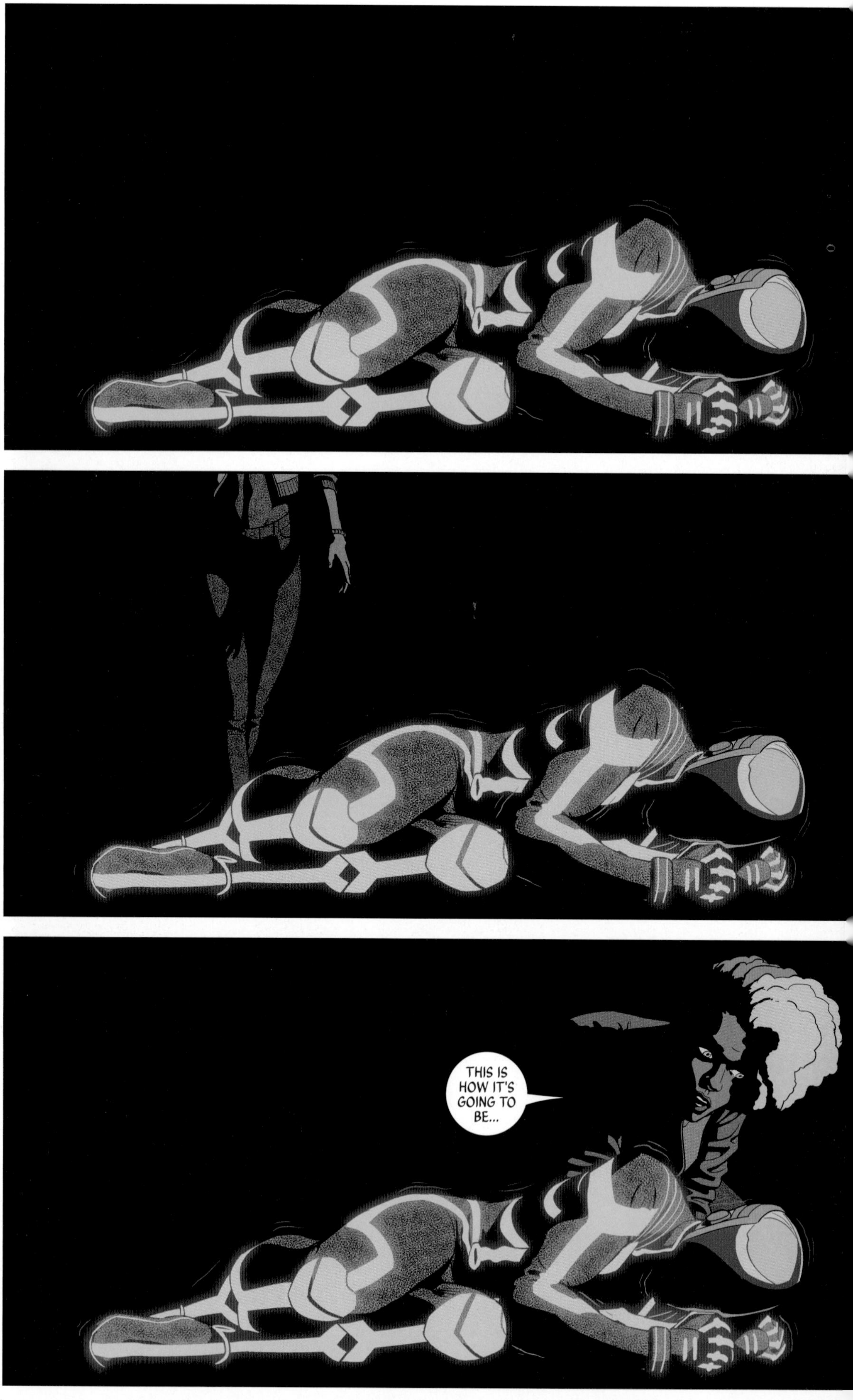
THIS IS HOW IT'S GOING TO BE...

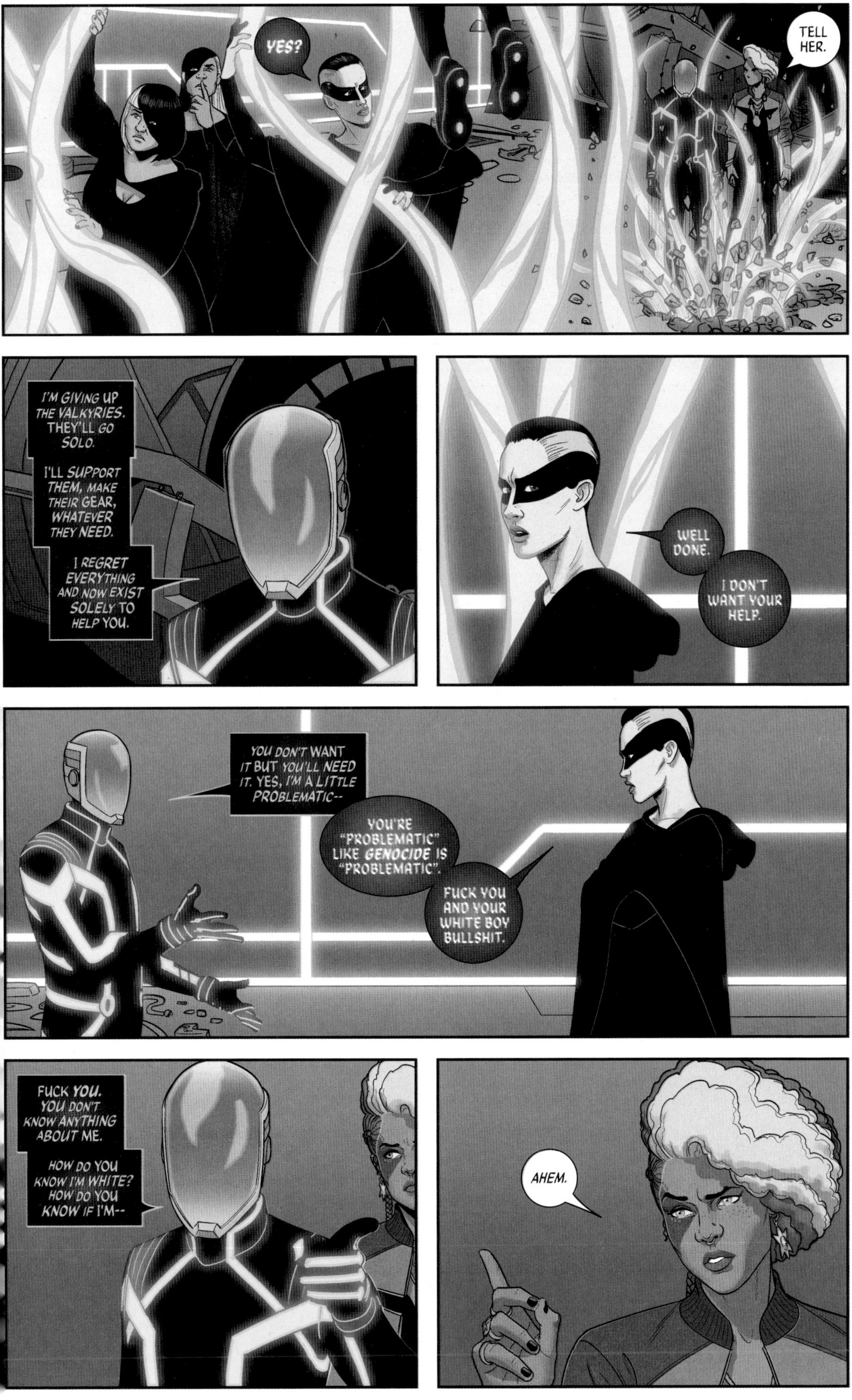
YES?
TELL HER.
I'M GIVING UP THE VALKYRIES. THEY'LL GO SOLO.
I'LL SUPPORT THEM, MAKE THEIR GEAR, WHATEVER THEY NEED.
I REGRET EVERYTHING AND NOW EXIST SOLELY TO HELP YOU.
WELL DONE.
I DON'T WANT YOUR HELP.
YOU DON'T WANT IT BUT YOU'LL NEED IT. YES, I'M A LITTLE PROBLEMATIC--
YOU'RE "PROBLEMATIC" LIKE GENOCIDE IS "PROBLEMATIC".
FUCK YOU AND YOUR WHITE BOY BULLSHIT.
FUCK YOU. YOU DON'T KNOW ANYTHING ABOUT ME.
HOW DO YOU KNOW I'M WHITE? HOW DO YOU KNOW IF I'M--
AHEM.

LISTEN. WE'RE THE CLEVER, PRACTICAL TWO. BAAL IS PRACTICAL. MINERVA IS CLEVER. WE'RE BOTH.

WHO ELSE IS GOING TO WORK OUT WHAT'S GOING ON? SAKHMET? DIONYSUS? I THINK AMATERASU ONLY WEARS SANDALS SO MUCH BECAUSE SHE HAS TROUBLE WITH SHOELACES...

AND I AM...?

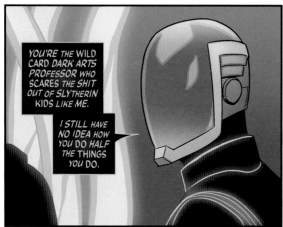

YOU'RE THE WILD CARD DARK ARTS PROFESSOR WHO SCARES THE SHIT OUT OF SLYTHERIN KIDS LIKE ME.

I STILL HAVE NO IDEA HOW YOU DO HALF THE THINGS YOU DO.

ME NEITHER. YOU'RE THE ONLY GOD WHO'S EVER AFFECTED ME. WHY?

YOU PROJECTED A PERFORMANCE THROUGH OWLY...

SHE DID? THAT'S IMPOSSIBLE.

AND...YOU SAID SOMETHING HAPPENED AFTER LUCIFER DIED.

WHAT WAS THAT?

NOTHING IMPORTANT.

SEE! THAT'S THE SORT OF ENIGMATIC WANKERY WE HAVEN'T GOT TIME FOR WHEN WE'RE ALL GOING TO BE DEAD WITHIN TWO YEARS!

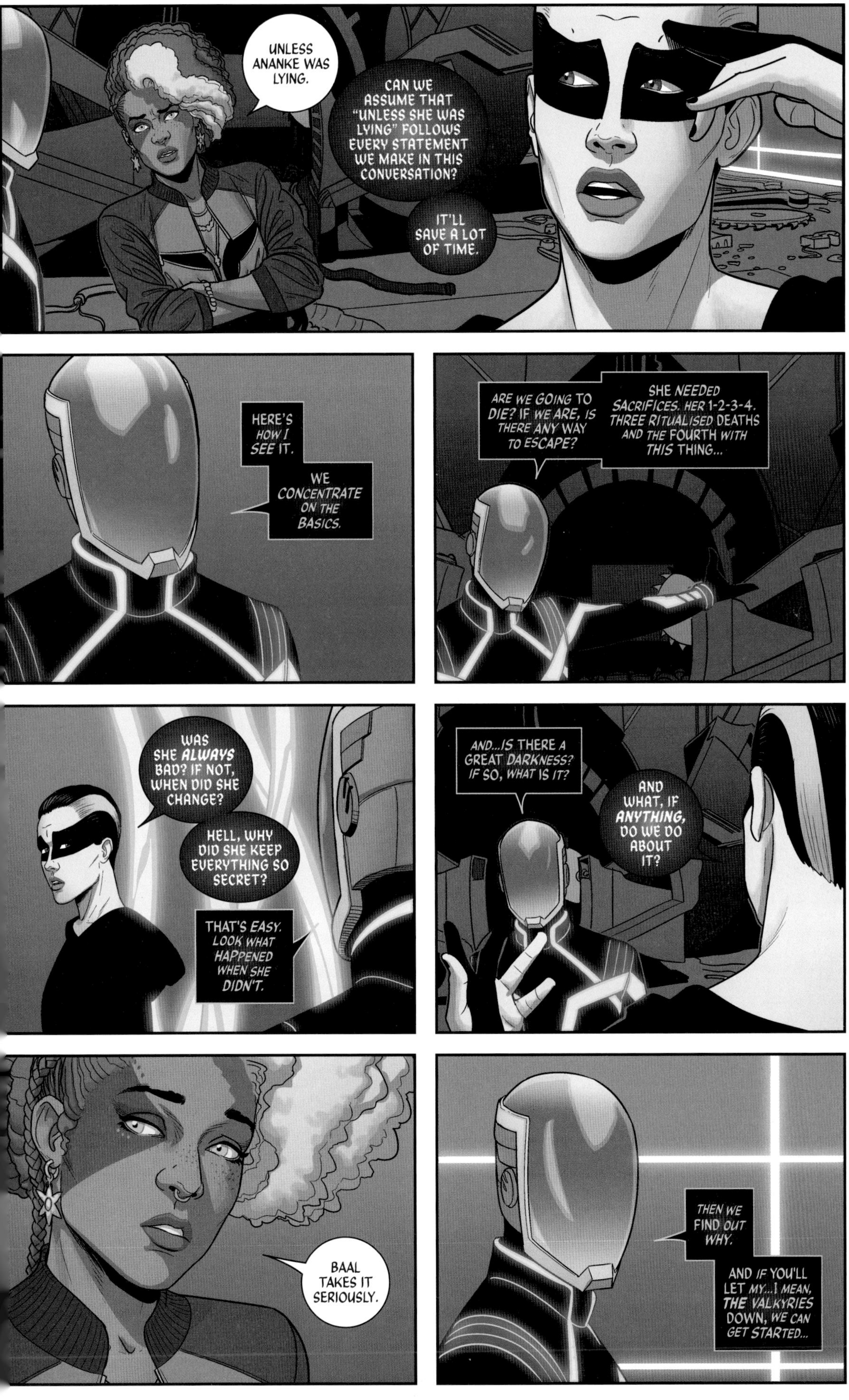
UNLESS ANANKE WAS LYING.
CAN WE ASSUME THAT "UNLESS SHE WAS LYING" FOLLOWS EVERY STATEMENT WE MAKE IN THIS CONVERSATION?
IT'LL SAVE A LOT OF TIME.
HERE'S HOW I SEE IT.
WE CONCENTRATE ON THE BASICS.
ARE WE GOING TO DIE? IF WE ARE, IS THERE ANY WAY TO ESCAPE?
SHE NEEDED SACRIFICES. HER 1-2-3-4. THREE RITUALISED DEATHS AND THE FOURTH WITH THIS THING...
WAS SHE ALWAYS BAD? IF NOT, WHEN DID SHE CHANGE?
HELL, WHY DID SHE KEEP EVERYTHING SO SECRET?
THAT'S EASY. LOOK WHAT HAPPENED WHEN SHE DIDN'T.
AND...IS THERE A GREAT DARKNESS? IF SO, WHAT IS IT?
AND WHAT, IF ANYTHING, DO WE DO ABOUT IT?
BAAL TAKES IT SERIOUSLY.
THEN WE FIND OUT WHY.
AND IF YOU'LL LET MY...I MEAN, THE VALKYRIES DOWN, WE CAN GET STARTED...

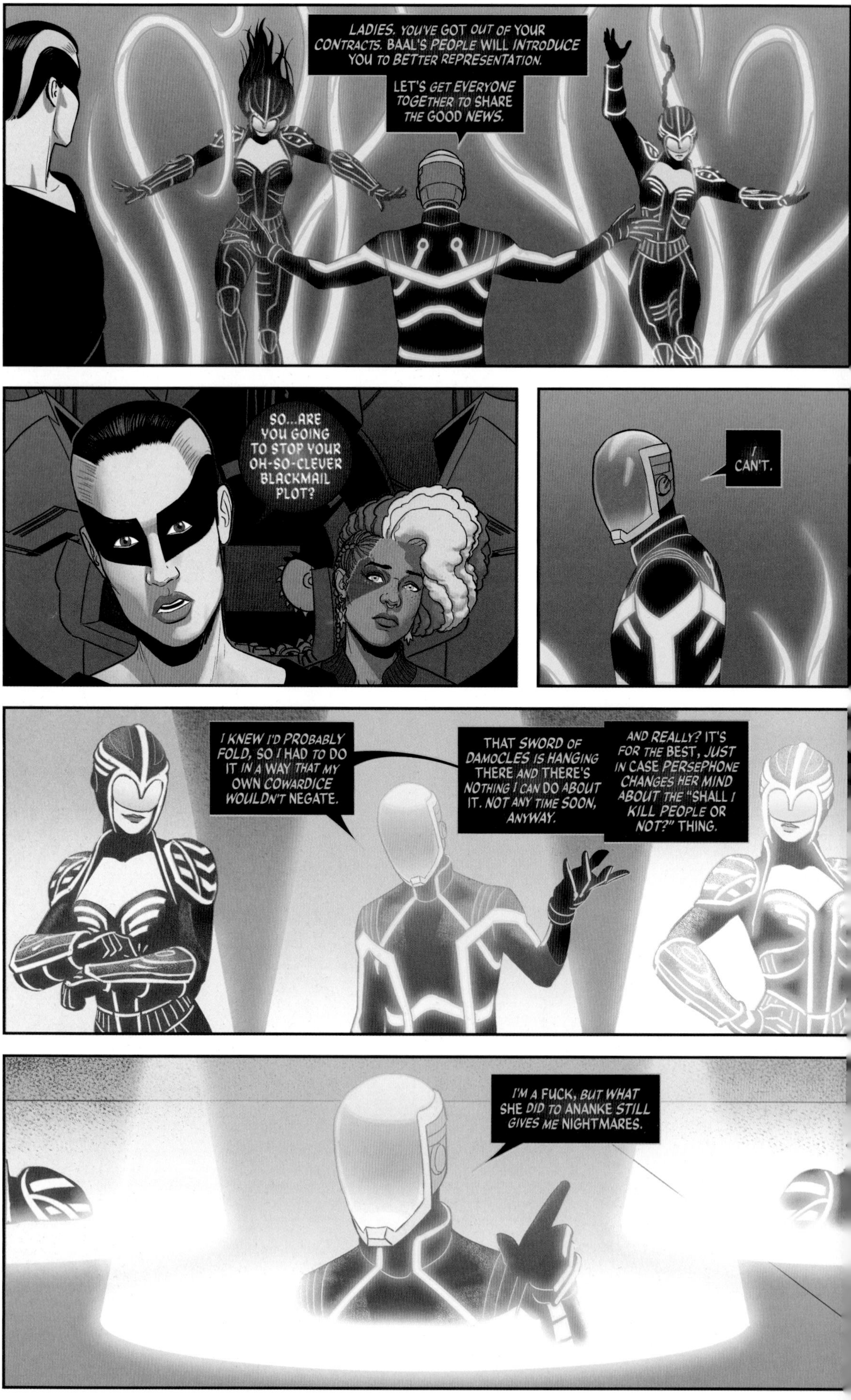

LADIES. YOU'VE GOT OUT OF YOUR CONTRACTS. BAAL'S PEOPLE WILL INTRODUCE YOU TO BETTER REPRESENTATION.
LET'S GET EVERYONE TOGETHER TO SHARE THE GOOD NEWS.
SO...ARE YOU GOING TO STOP YOUR OH-SO-CLEVER BLACKMAIL PLOT?
I CAN'T.
I KNEW I'D PROBABLY FOLD, SO I HAD TO DO IT IN A WAY THAT MY OWN COWARDICE WOULDN'T NEGATE.
THAT SWORD OF DAMOCLES IS HANGING THERE AND THERE'S NOTHING I CAN DO ABOUT IT. NOT ANY TIME SOON, ANYWAY.
AND REALLY? IT'S FOR THE BEST, JUST IN CASE PERSEPHONE CHANGES HER MIND ABOUT THE "SHALL I KILL PEOPLE OR NOT?" THING.
I'M A FUCK, BUT WHAT SHE DID TO ANANKE STILL GIVES ME NIGHTMARES.

‹DEFAULT ELEUSINIA RINGTONE!›
3G
Cass
Before I forget...what the fuck was all that about?
How many people you willing to kill?
I--
3G
Cass
And don't you dare say as many as it takes. It doesn't make you badass.
Wrong question anyway: how many people are you willing to GET killed just by being near you?
Because that's what this means. It escalates.
What kind of person would think that was a good idea, Laura?
12.27
Laura Fangirl
Details
many people are you willing to GET killed just by being near you?
Because that's what this means. It escalates.
What kind of person would think that was a good idea, Laura?
No person.

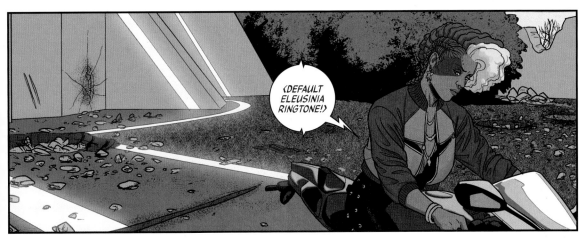

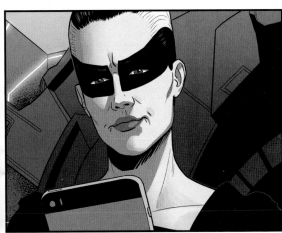

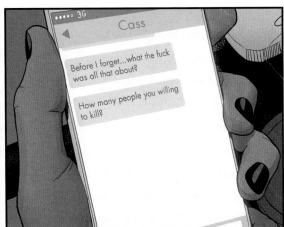

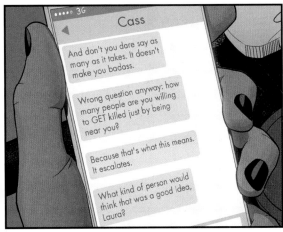

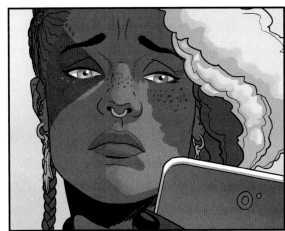

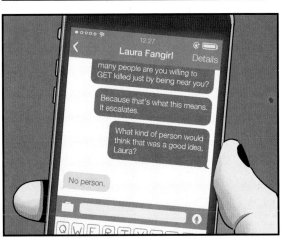

ALL HAPPY
FAMILIES ARE
ALIKE

1 JANUARY 2015

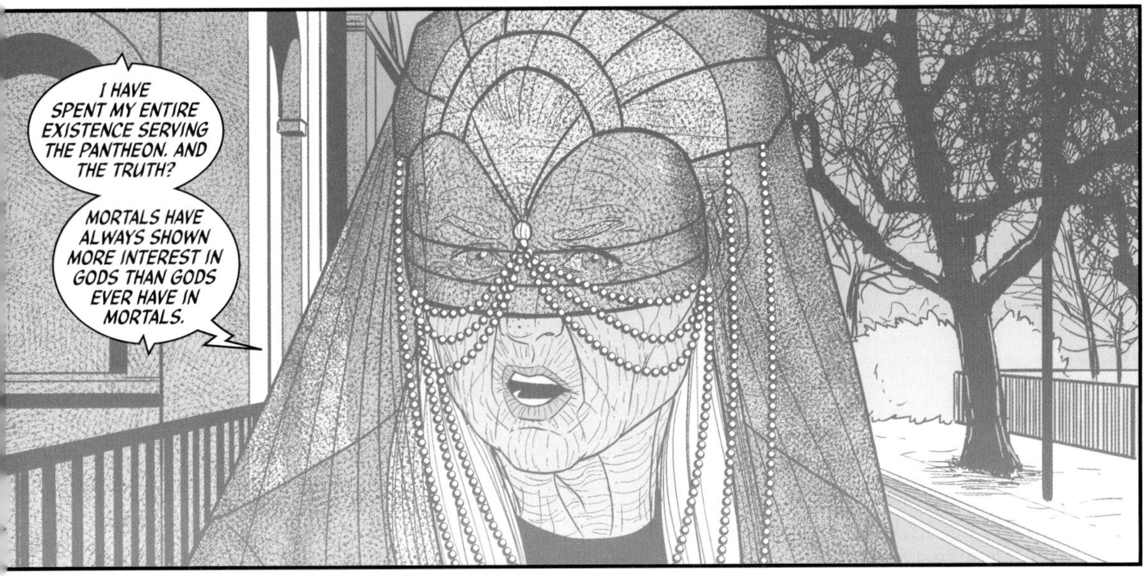
I HAVE SPENT MY ENTIRE EXISTENCE SERVING THE PANTHEON. AND THE TRUTH?
MORTALS HAVE ALWAYS SHOWN MORE INTEREST IN GODS THAN GODS EVER HAVE IN MORTALS.

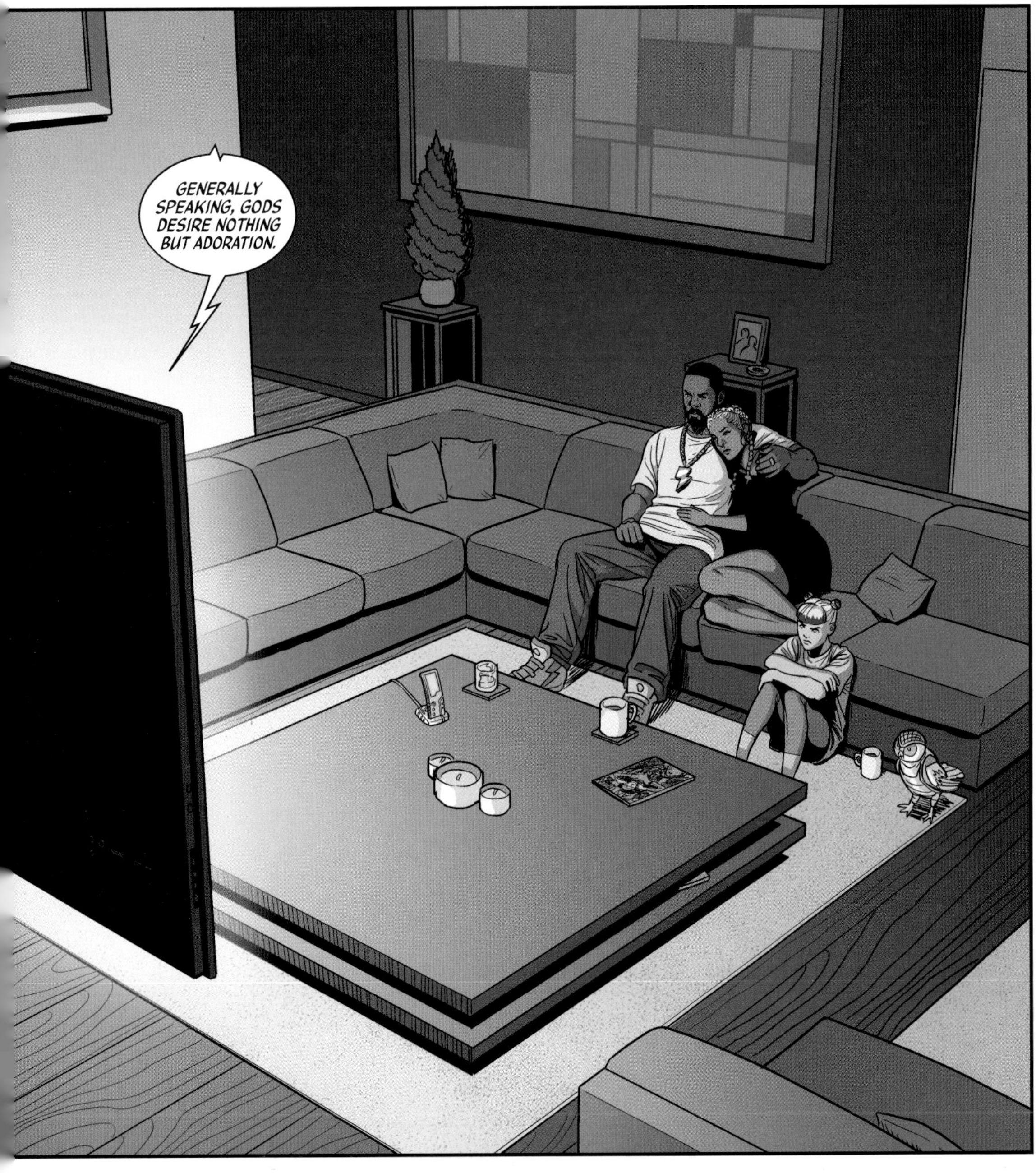
GENERALLY SPEAKING, GODS DESIRE NOTHING BUT ADORATION.

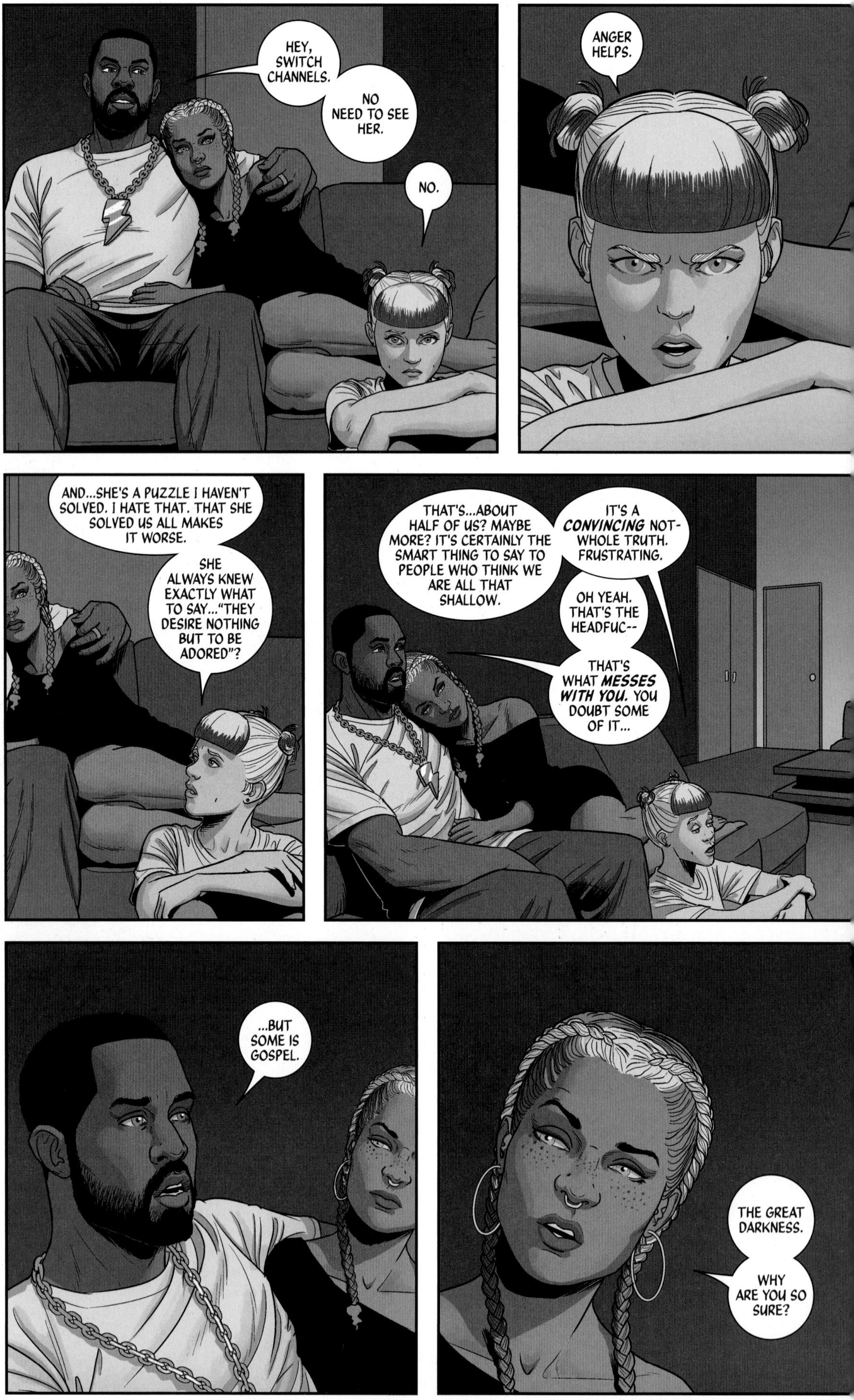
HEY, SWITCH CHANNELS.
NO NEED TO SEE HER.
NO.
ANGER HELPS.
AND...SHE'S A PUZZLE I HAVEN'T SOLVED. I HATE THAT. THAT SHE SOLVED US ALL MAKES IT WORSE.
SHE ALWAYS KNEW EXACTLY WHAT TO SAY..."THEY DESIRE NOTHING BUT TO BE ADORED"?
THAT'S...ABOUT HALF OF US? MAYBE MORE? IT'S CERTAINLY THE SMART THING TO SAY TO PEOPLE WHO THINK WE ARE ALL THAT SHALLOW.
IT'S A CONVINCING NOT-WHOLE TRUTH. FRUSTRATING.
OH YEAH. THAT'S THE HEADFUC--
THAT'S WHAT MESSES WITH YOU. YOU DOUBT SOME OF IT...
...BUT SOME IS GOSPEL.
THE GREAT DARKNESS.
WHY ARE YOU SO SURE?

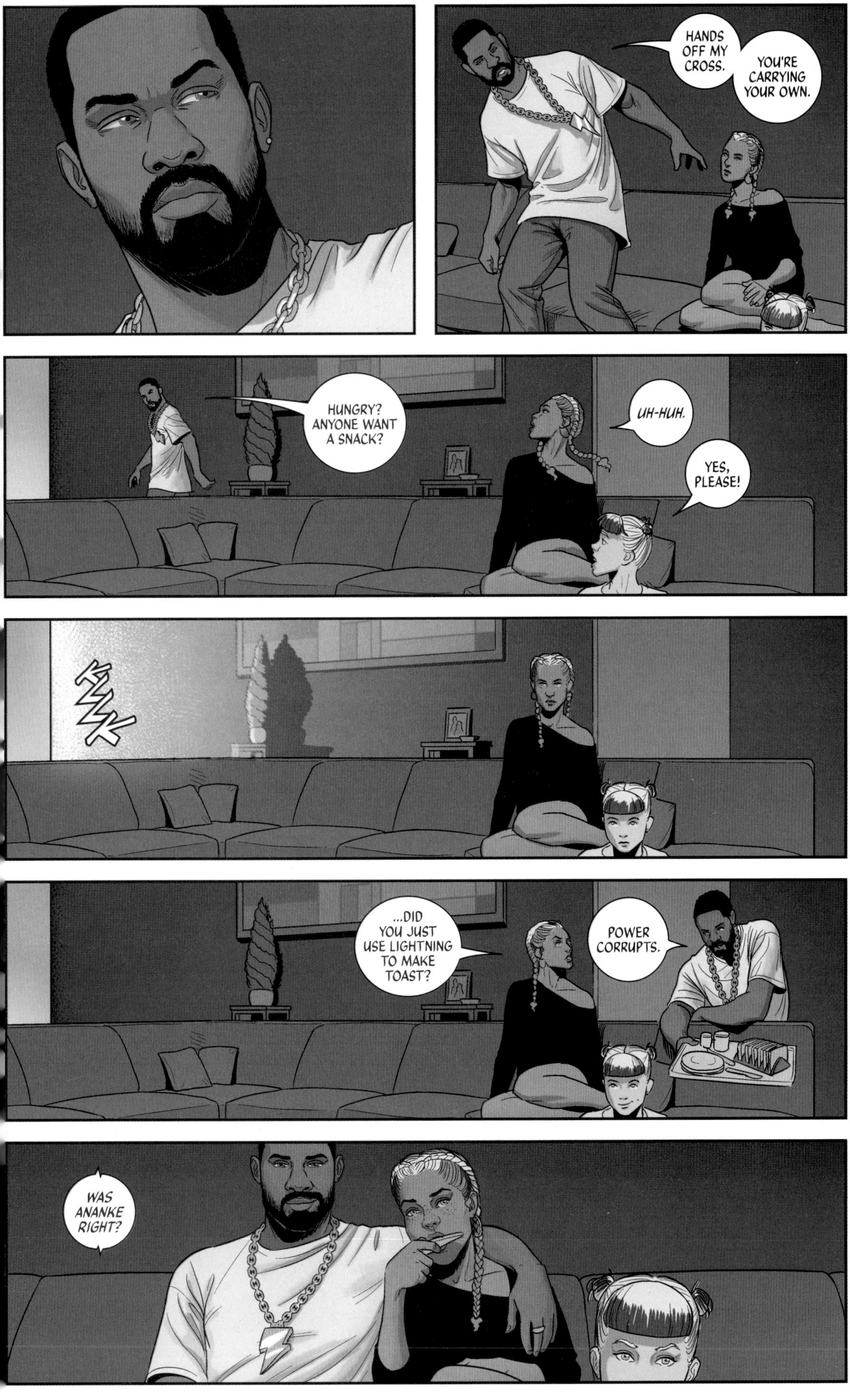
HANDS OFF MY CROSS.
YOU'RE CARRYING YOUR OWN.
HUNGRY? ANYONE WANT A SNACK?
UH-HUH.
YES, PLEASE!
KZZK
...DID YOU JUST USE LIGHTNING TO MAKE TOAST?
POWER CORRUPTS.
WAS ANANKE RIGHT?

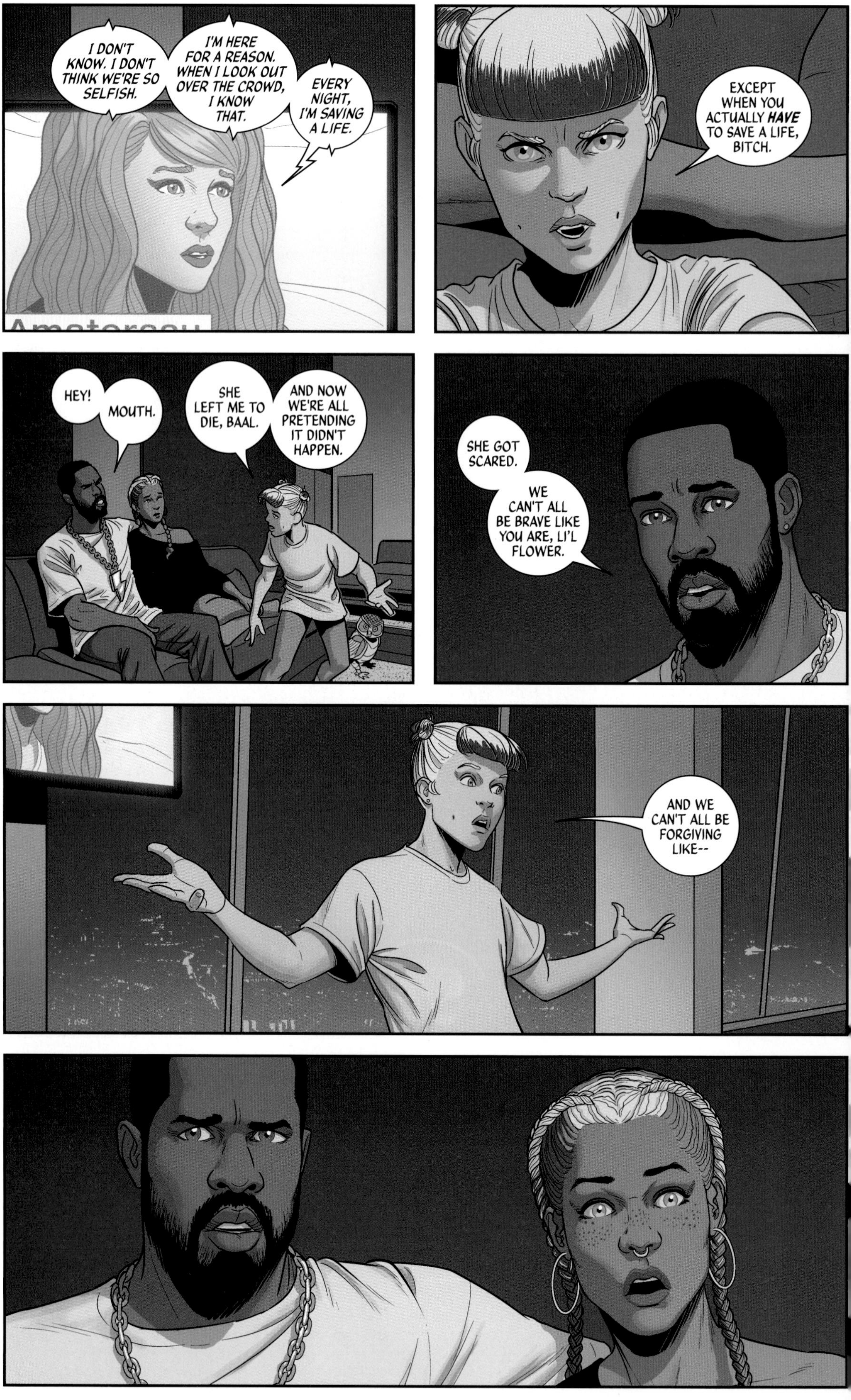
I DON'T KNOW. I DON'T THINK WE'RE SO SELFISH.
I'M HERE FOR A REASON. WHEN I LOOK OUT OVER THE CROWD, I KNOW THAT.
EVERY NIGHT, I'M SAVING A LIFE.
EXCEPT WHEN YOU ACTUALLY **HAVE** TO SAVE A LIFE, BITCH.
HEY!
MOUTH.
SHE LEFT ME TO DIE, BAAL.
AND NOW WE'RE ALL PRETENDING IT DIDN'T HAPPEN.
SHE GOT SCARED.
WE CAN'T ALL BE BRAVE LIKE YOU ARE, LI'L FLOWER.
AND WE CAN'T ALL BE FORGIVING LIKE--

WHAT'S WRONG?

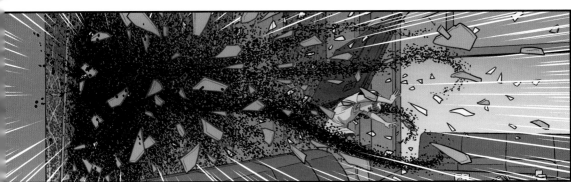

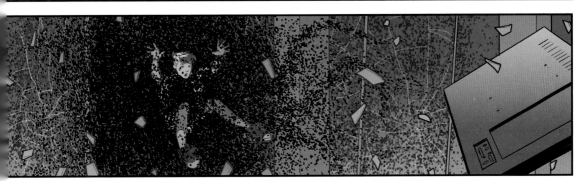

WHY AM I SO SURE THE GREAT DARKNESS EXISTS?

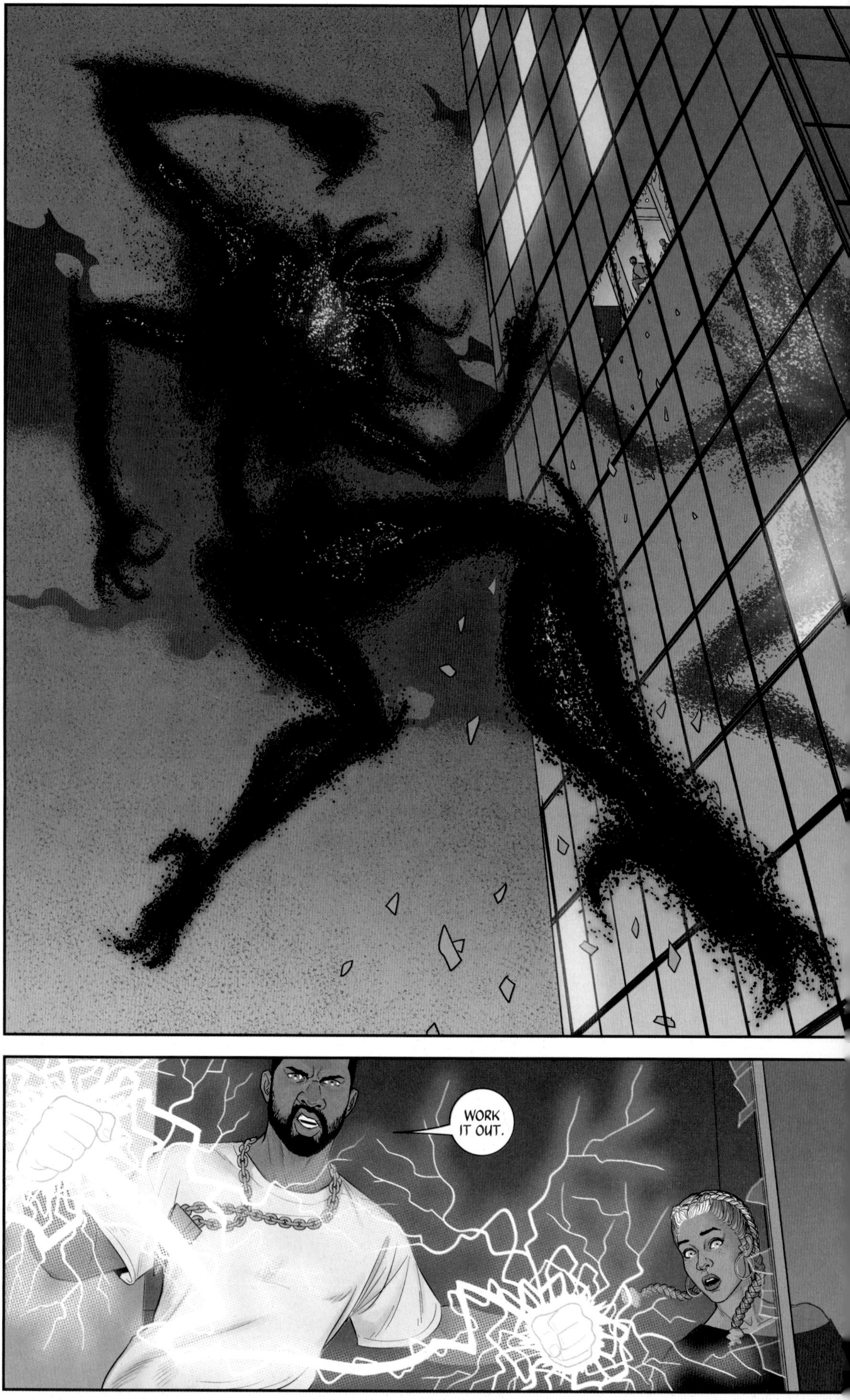
WORK IT OUT.

CHAOTIC EVIL IS
THE NEW BLACK

1 JANUARY 2015

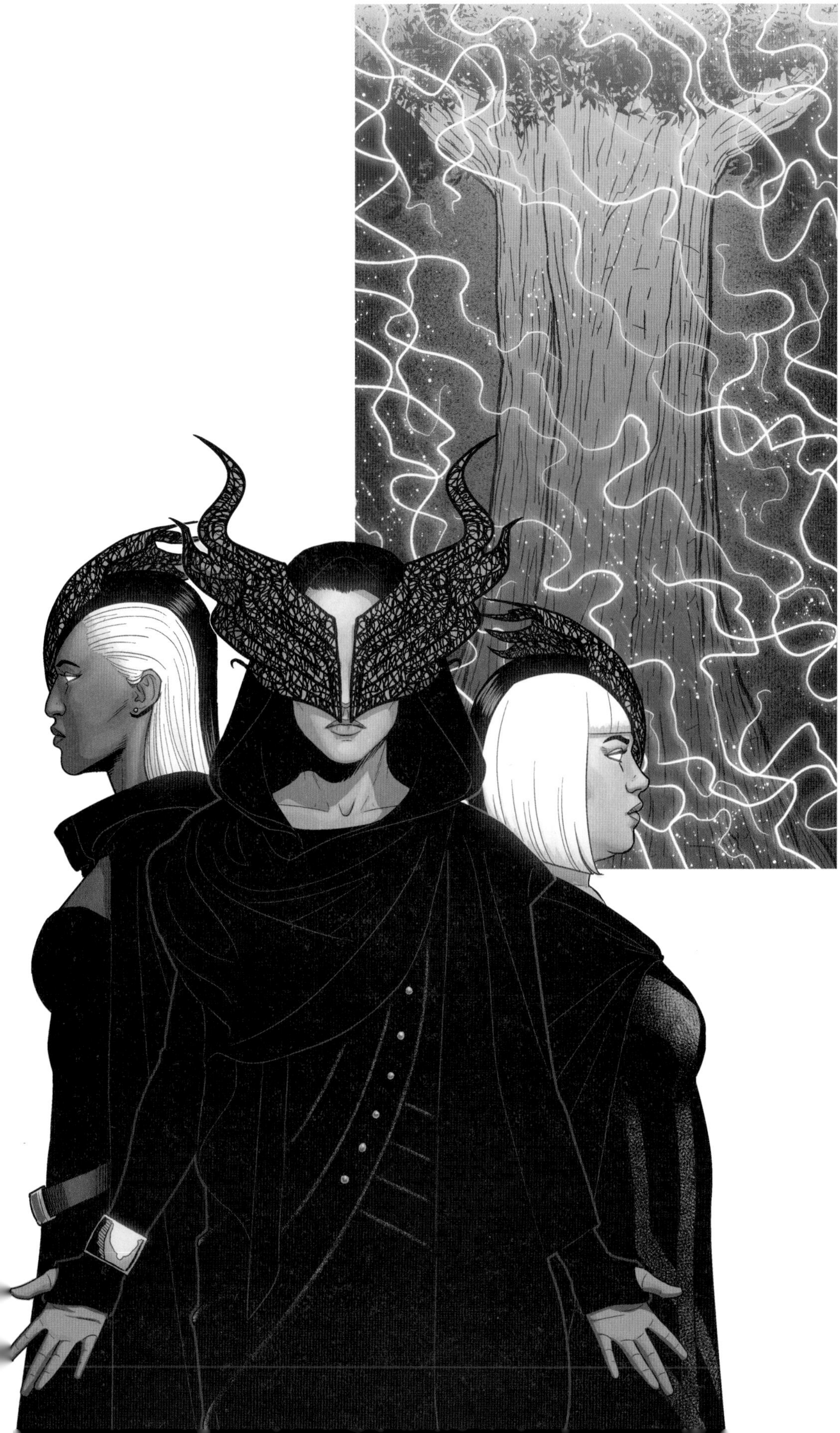

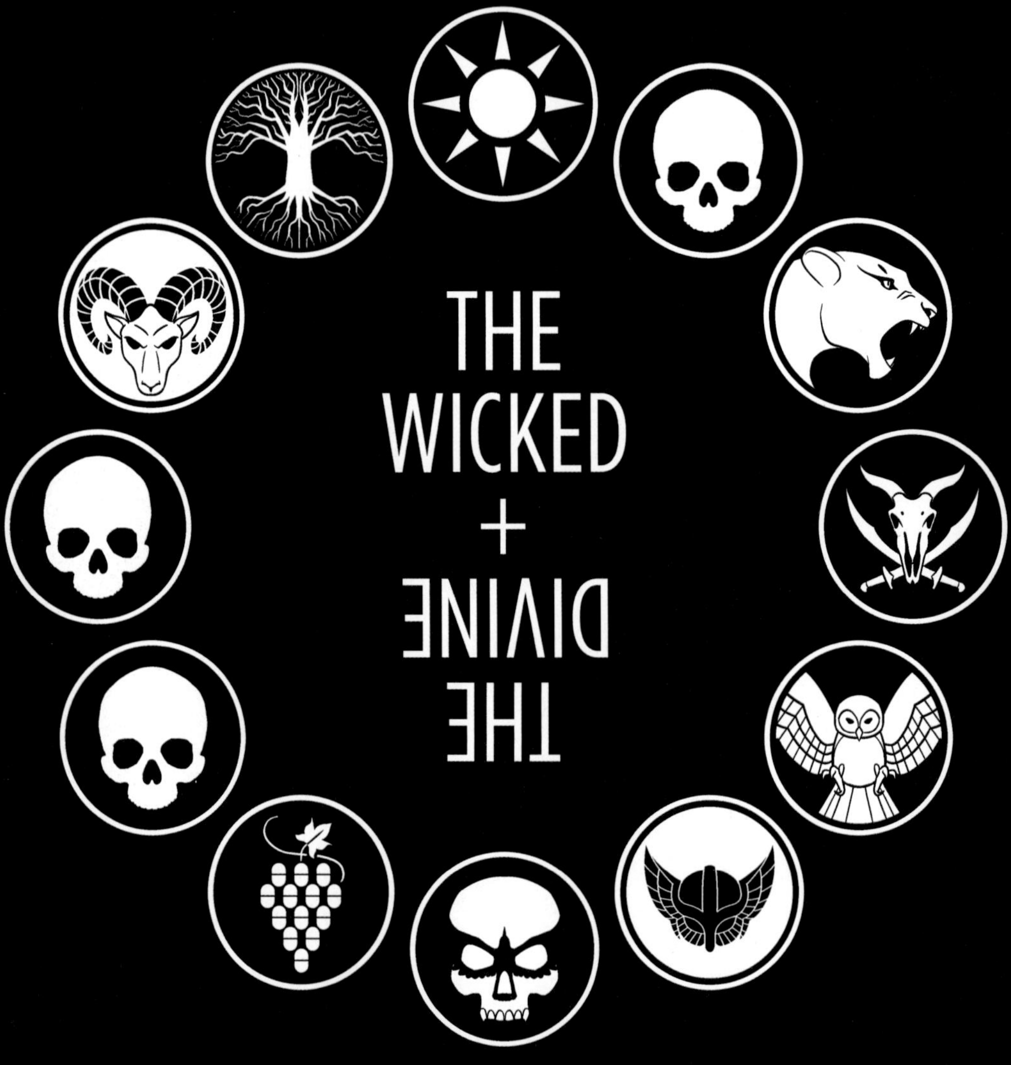
THE
WICKED
+
THE
DIVINE

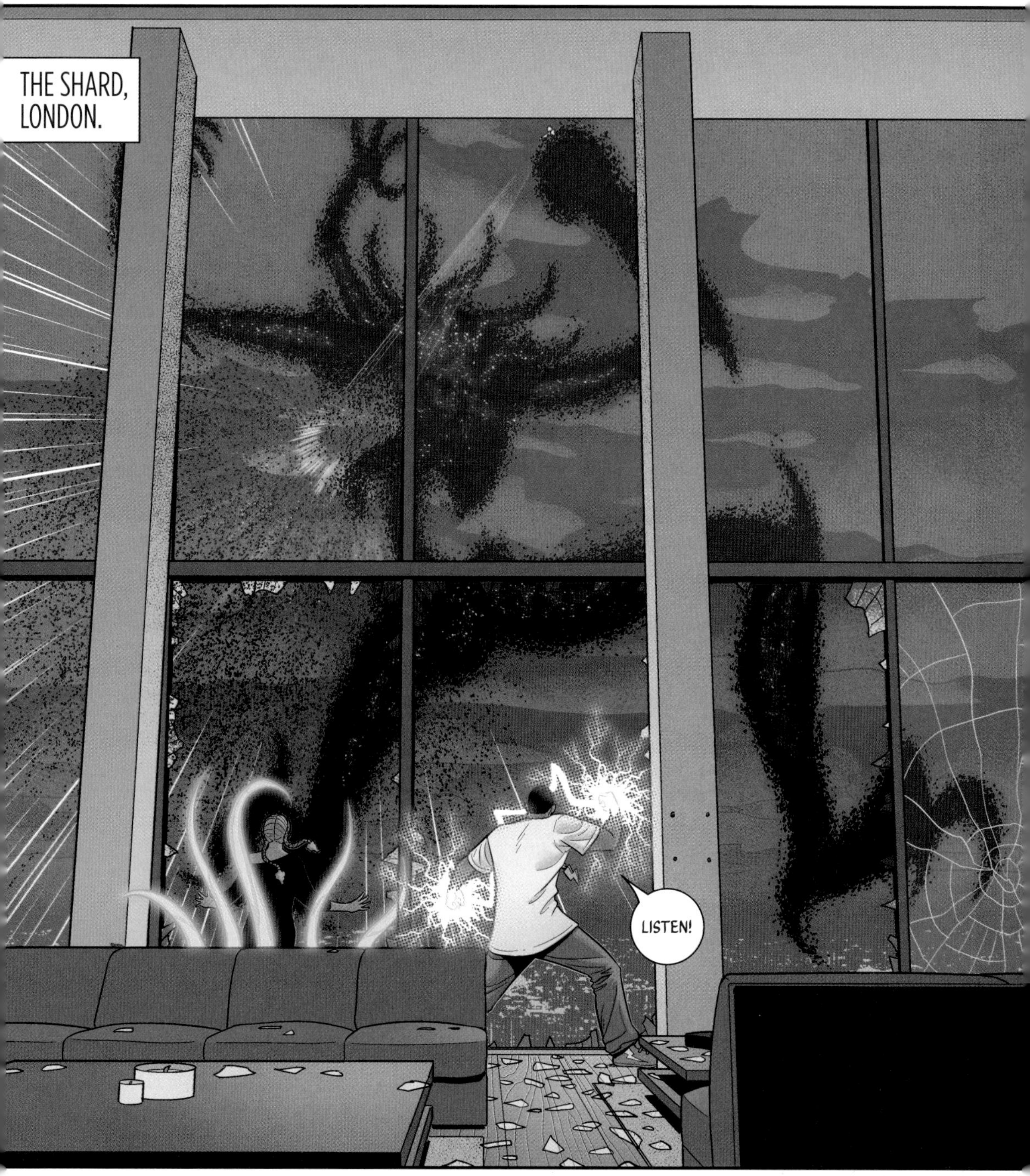
THE SHARD, LONDON.
LISTEN!

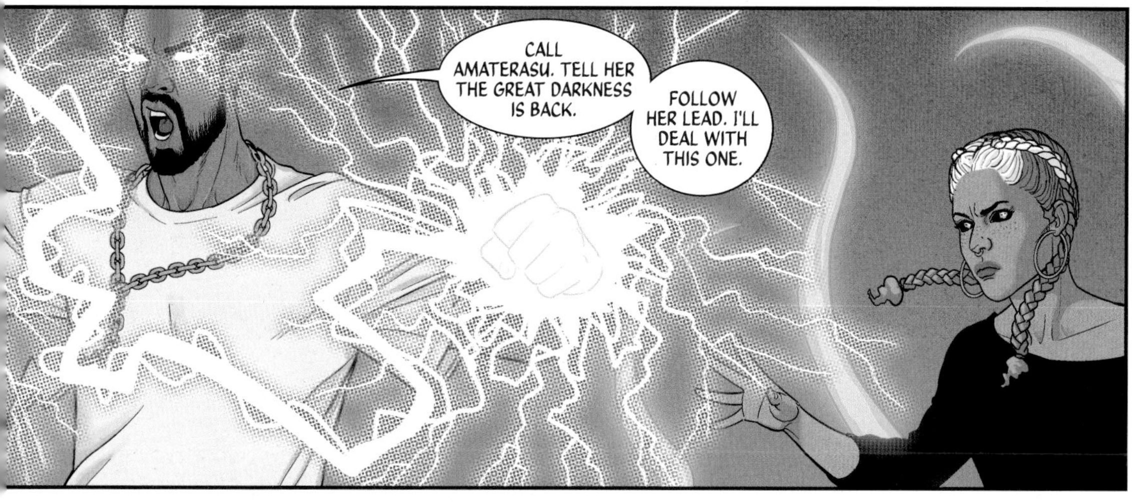
CALL AMATERASU. TELL HER THE GREAT DARKNESS IS BACK.
FOLLOW HER LEAD. I'LL DEAL WITH THIS ONE.

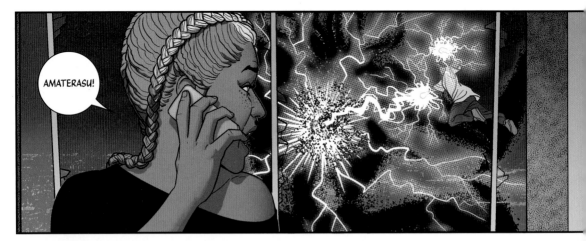

AMATERASU!

HEY, PERSY-POO. I'M WATCHING *THE WALKING DEAD.* I'VE JUST REALISED!

THE *HUMANS* ARE THE WALKING D--

THE GREAT DARKNESS! IT'S HERE!

GOSH.

MUMMY! THAT GLOWING ARM-PIECE!

WHERE DID YOU PUT IT?

≈KLLK≈

HUH?

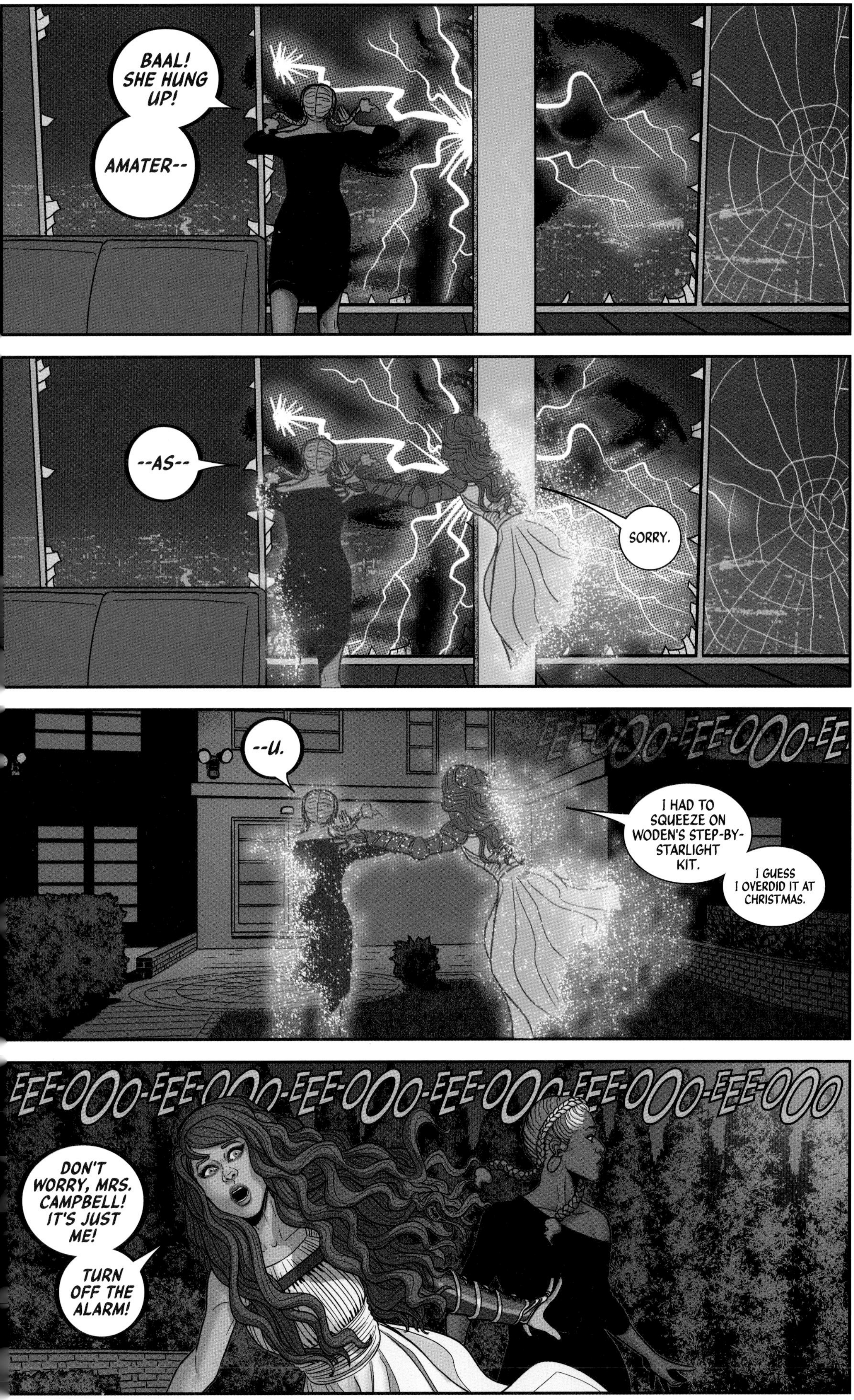
BAAL! SHE HUNG UP!
AMATER--
--AS--
SORRY.
--U.
EEE-OOO-EEE-OOO-EE
I HAD TO SQUEEZE ON WODEN'S STEP-BY-STARLIGHT KIT.
I GUESS I OVERDID IT AT CHRISTMAS.
EEE-OOO-EEE-OOO-EEE-OOO-EEE-OOO-EEE-OOO-EEE-OOO
DON'T WORRY, MRS. CAMPBELL! IT'S JUST ME!
TURN OFF THE ALARM!

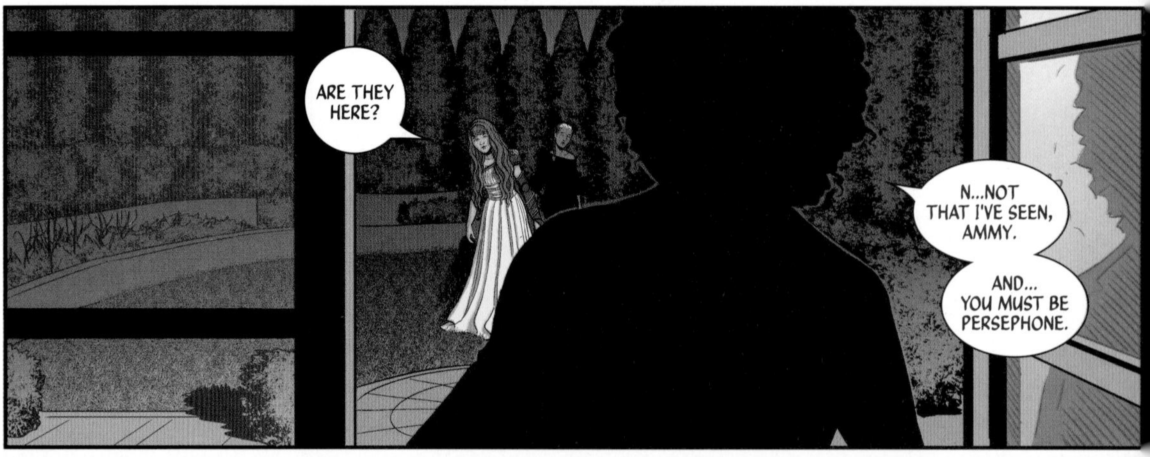
ARE THEY HERE?
N...NOT THAT I'VE SEEN, AMMY.
AND... YOU MUST BE PERSEPHONE.
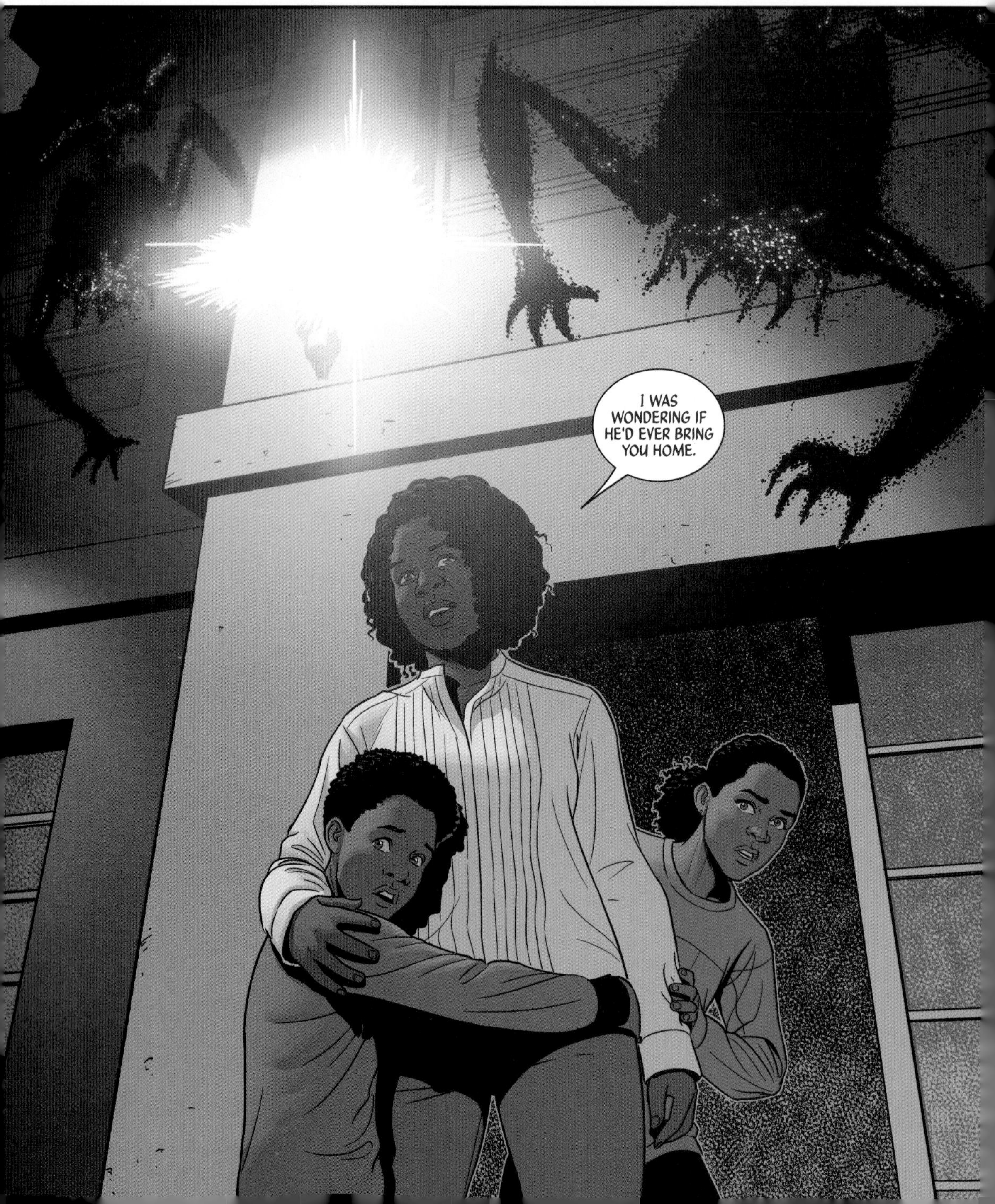
I WAS WONDERING IF HE'D EVER BRING YOU HOME.

PARENTAL
GUIDANCE

1 JANUARY 2015

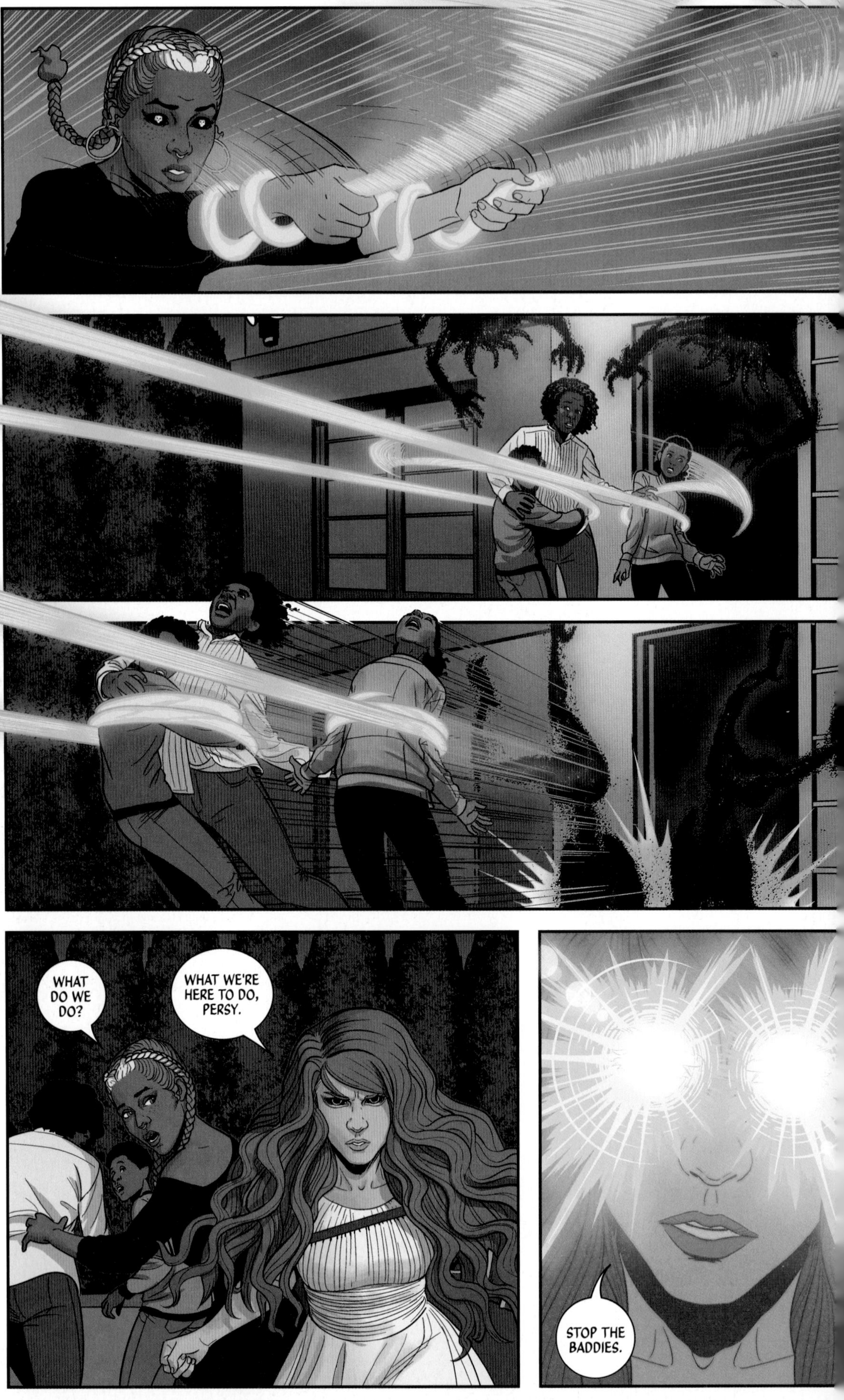
WHAT DO WE DO?
WHAT WE'RE HERE TO DO, PERSY.
STOP THE BADDIES.

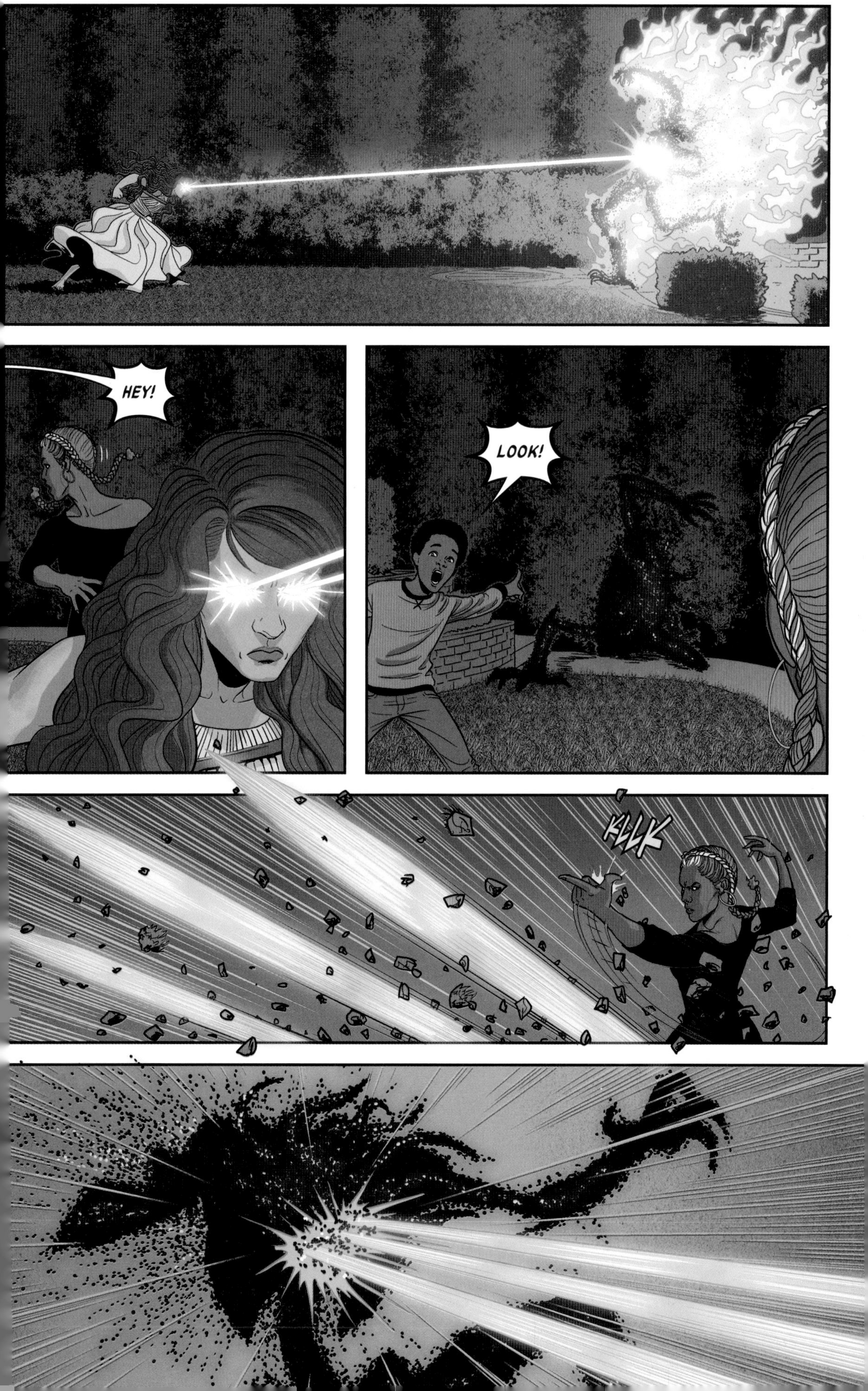
HEY!
LOOK!
KLLK

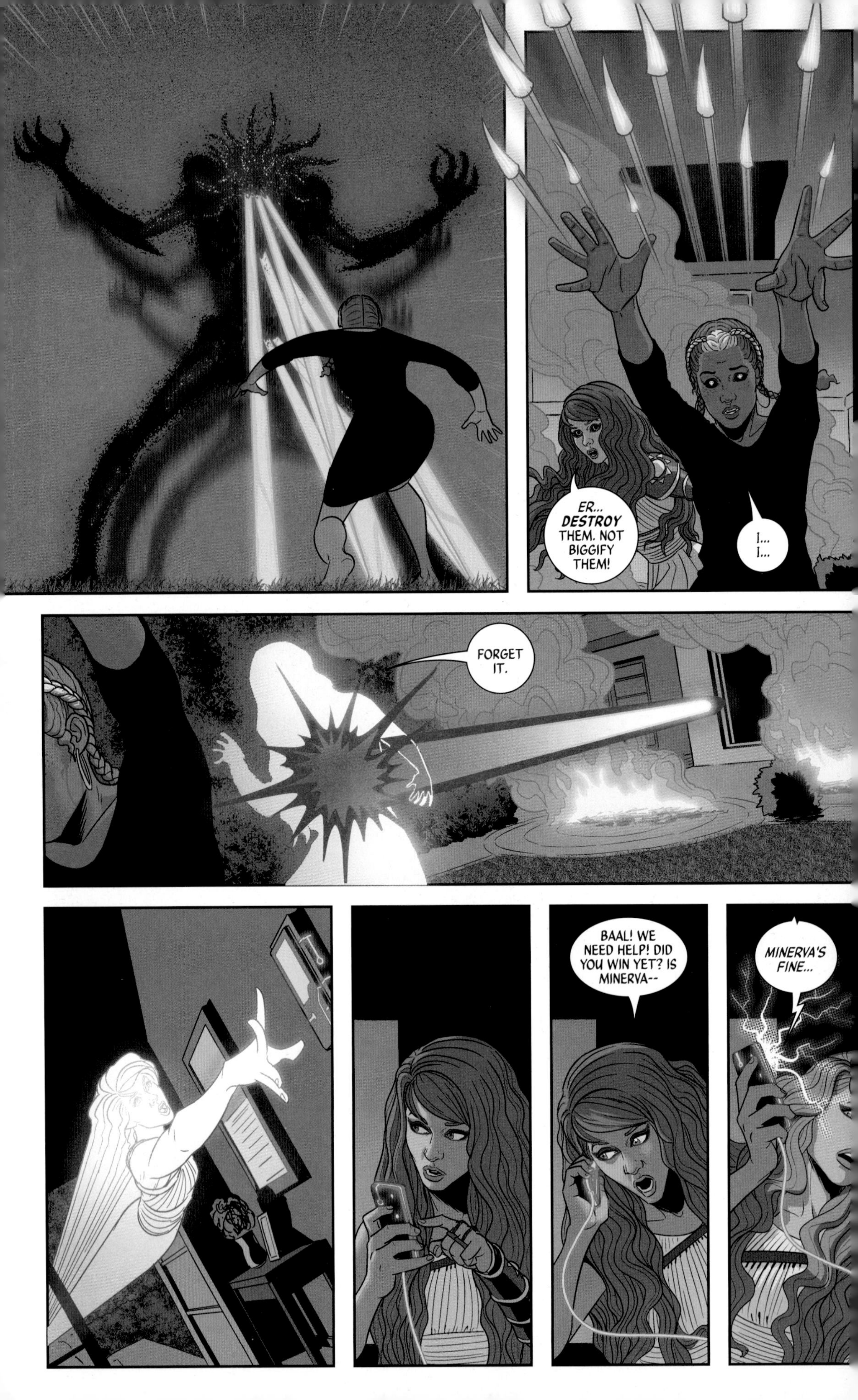
ER...
DESTROY
THEM. NOT
BIGGIFY
THEM!
I...
I...
FORGET
IT.
BAAL! WE
NEED HELP! DID
YOU WIN YET? IS
MINERVA--
MINERVA'S
FINE...

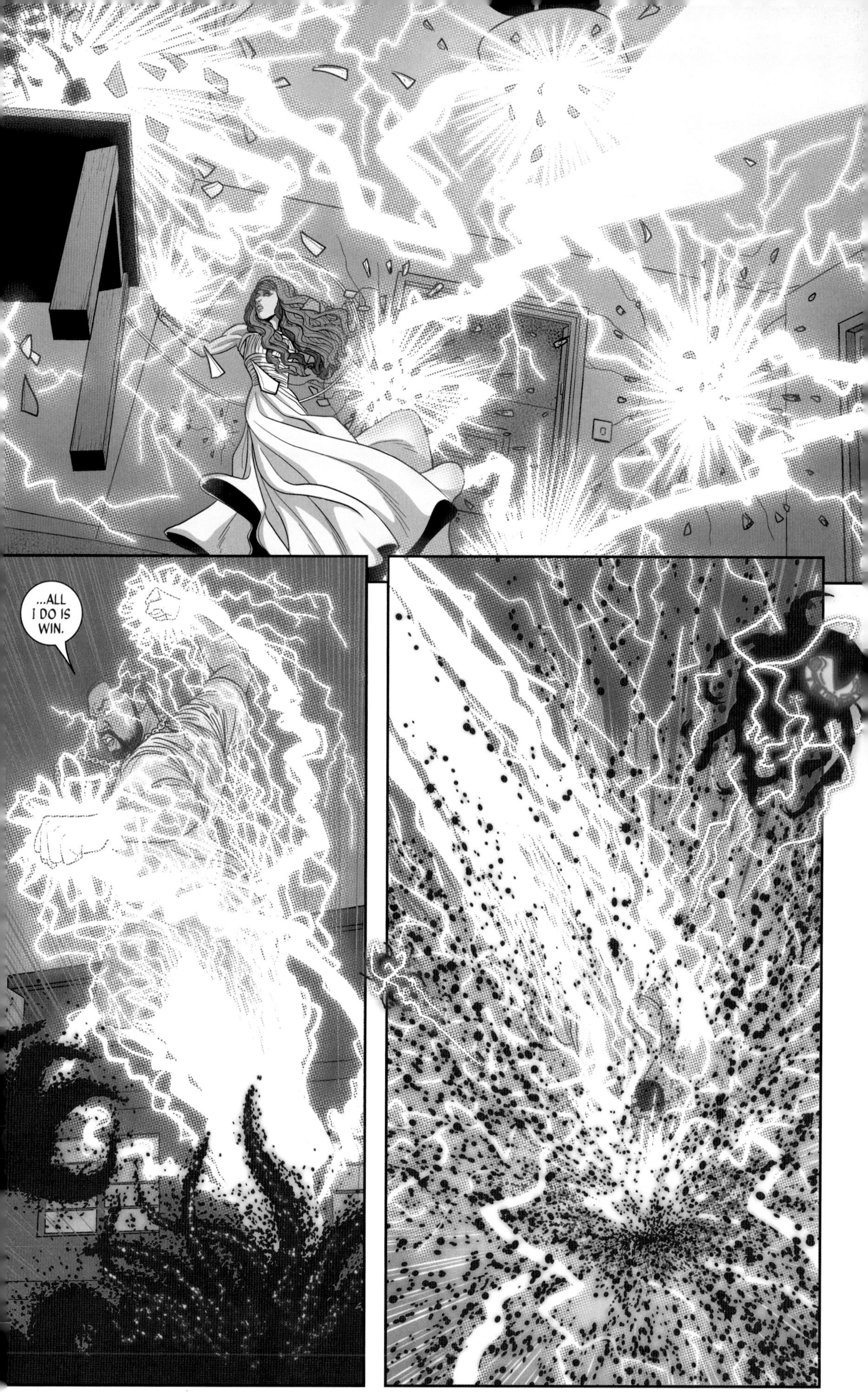
...ALL I DO IS WIN.

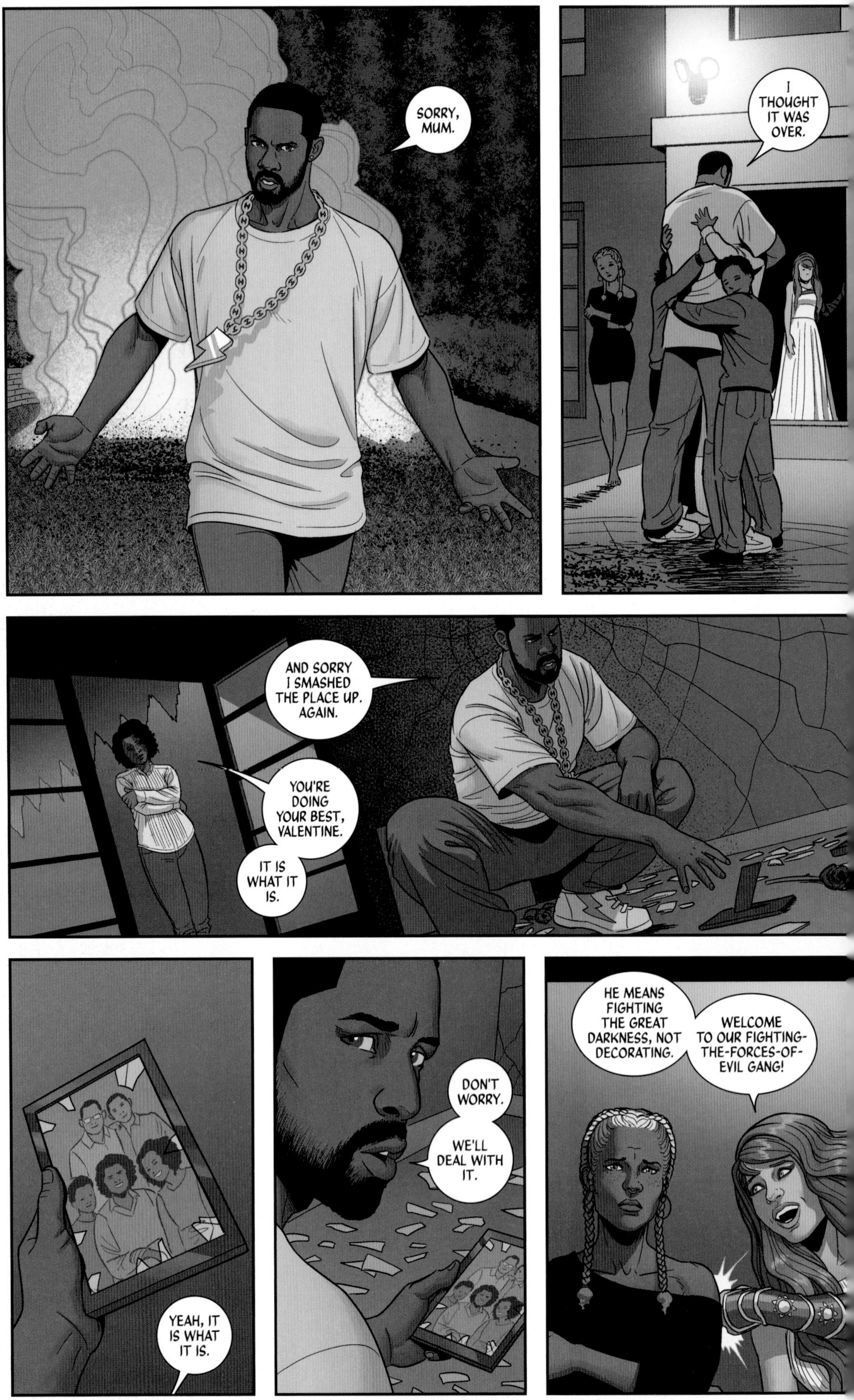
SORRY, MUM.
I THOUGHT IT WAS OVER.
AND SORRY I SMASHED THE PLACE UP. AGAIN.
YOU'RE DOING YOUR BEST, VALENTINE.
IT IS WHAT IT IS.
YEAH, IT IS WHAT IT IS.
DON'T WORRY.
WE'LL DEAL WITH IT.
HE MEANS FIGHTING THE GREAT DARKNESS, NOT DECORATING.
WELCOME TO OUR FIGHTING-THE-FORCES-OF-EVIL GANG!

THE WATCH

2 JANUARY 2015

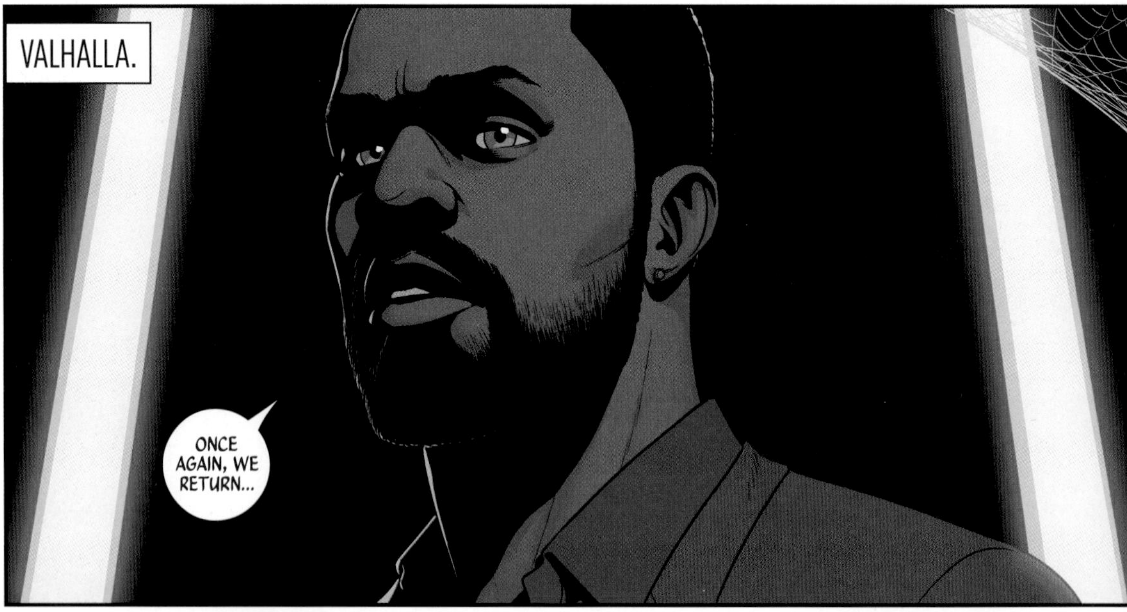
VALHALLA.
ONCE AGAIN, WE RETURN...

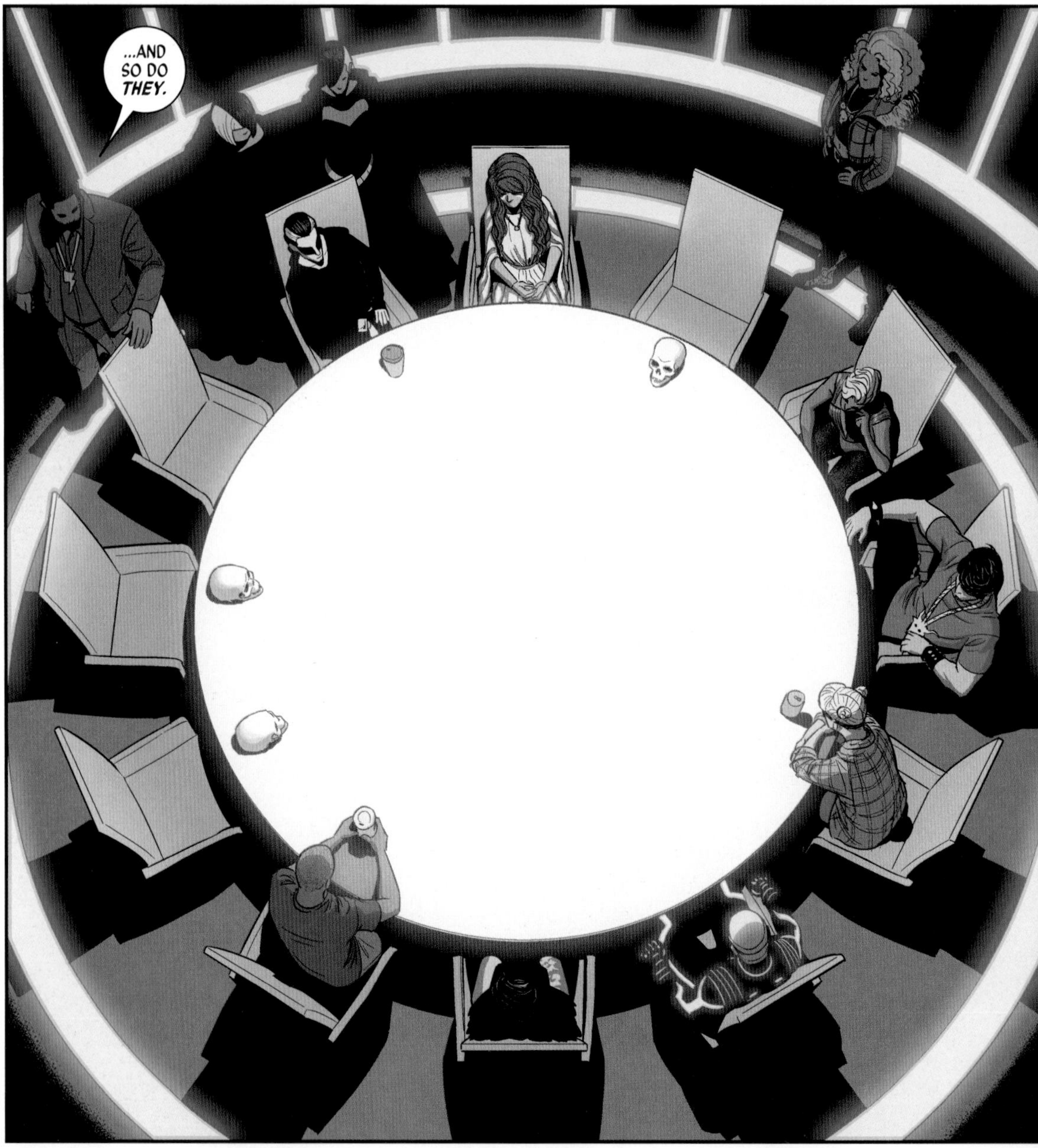
...AND SO DO *THEY.*

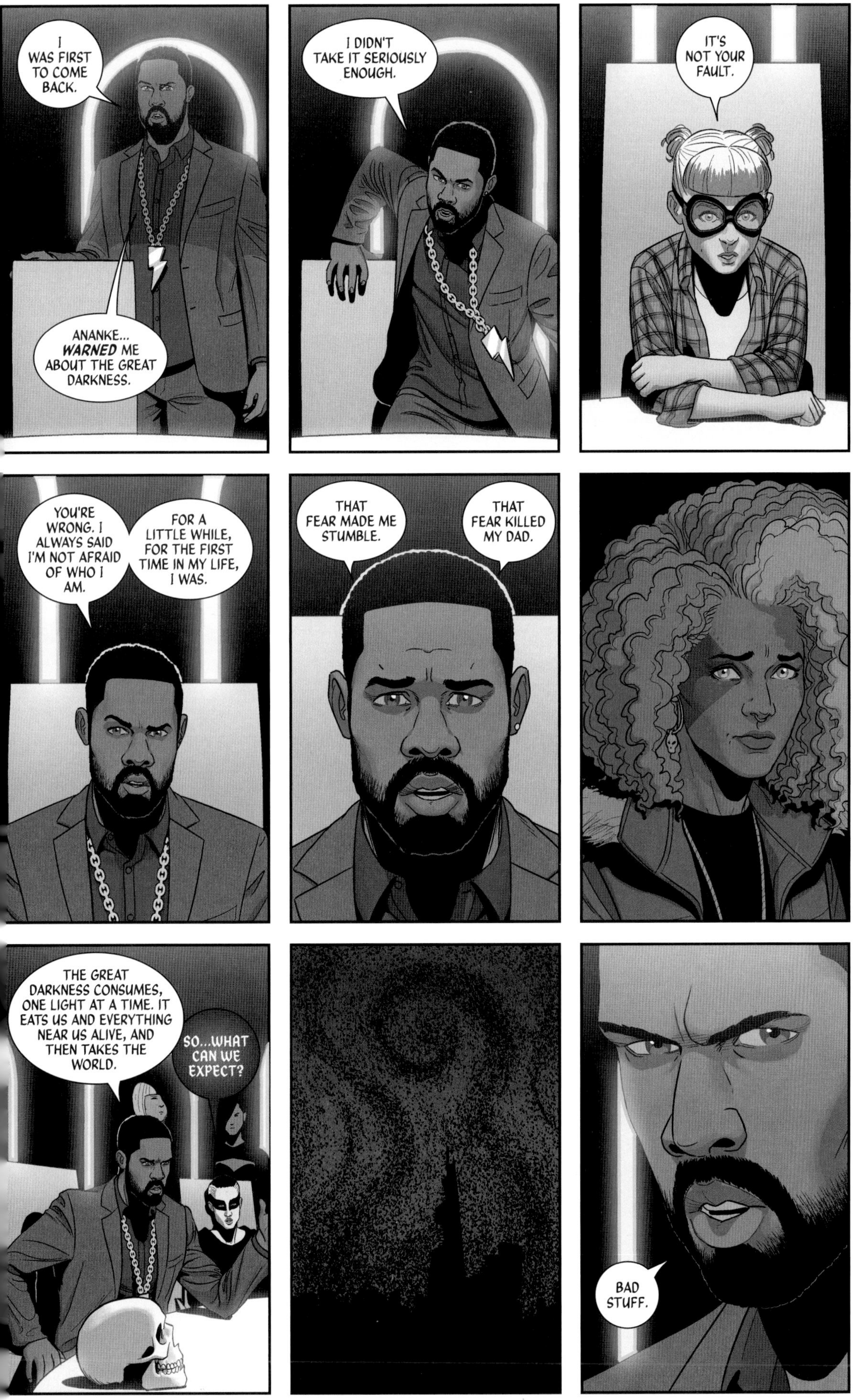
I WAS FIRST TO COME BACK.
ANANKE... **WARNED** ME ABOUT THE GREAT DARKNESS.
I DIDN'T TAKE IT SERIOUSLY ENOUGH.
IT'S NOT YOUR FAULT.
YOU'RE WRONG. I ALWAYS SAID I'M NOT AFRAID OF WHO I AM.
FOR A LITTLE WHILE, FOR THE FIRST TIME IN MY LIFE, I WAS.
THAT FEAR MADE ME STUMBLE.
THAT FEAR KILLED MY DAD.
THE GREAT DARKNESS CONSUMES, ONE LIGHT AT A TIME. IT EATS US AND EVERYTHING NEAR US ALIVE, AND THEN TAKES THE WORLD.
SO...WHAT CAN WE EXPECT?
BAD STUFF.

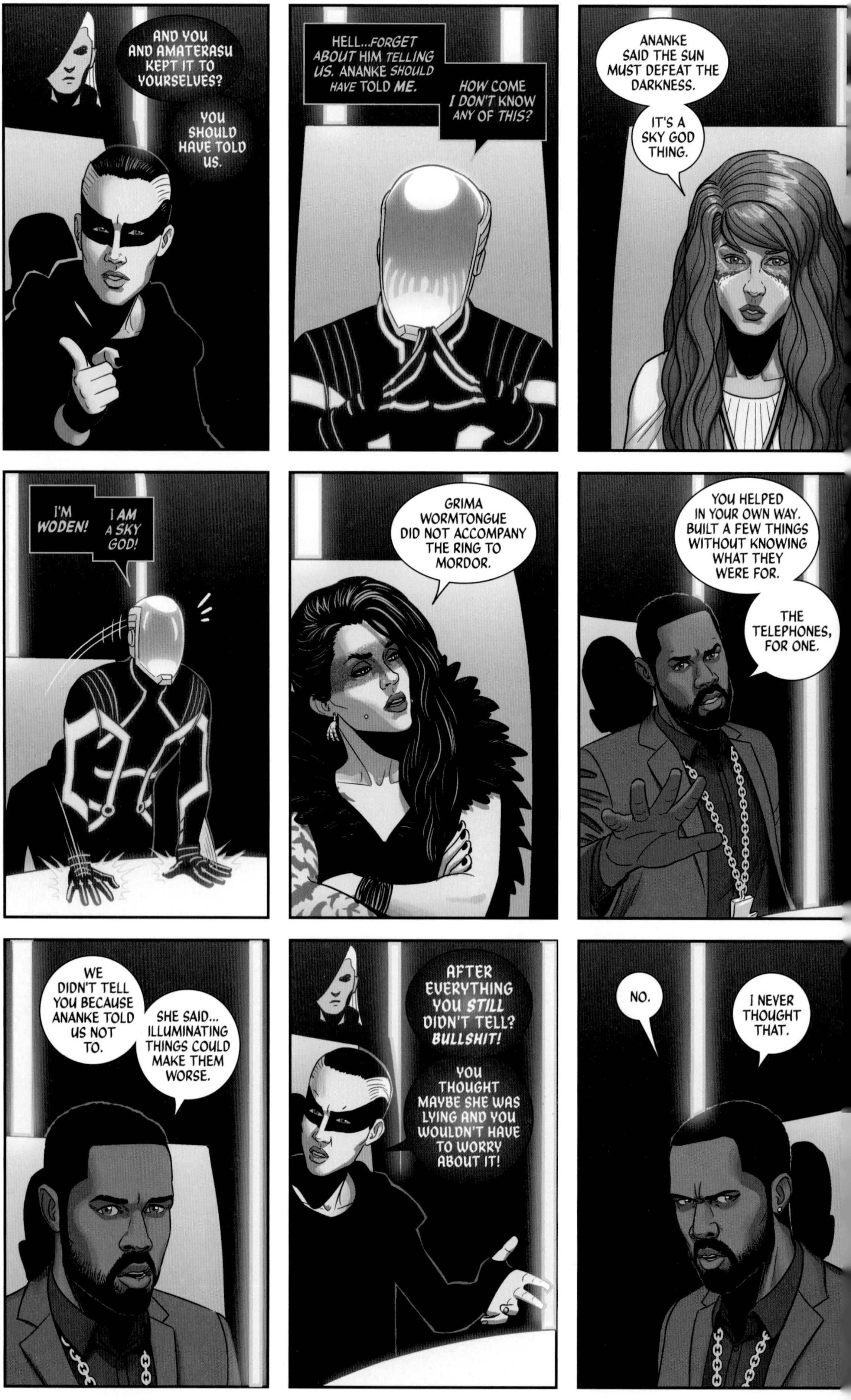
AND YOU AND AMATERASU KEPT IT TO YOURSELVES?
YOU SHOULD HAVE TOLD US.
HELL...FORGET ABOUT HIM TELLING US. ANANKE SHOULD HAVE TOLD ME.
HOW COME I DON'T KNOW ANY OF THIS?
ANANKE SAID THE SUN MUST DEFEAT THE DARKNESS.
IT'S A SKY GOD THING.
I'M WODEN!
I AM A SKY GOD!
GRIMA WORMTONGUE DID NOT ACCOMPANY THE RING TO MORDOR.
YOU HELPED IN YOUR OWN WAY. BUILT A FEW THINGS WITHOUT KNOWING WHAT THEY WERE FOR.
THE TELEPHONES, FOR ONE.
WE DIDN'T TELL YOU BECAUSE ANANKE TOLD US NOT TO.
SHE SAID... ILLUMINATING THINGS COULD MAKE THEM WORSE.
AFTER EVERYTHING YOU STILL DIDN'T TELL? BULLSHIT!
YOU THOUGHT MAYBE SHE WAS LYING AND YOU WOULDN'T HAVE TO WORRY ABOUT IT!
NO.
I NEVER THOUGHT THAT.

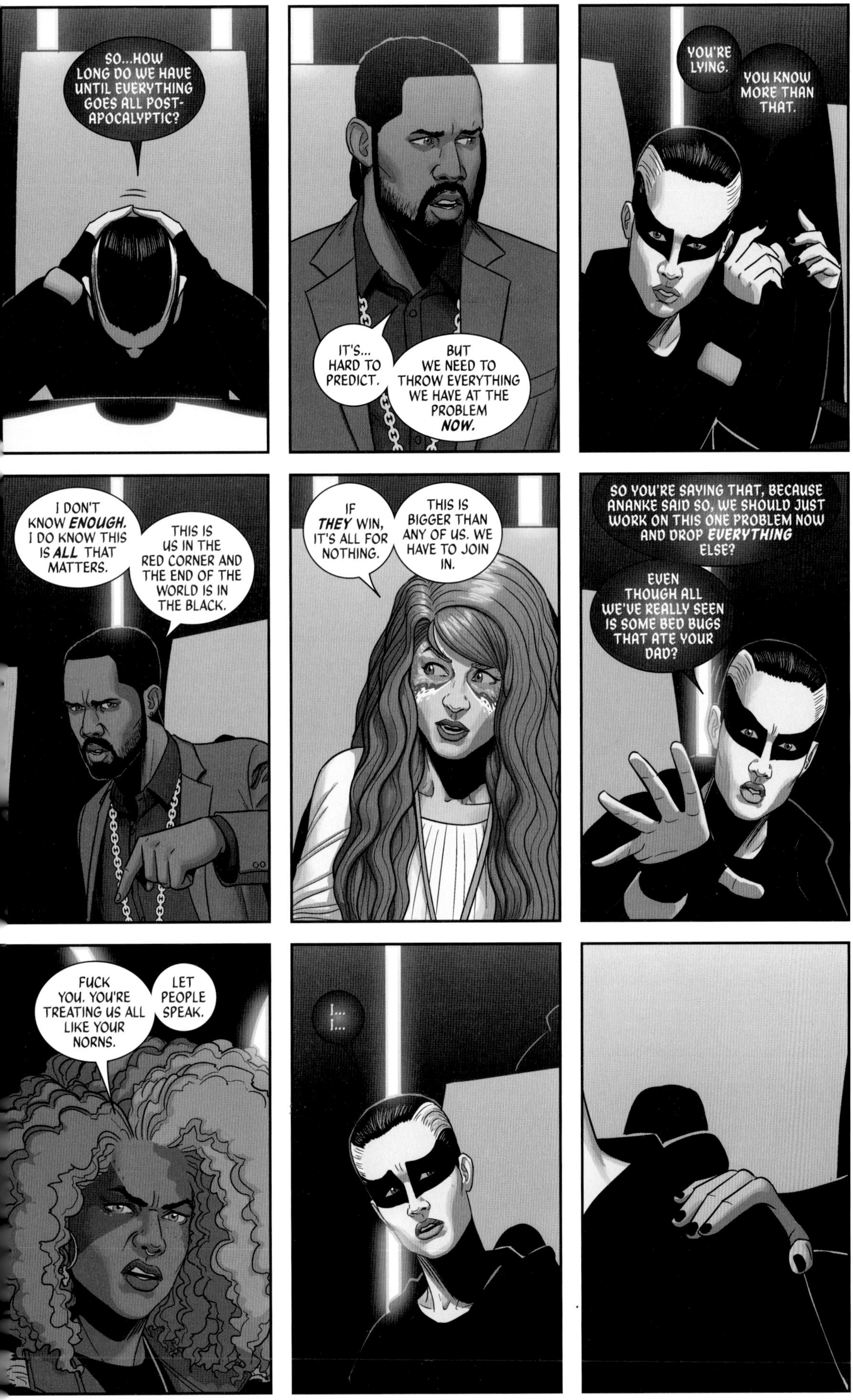
SO...HOW LONG DO WE HAVE UNTIL EVERYTHING GOES ALL POST-APOCALYPTIC?
IT'S... HARD TO PREDICT.
BUT WE NEED TO THROW EVERYTHING WE HAVE AT THE PROBLEM NOW.
YOU'RE LYING.
YOU KNOW MORE THAN THAT.
I DON'T KNOW ENOUGH. I DO KNOW THIS IS ALL THAT MATTERS.
THIS IS US IN THE RED CORNER AND THE END OF THE WORLD IS IN THE BLACK.
IF THEY WIN, IT'S ALL FOR NOTHING.
THIS IS BIGGER THAN ANY OF US. WE HAVE TO JOIN IN.
SO YOU'RE SAYING THAT, BECAUSE ANANKE SAID SO, WE SHOULD JUST WORK ON THIS ONE PROBLEM NOW AND DROP EVERYTHING ELSE?
EVEN THOUGH ALL WE'VE REALLY SEEN IS SOME BED BUGS THAT ATE YOUR DAD?
FUCK YOU. YOU'RE TREATING US ALL LIKE YOUR NORNS.
LET PEOPLE SPEAK.
I... I...

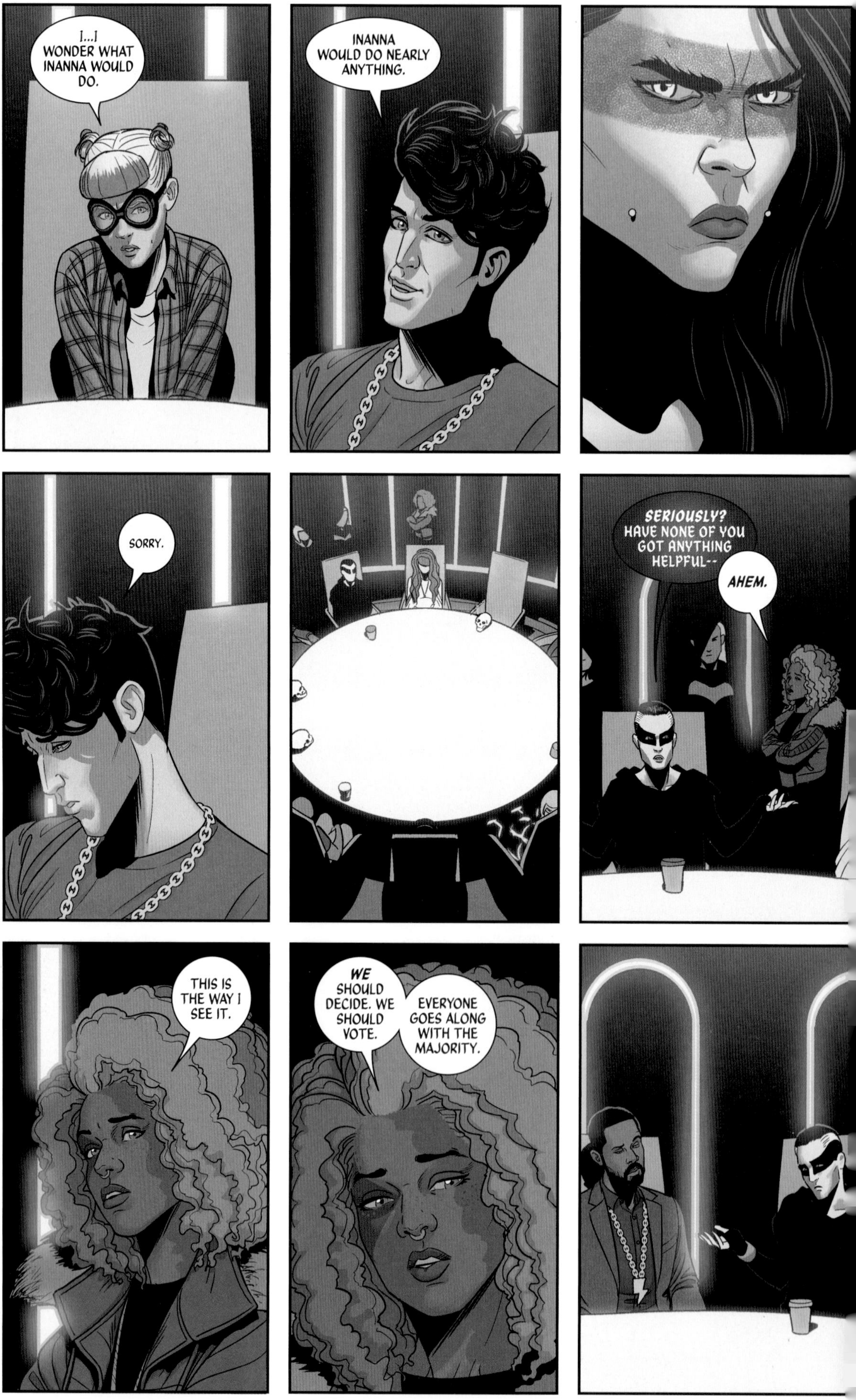
[...] WONDER WHAT INANNA WOULD DO.
INANNA WOULD DO NEARLY ANYTHING.
SORRY.
SERIOUSLY? HAVE NONE OF YOU GOT ANYTHING HELPFUL--
AHEM.
THIS IS THE WAY I SEE IT.
WE SHOULD DECIDE. WE SHOULD VOTE.
EVERYONE GOES ALONG WITH THE MAJORITY.

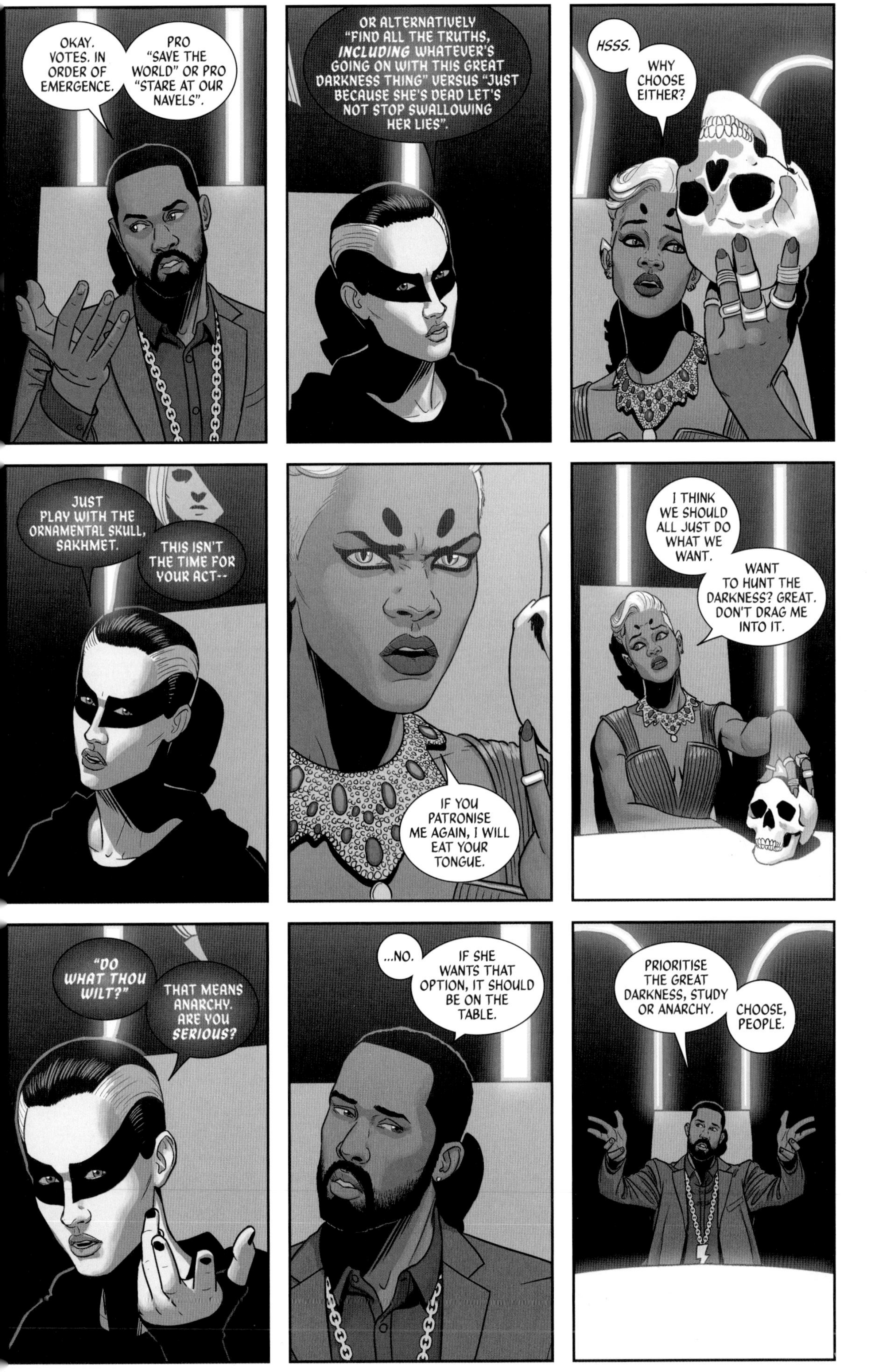

OKAY. VOTES. IN ORDER OF EMERGENCE.
PRO "SAVE THE WORLD" OR PRO "STARE AT OUR NAVELS".
OR ALTERNATIVELY "FIND ALL THE TRUTHS, *INCLUDING* WHATEVER'S GOING ON WITH THIS GREAT DARKNESS THING" VERSUS "JUST BECAUSE SHE'S DEAD LET'S NOT STOP SWALLOWING HER LIES".
HSSS.
WHY CHOOSE EITHER?
JUST PLAY WITH THE ORNAMENTAL SKULL, SAKHMET.
THIS ISN'T THE TIME FOR YOUR ACT--
IF YOU PATRONISE ME AGAIN, I WILL EAT YOUR TONGUE.
I THINK WE SHOULD ALL JUST DO WHAT WE WANT.
WANT TO HUNT THE DARKNESS? GREAT. DON'T DRAG ME INTO IT.
"DO WHAT THOU WILT?"
THAT MEANS ANARCHY. ARE YOU *SERIOUS?*
...NO.
IF SHE WANTS THAT OPTION, IT SHOULD BE ON THE TABLE.
PRIORITISE THE GREAT DARKNESS, STUDY OR ANARCHY.
CHOOSE, PEOPLE.

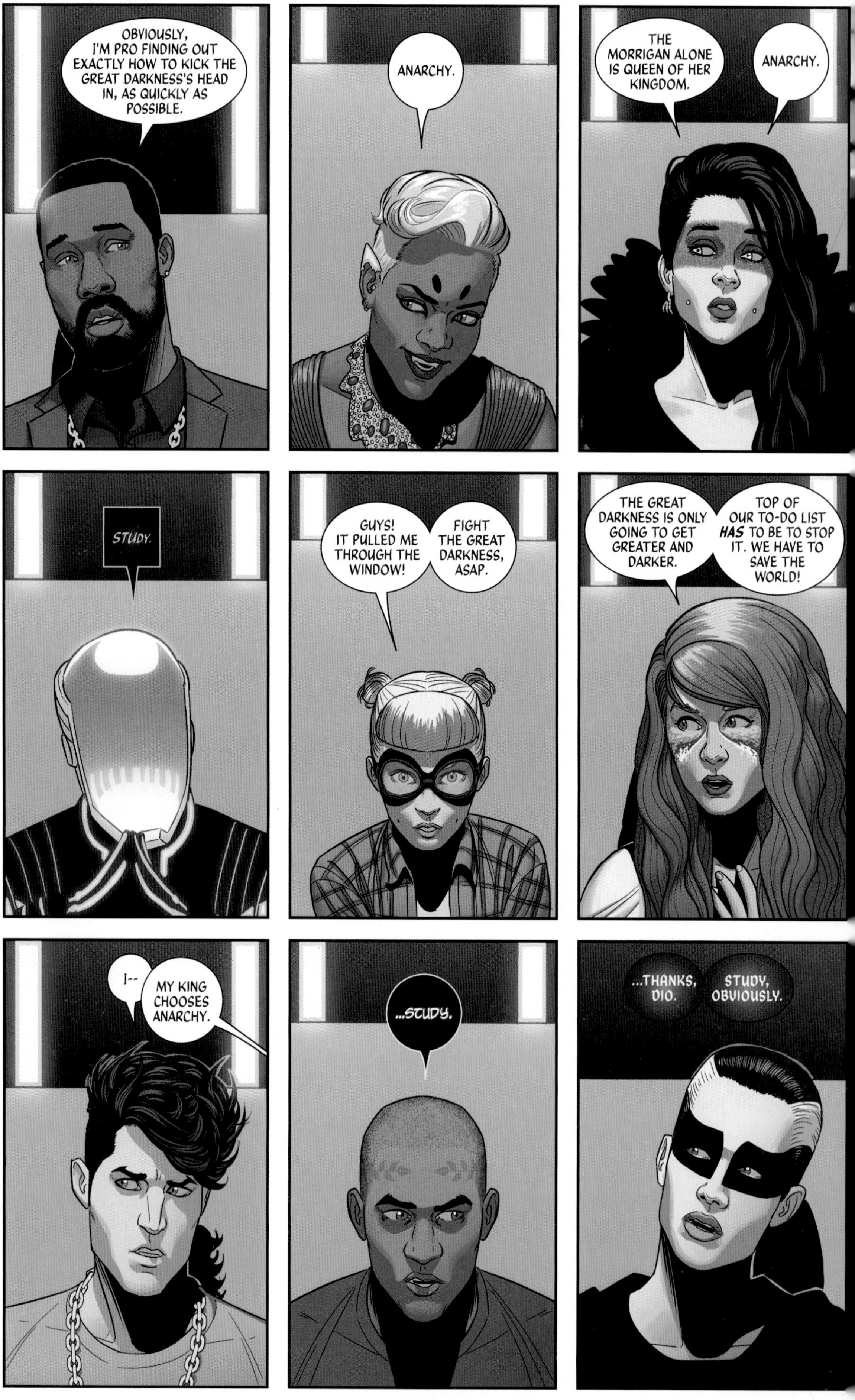
OBVIOUSLY, I'M PRO FINDING OUT EXACTLY HOW TO KICK THE GREAT DARKNESS'S HEAD IN, AS QUICKLY AS POSSIBLE.
ANARCHY.
THE MORRIGAN ALONE IS QUEEN OF HER KINGDOM.
ANARCHY.
STUDY.
GUYS! IT PULLED ME THROUGH THE WINDOW!
FIGHT THE GREAT DARKNESS, ASAP.
THE GREAT DARKNESS IS ONLY GOING TO GET GREATER AND DARKER.
TOP OF OUR TO-DO LIST HAS TO BE TO STOP IT. WE HAVE TO SAVE THE WORLD!
I--
MY KING CHOOSES ANARCHY.
...STUDY.
...THANKS, DIO.
STUDY, OBVIOUSLY.

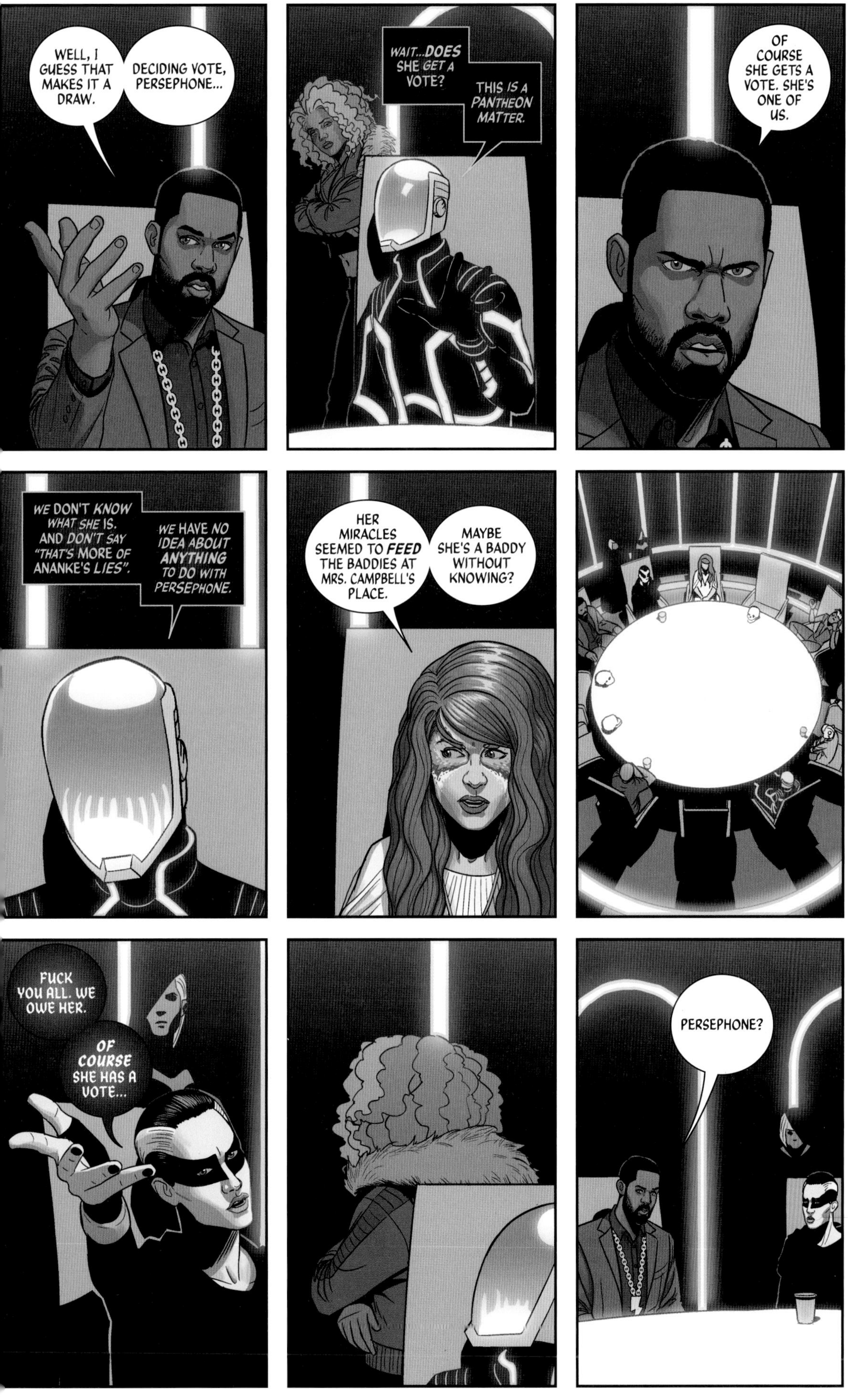
WELL, I GUESS THAT MAKES IT A DRAW.
DECIDING VOTE, PERSEPHONE...
WAIT...DOES SHE GET A VOTE?
THIS IS A PANTHEON MATTER.
OF COURSE SHE GETS A VOTE. SHE'S ONE OF US.
WE DON'T KNOW WHAT SHE IS. AND DON'T SAY "THAT'S MORE OF ANANKE'S LIES".
WE HAVE NO IDEA ABOUT ANYTHING TO DO WITH PERSEPHONE.
HER MIRACLES SEEMED TO FEED THE BADDIES AT MRS. CAMPBELL'S PLACE.
MAYBE SHE'S A BADDY WITHOUT KNOWING?
FUCK YOU ALL. WE OWE HER.
OF COURSE SHE HAS A VOTE...
PERSEPHONE?

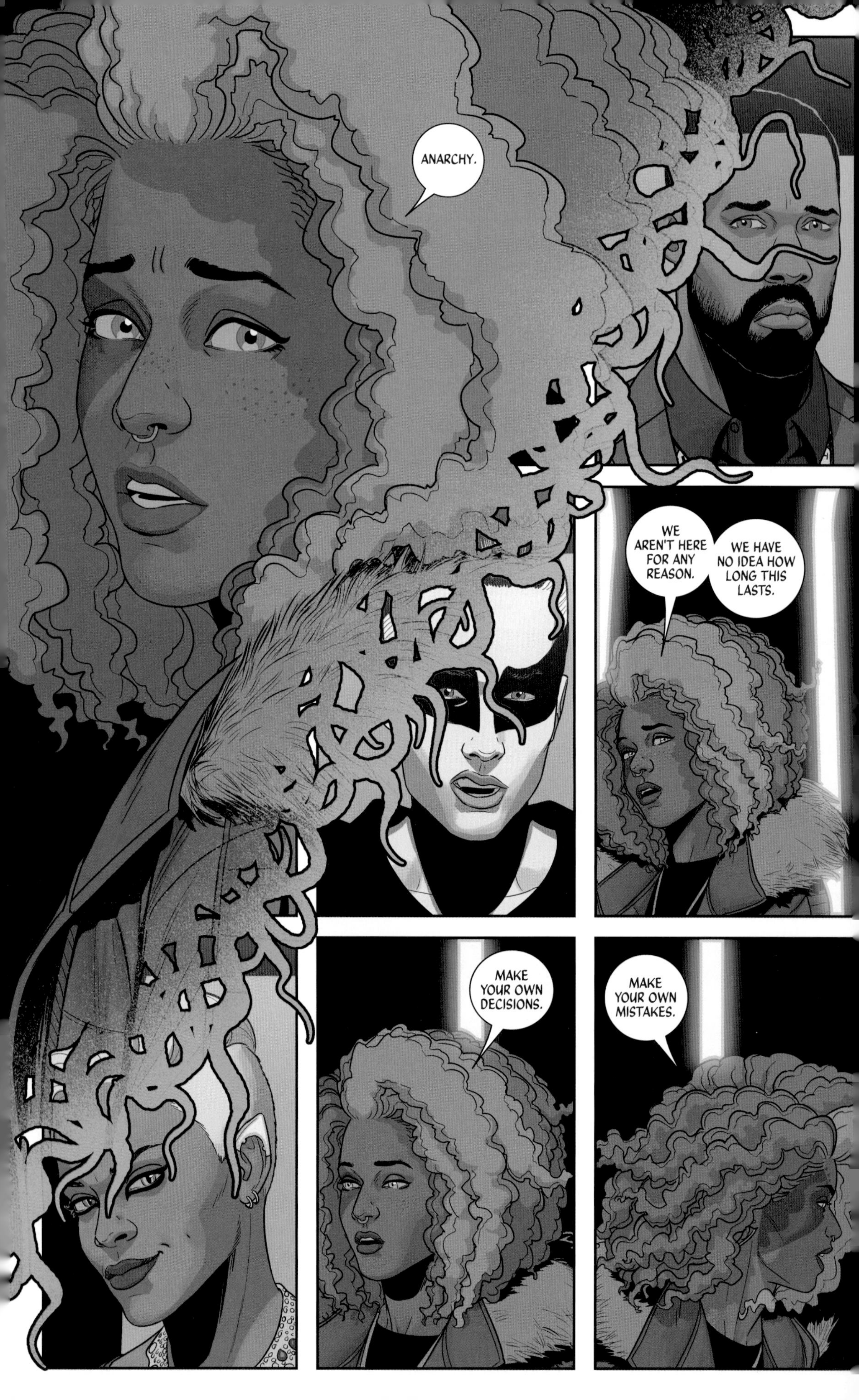
ANARCHY.
WE AREN'T HERE FOR ANY REASON.
WE HAVE NO IDEA HOW LONG THIS LASTS.
MAKE YOUR OWN DECISIONS.
MAKE YOUR OWN MISTAKES.

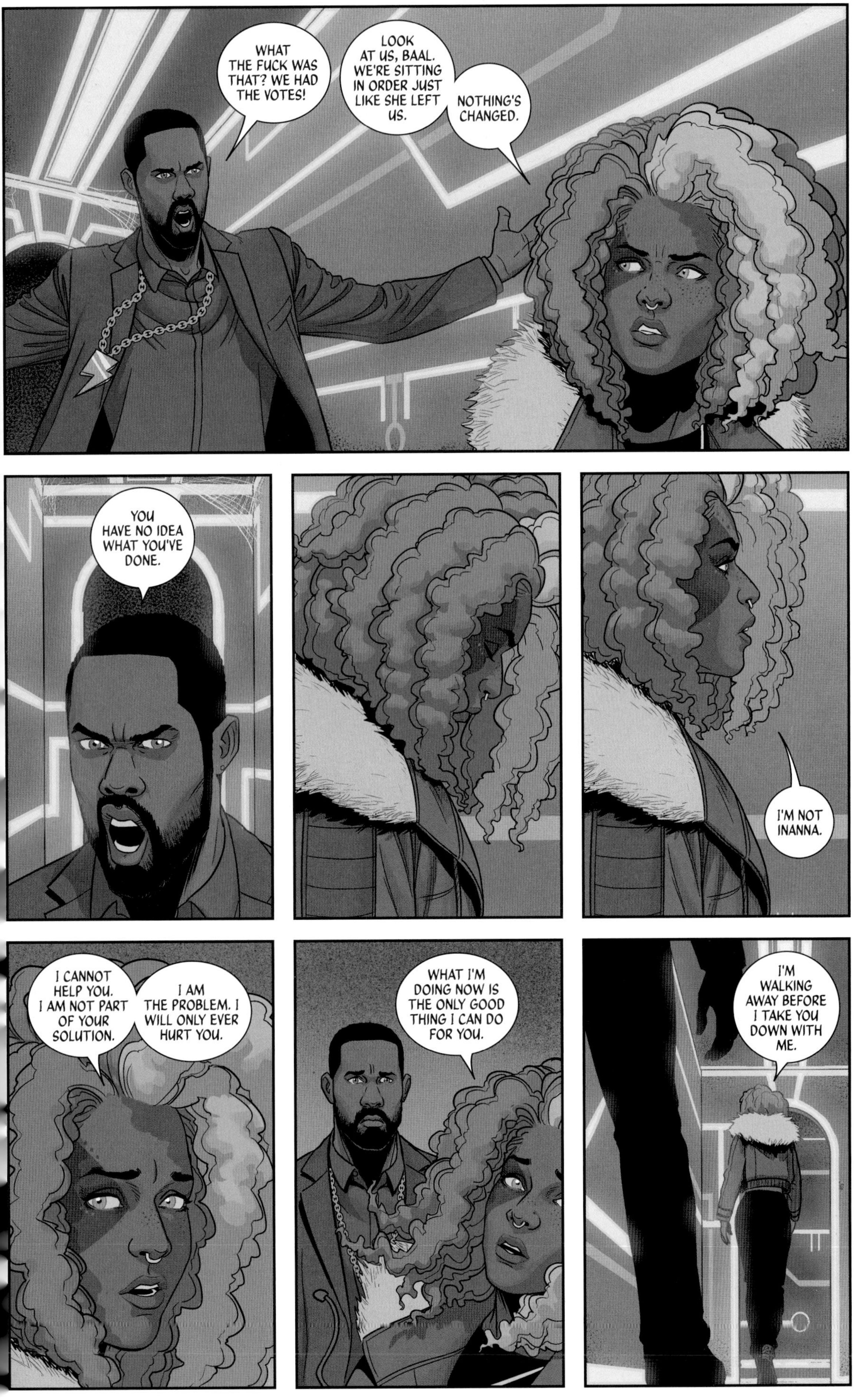
WHAT THE FUCK WAS THAT? WE HAD THE VOTES!
LOOK AT US, BAAL. WE'RE SITTING IN ORDER JUST LIKE SHE LEFT US.
NOTHING'S CHANGED.
YOU HAVE NO IDEA WHAT YOU'VE DONE.
I'M NOT INANNA.
I CANNOT HELP YOU. I AM NOT PART OF YOUR SOLUTION.
I AM THE PROBLEM. I WILL ONLY EVER HURT YOU.
WHAT I'M DOING NOW IS THE ONLY GOOD THING I CAN DO FOR YOU.
I'M WALKING AWAY BEFORE I TAKE YOU DOWN WITH ME.

FUCKING LAURA FUCKING WILSON FUCKING *FUCKING* FUCKING!

HEY, CASS. I *DID* TRY AND STOP HER...

...BUT *IT COULD BE WORSE.* ONLY MINERVA WOULD BE OF ANY USE *TO US,* AND IT'S NOT AS IF THEY'VE TOLD US TO STOP RESEARCHING.

AND IF WE'RE ALL FREE, WE'RE FREE TO IMPRESS THEM. WE CAN MAKE THEM *WANT* TO JOIN US.

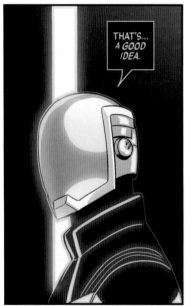

THAT'S... A *GOOD* IDEA.

WHAT'S *THE SAYING* ABOUT THE *ACCURACY* OF STOPPED *CLOCKS?*

I *SWEAR* THERE WAS ONE...

IGNORE HIM.

THANKS FOR SEEING SENSE.

THOUGH... WHY *DID* YOU PICK US?

DON'T TAKE THIS WRONG, BUT YOU'VE *NEVER* COME ACROSS AS PARTICULARLY STUDIOUS.

A *CHOICE* BETWEEN SOMETHING WE KNOW *NOTHING* ABOUT, DISCOVERING WHAT WE CAN *ACTUALLY* DO, AND JUST BEING *SELFISH?*

NOT REALLY A CHOICE.

OH GOOD.

THE WAY TODAY'S BEEN GOING, I'D THINK IT WAS SOMETHING AWFUL LIKE "I WANT TO BANG YOU."

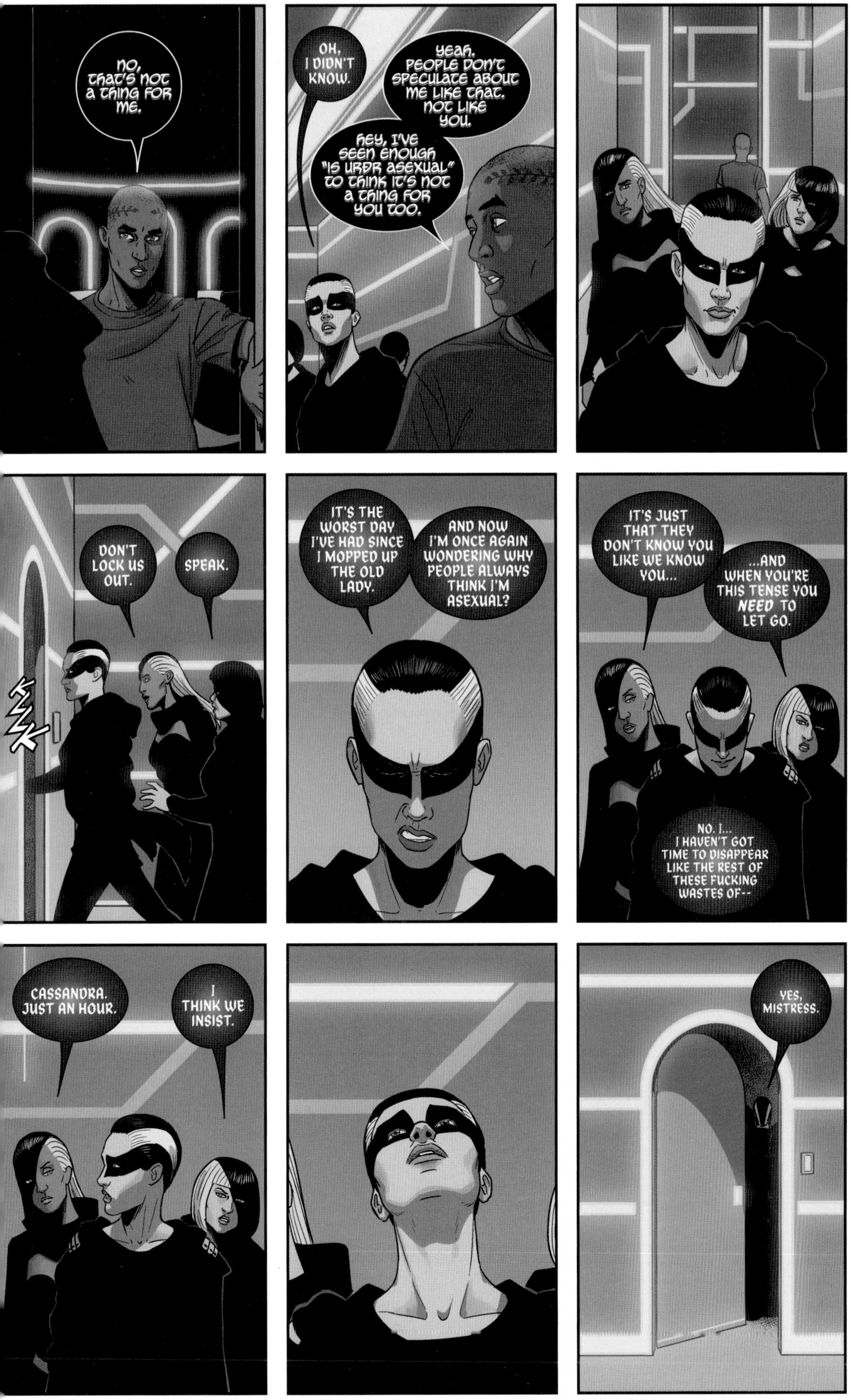

NO, THAT'S NOT A THING FOR ME.
OH, I DIDN'T KNOW.
YEAH. PEOPLE DON'T SPECULATE ABOUT ME LIKE THAT. NOT LIKE YOU.
HEY, I'VE SEEN ENOUGH "IS URDR ASEXUAL" TO THINK IT'S NOT A THING FOR YOU TOO.
DON'T LOCK US OUT.
SPEAK.
KLIK
IT'S THE WORST DAY I'VE HAD SINCE I MOPPED UP THE OLD LADY.
AND NOW I'M ONCE AGAIN WONDERING WHY PEOPLE ALWAYS THINK I'M ASEXUAL?
IT'S JUST THAT THEY DON'T KNOW YOU LIKE WE KNOW YOU...
...AND WHEN YOU'RE THIS TENSE YOU NEED TO LET GO.
NO. I... I HAVEN'T GOT TIME TO DISAPPEAR LIKE THE REST OF THESE FUCKING WASTES OF--
CASSANDRA. JUST AN HOUR.
I THINK WE INSIST.
YES, MISTRESS.

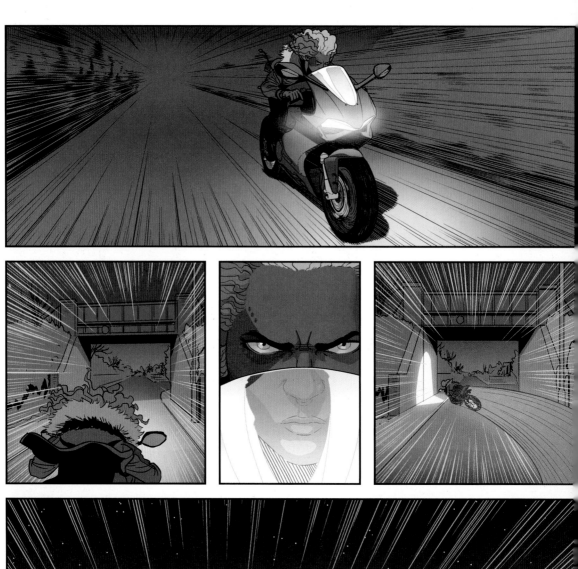

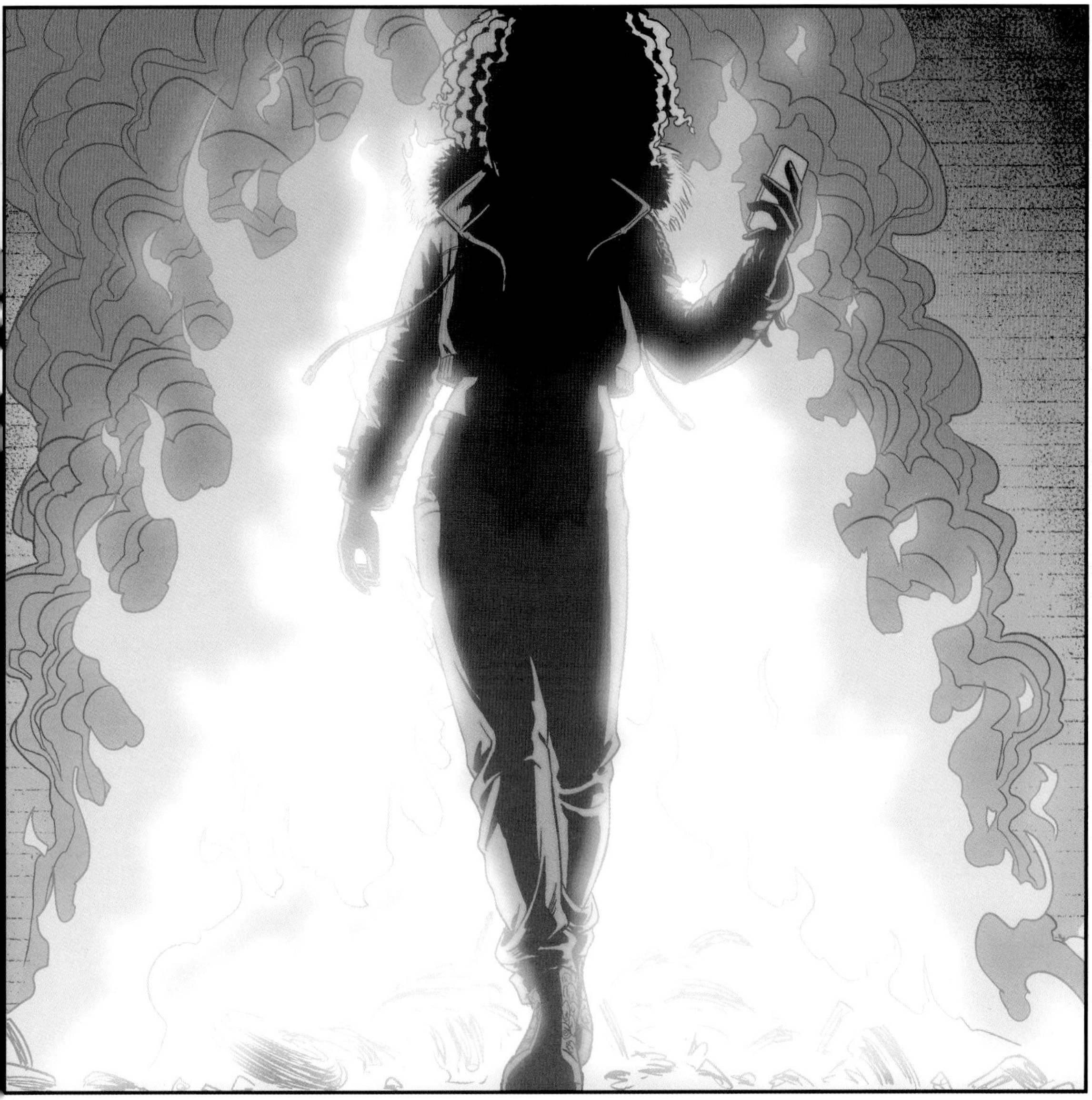

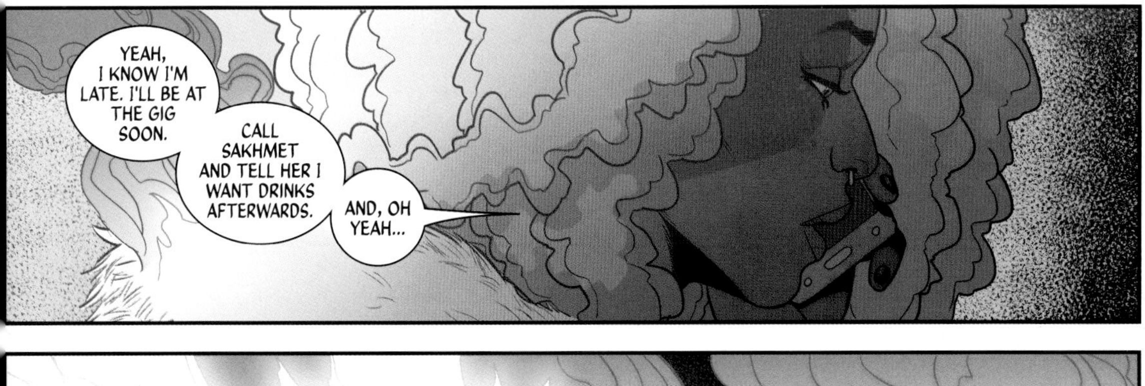
YEAH, I KNOW I'M LATE. I'LL BE AT THE GIG SOON.
CALL SAKHMET AND TELL HER I WANT DRINKS AFTERWARDS.
AND, OH YEAH...

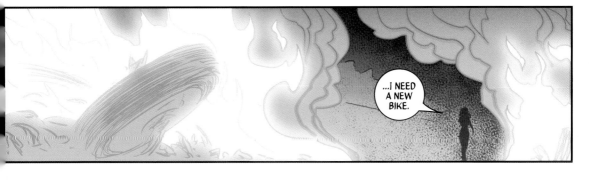

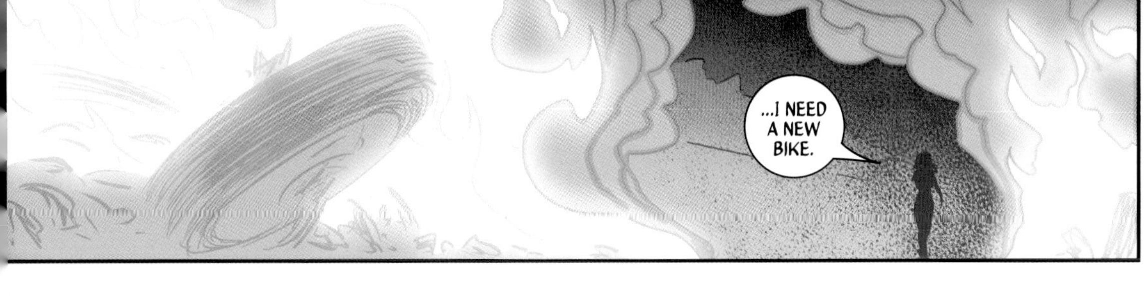
...I NEED A NEW BIKE.

TIK-TOK
TIK-TOK

2 JANUARY 2015

THE
WICKED
+
THE DIVINE

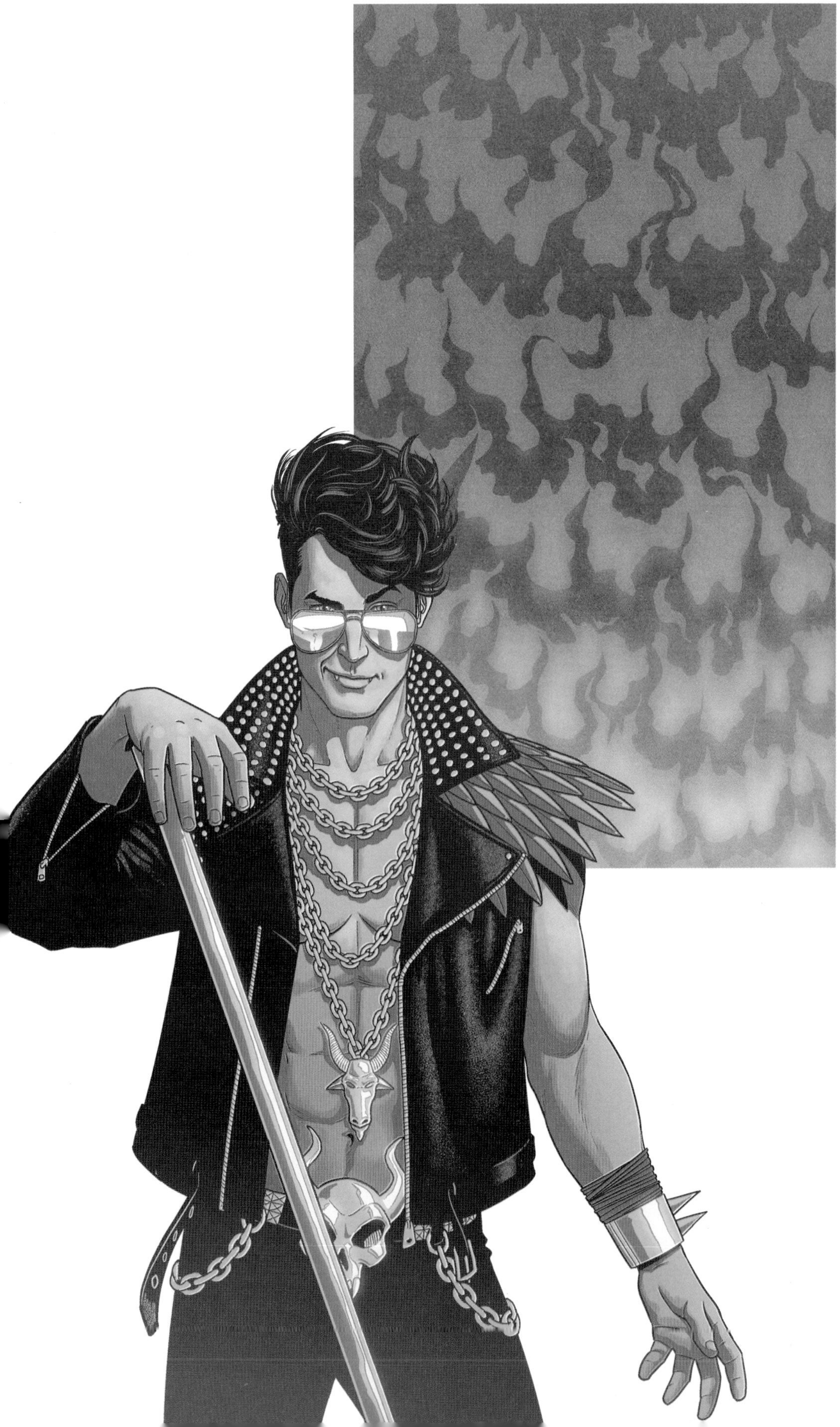

THE
WICKED
+
THE DIVINE

WHAT'S THAT, LI'L FLOWER?

THE SHARD, LONDON.

JUST SOMETHING PERSEPHONE BOUGHT FOR THE HOUSE. MAY AS WELL USE IT.

PANTHEON OFFICIAL CALENDAR

WHAT'S WRONG?

NOTHING. JUST OCTOBER TO DECEMBER.

I'LL USE THEM AS POSTERS.

September 2015

Sunday	Monday	Tuesday	Wednesday
		1	2
7	8	9	
	15	16	1
21	22	23	24
28	29	30	

I MEAN, WE WON'T BE NEEDING THEM.

MINERVA'S DEATH DAY

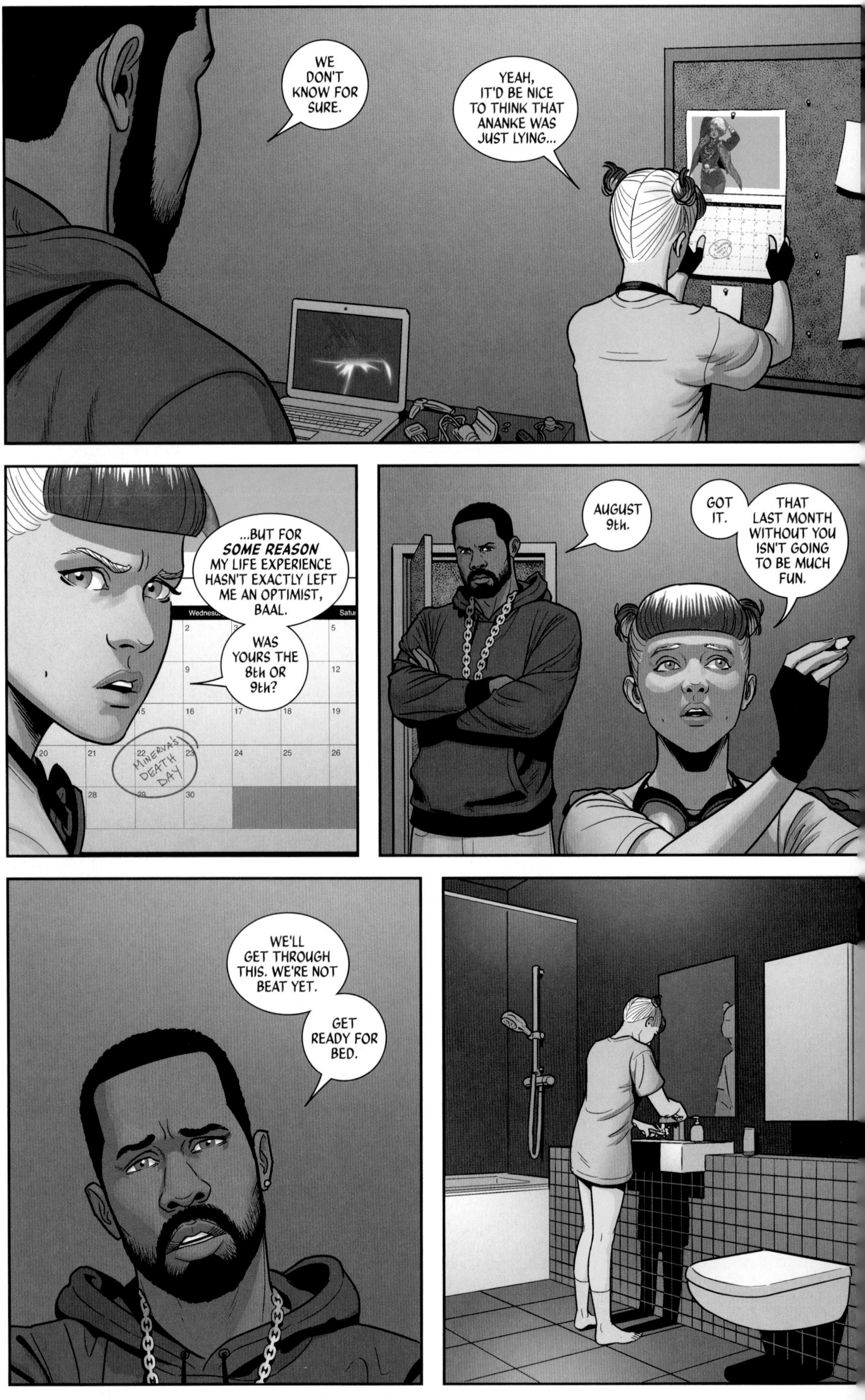
WE DON'T KNOW FOR SURE.
YEAH, IT'D BE NICE TO THINK THAT ANANKE WAS JUST LYING...
...BUT FOR *SOME REASON* MY LIFE EXPERIENCE HASN'T EXACTLY LEFT ME AN OPTIMIST, BAAL.
WAS YOURS THE 8th OR 9th?
MINERVA'S DEATH DAY
AUGUST 9th.
GOT IT.
THAT LAST MONTH WITHOUT YOU ISN'T GOING TO BE MUCH FUN.
WE'LL GET THROUGH THIS. WE'RE NOT BEAT YET.
GET READY FOR BED.

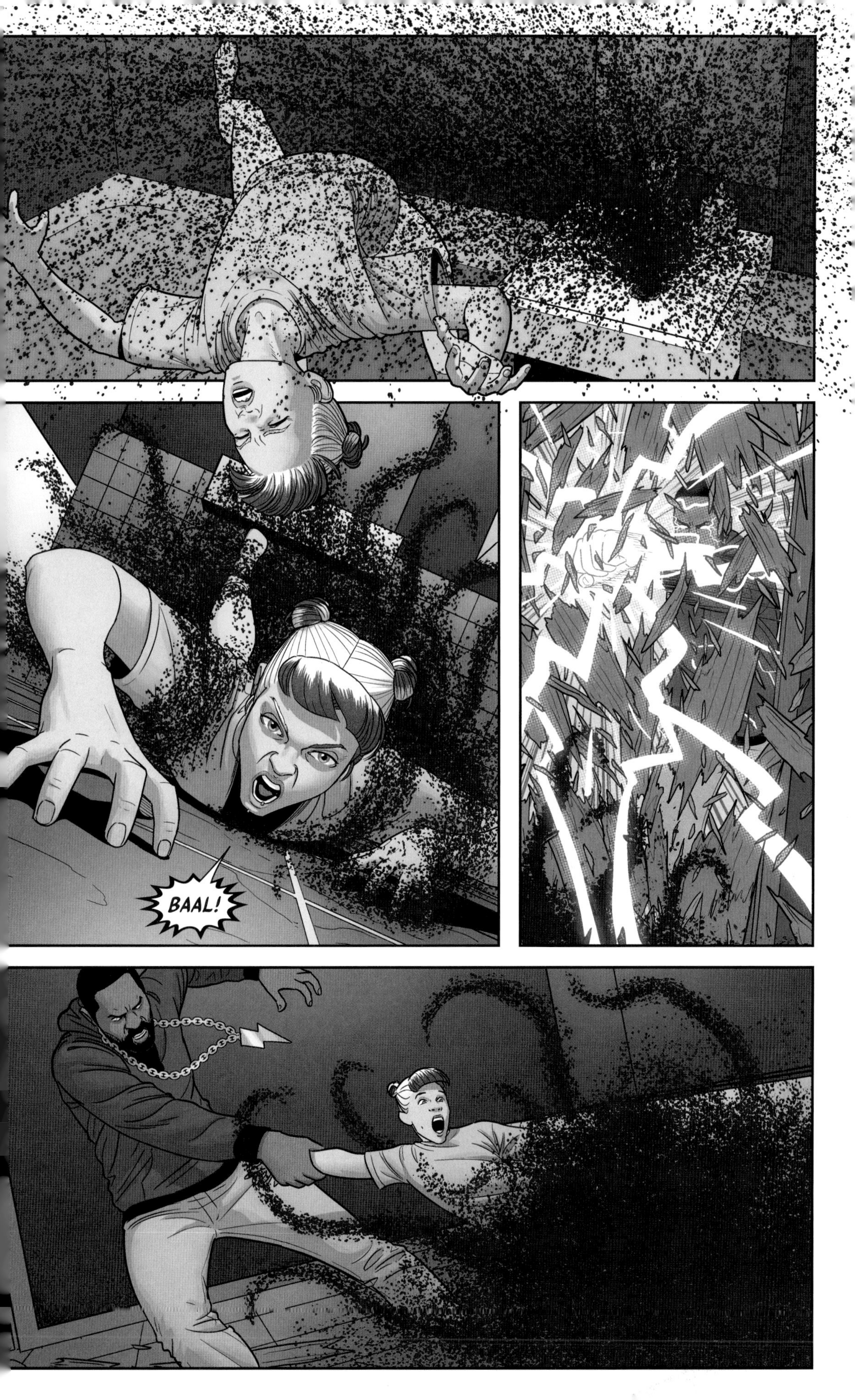
BAAL!

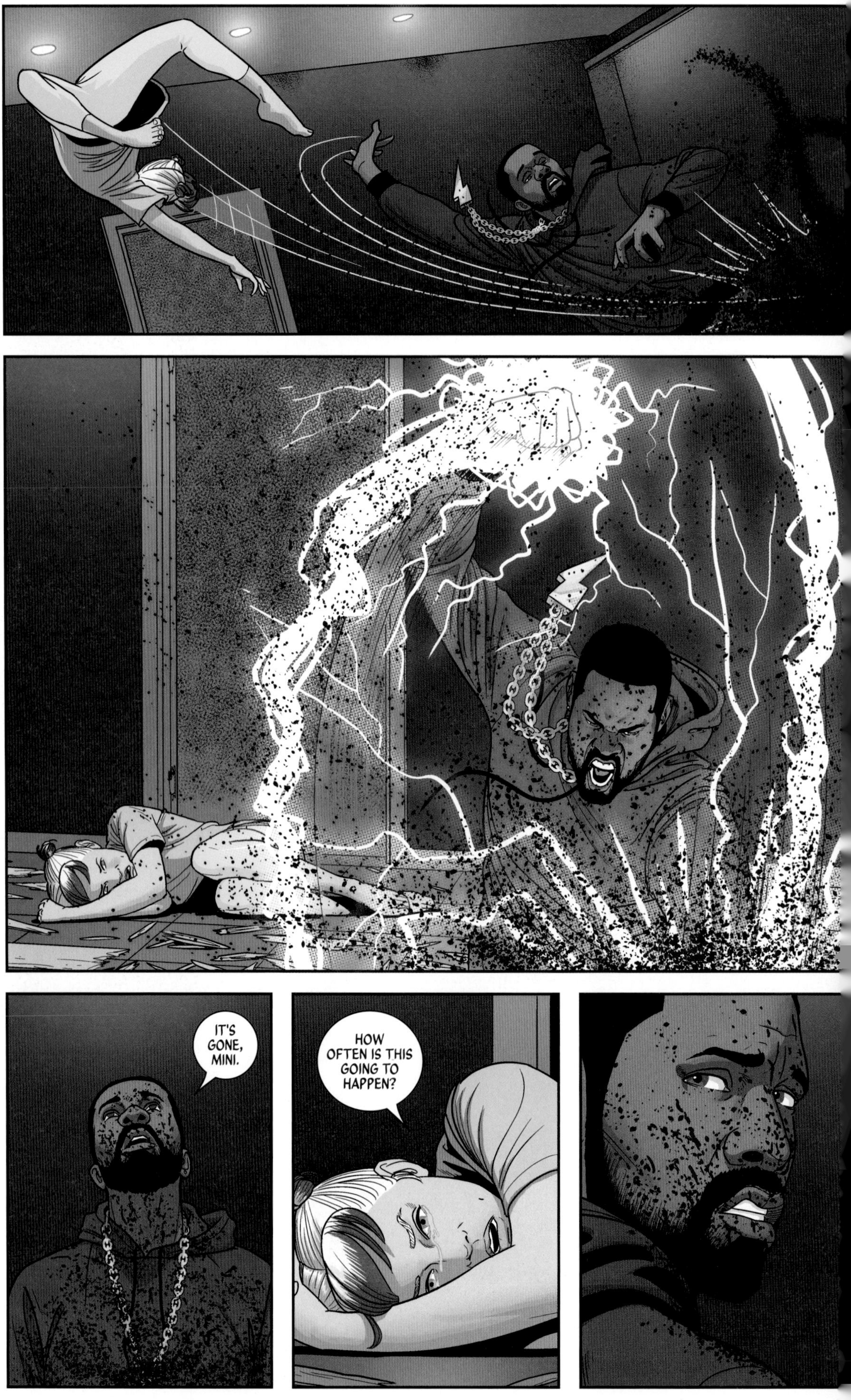
IT'S GONE, MINI.
HOW OFTEN IS THIS GOING TO HAPPEN?

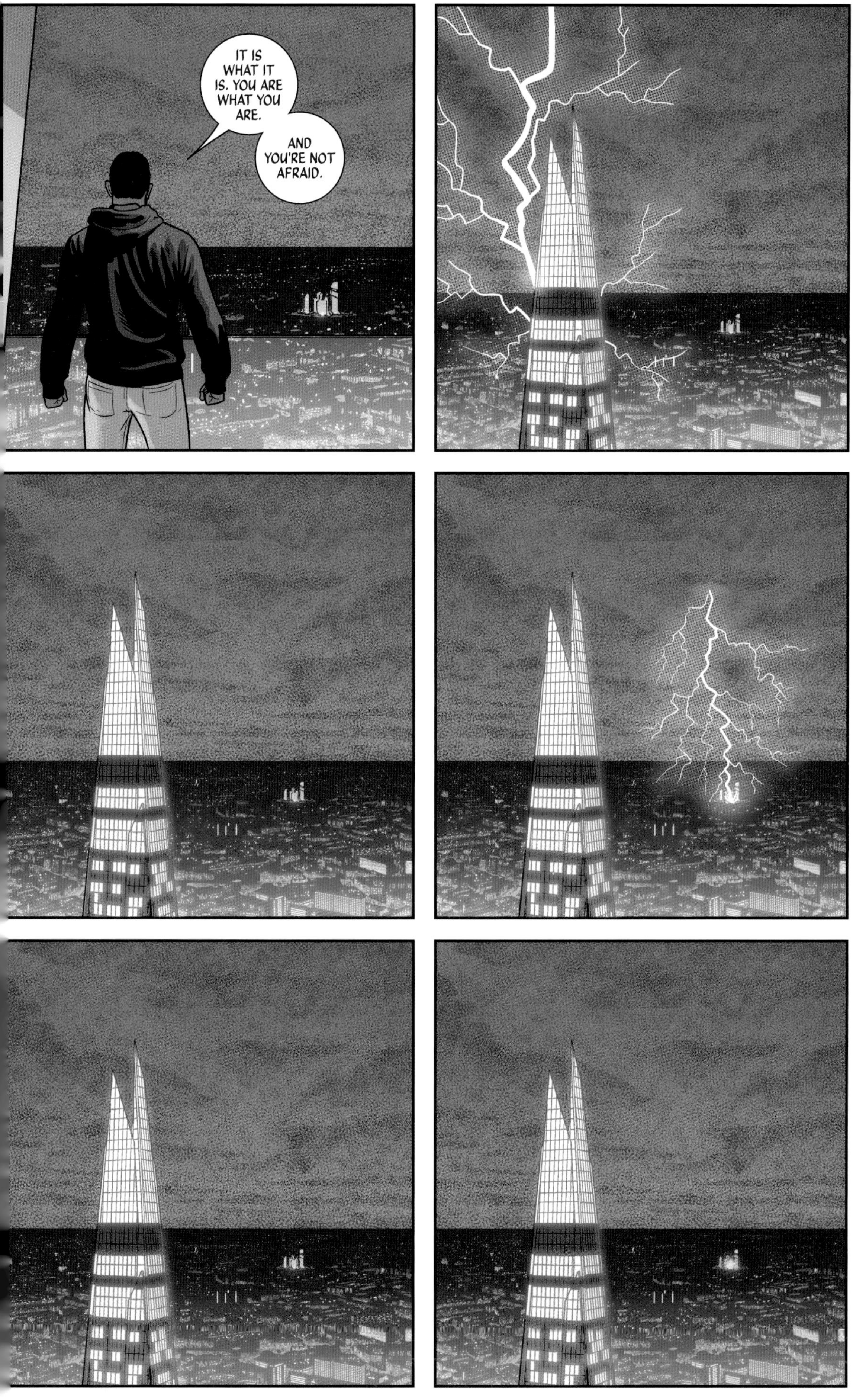
IT IS WHAT IT IS. YOU ARE WHAT YOU ARE.
AND YOU'RE NOT AFRAID.

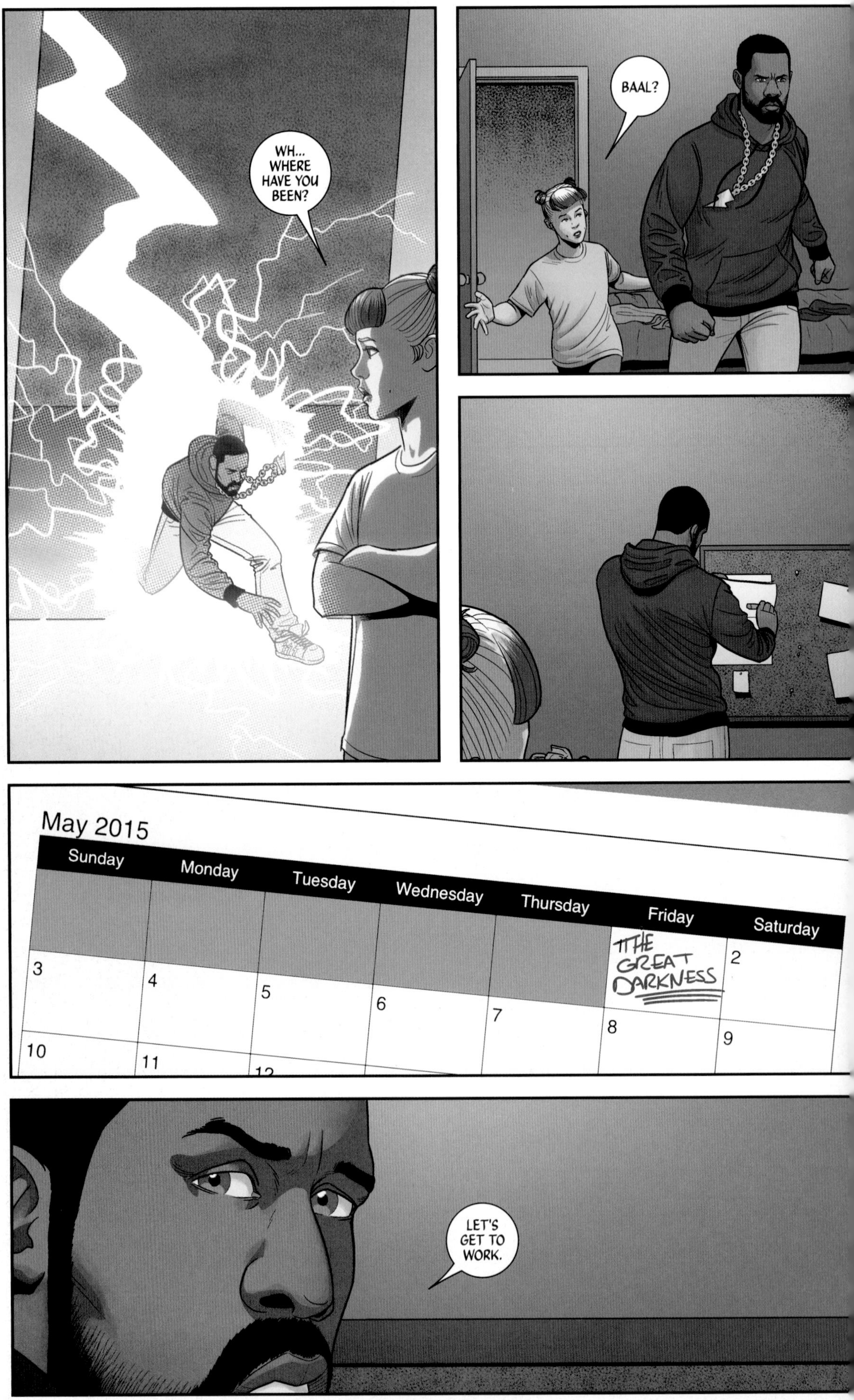
WH... WHERE HAVE YOU BEEN?
BAAL?
May 2015
Sunday
Monday
Tuesday
Wednesday
Thursday
Friday
Saturday
THE GREAT DARKNESS
2
3
4
5
6
7
8
9
10
11
LET'S GET TO WORK.

PHASED

JANUARY TO FEBRUARY 2015

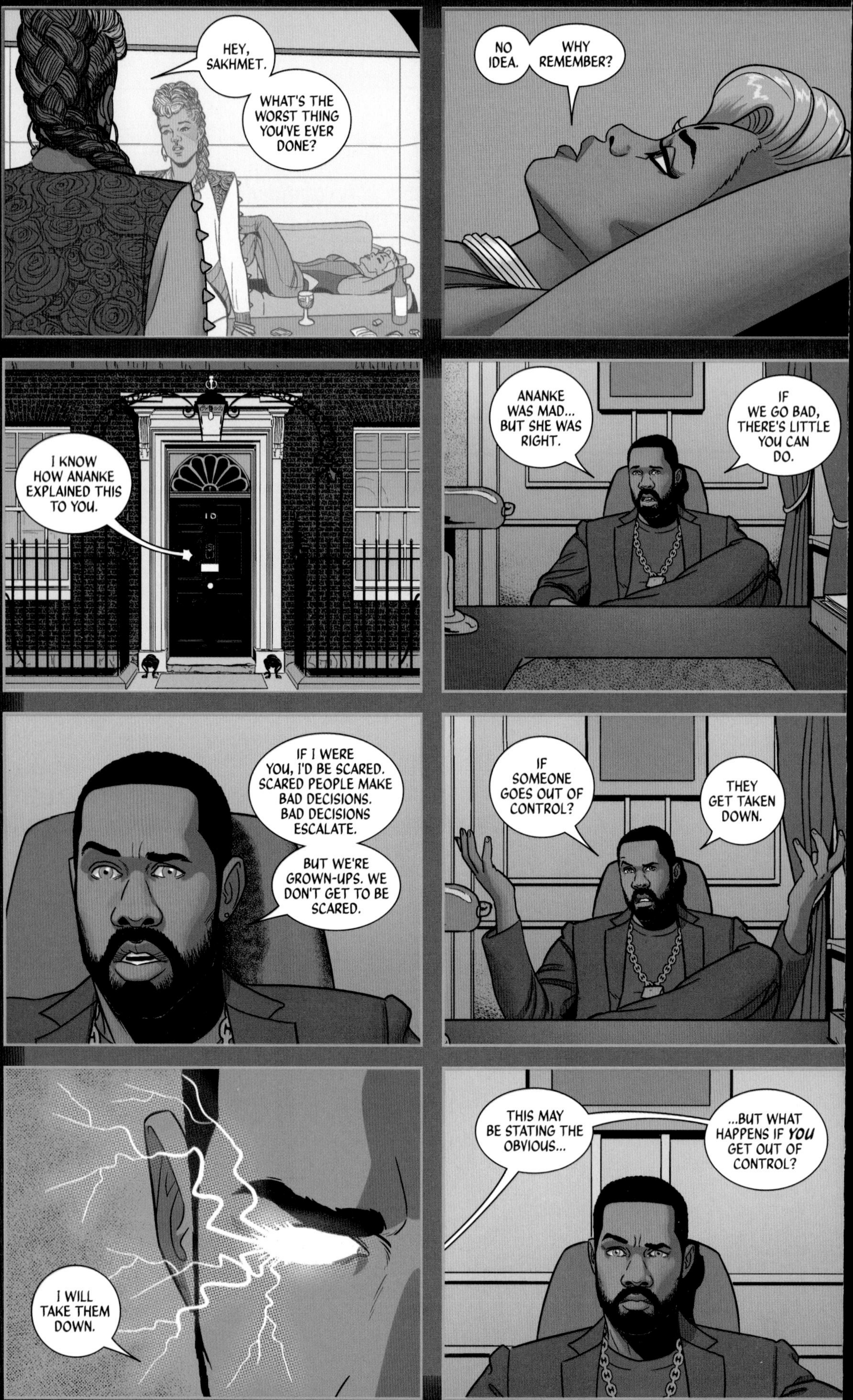
HEY, SAKHMET.
WHAT'S THE WORST THING YOU'VE EVER DONE?
NO IDEA.
WHY REMEMBER?
I KNOW HOW ANANKE EXPLAINED THIS TO YOU.
ANANKE WAS MAD... BUT SHE WAS RIGHT.
IF WE GO BAD, THERE'S LITTLE YOU CAN DO.
IF I WERE YOU, I'D BE SCARED. SCARED PEOPLE MAKE BAD DECISIONS. BAD DECISIONS ESCALATE.
BUT WE'RE GROWN-UPS. WE DON'T GET TO BE SCARED.
IF SOMEONE GOES OUT OF CONTROL?
THEY GET TAKEN DOWN.
I WILL TAKE THEM DOWN.
THIS MAY BE STATING THE OBVIOUS...
...BUT WHAT HAPPENS IF *YOU* GET OUT OF CONTROL?

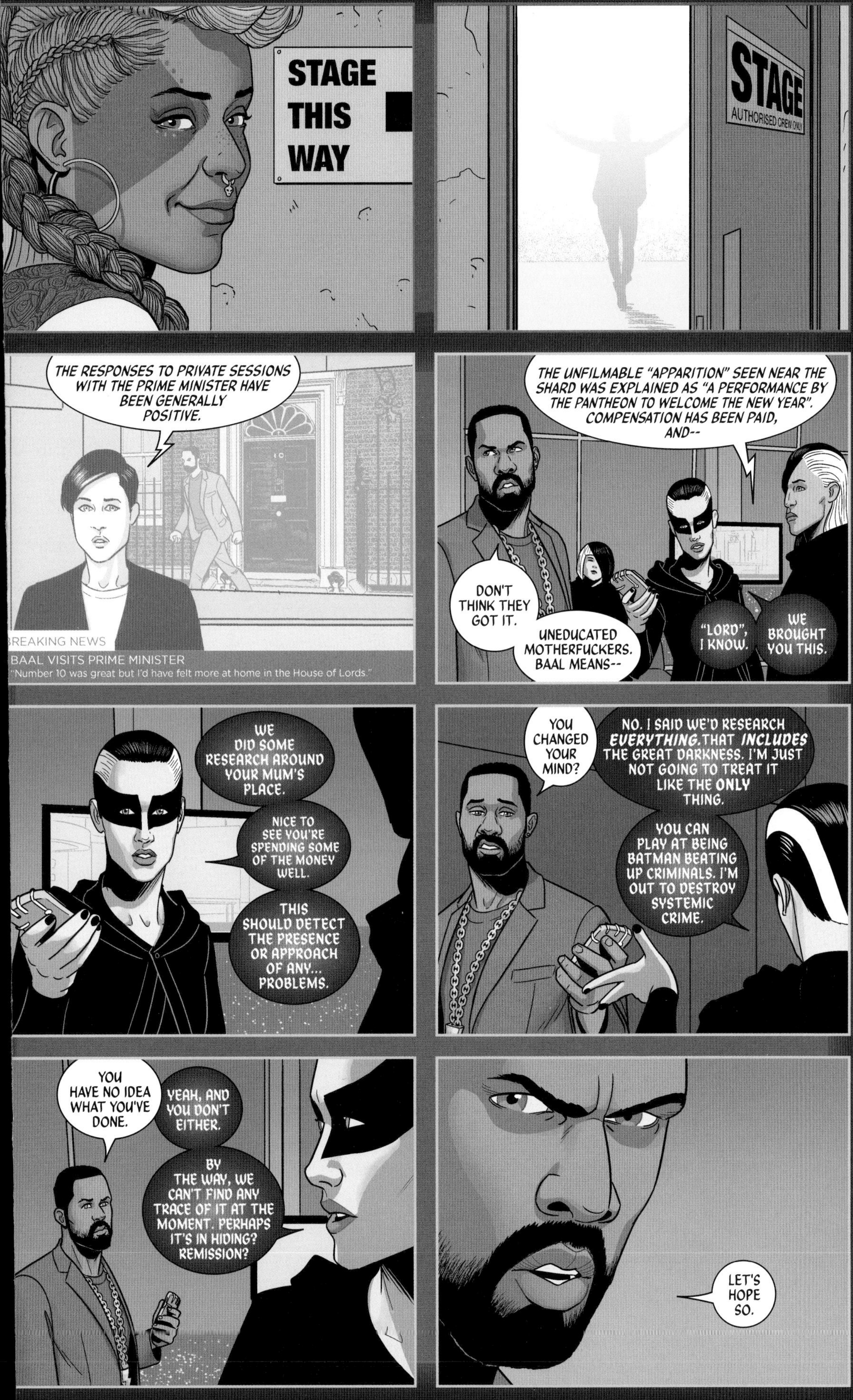
STAGE
THIS
WAY
STAGE
AUTHORISED CREW ONLY
THE RESPONSES TO PRIVATE SESSIONS WITH THE PRIME MINISTER HAVE BEEN GENERALLY POSITIVE.
BREAKING NEWS
BAAL VISITS PRIME MINISTER
"Number 10 was great but I'd have felt more at home in the House of Lords."
THE UNFILMABLE "APPARITION" SEEN NEAR THE SHARD WAS EXPLAINED AS "A PERFORMANCE BY THE PANTHEON TO WELCOME THE NEW YEAR". COMPENSATION HAS BEEN PAID, AND--
DON'T THINK THEY GOT IT.
UNEDUCATED MOTHERFUCKERS. BAAL MEANS--
"LORD", I KNOW.
WE BROUGHT YOU THIS.
WE DID SOME RESEARCH AROUND YOUR MUM'S PLACE.
NICE TO SEE YOU'RE SPENDING SOME OF THE MONEY WELL.
THIS SHOULD DETECT THE PRESENCE OR APPROACH OF ANY... PROBLEMS.
YOU CHANGED YOUR MIND?
NO. I SAID WE'D RESEARCH EVERYTHING. THAT INCLUDES THE GREAT DARKNESS. I'M JUST NOT GOING TO TREAT IT LIKE THE ONLY THING.
YOU CAN PLAY AT BEING BATMAN BEATING UP CRIMINALS. I'M OUT TO DESTROY SYSTEMIC CRIME.
YOU HAVE NO IDEA WHAT YOU'VE DONE.
YEAH, AND YOU DON'T EITHER.
BY THE WAY, WE CAN'T FIND ANY TRACE OF IT AT THE MOMENT. PERHAPS IT'S IN HIDING? REMISSION?
LET'S HOPE SO.

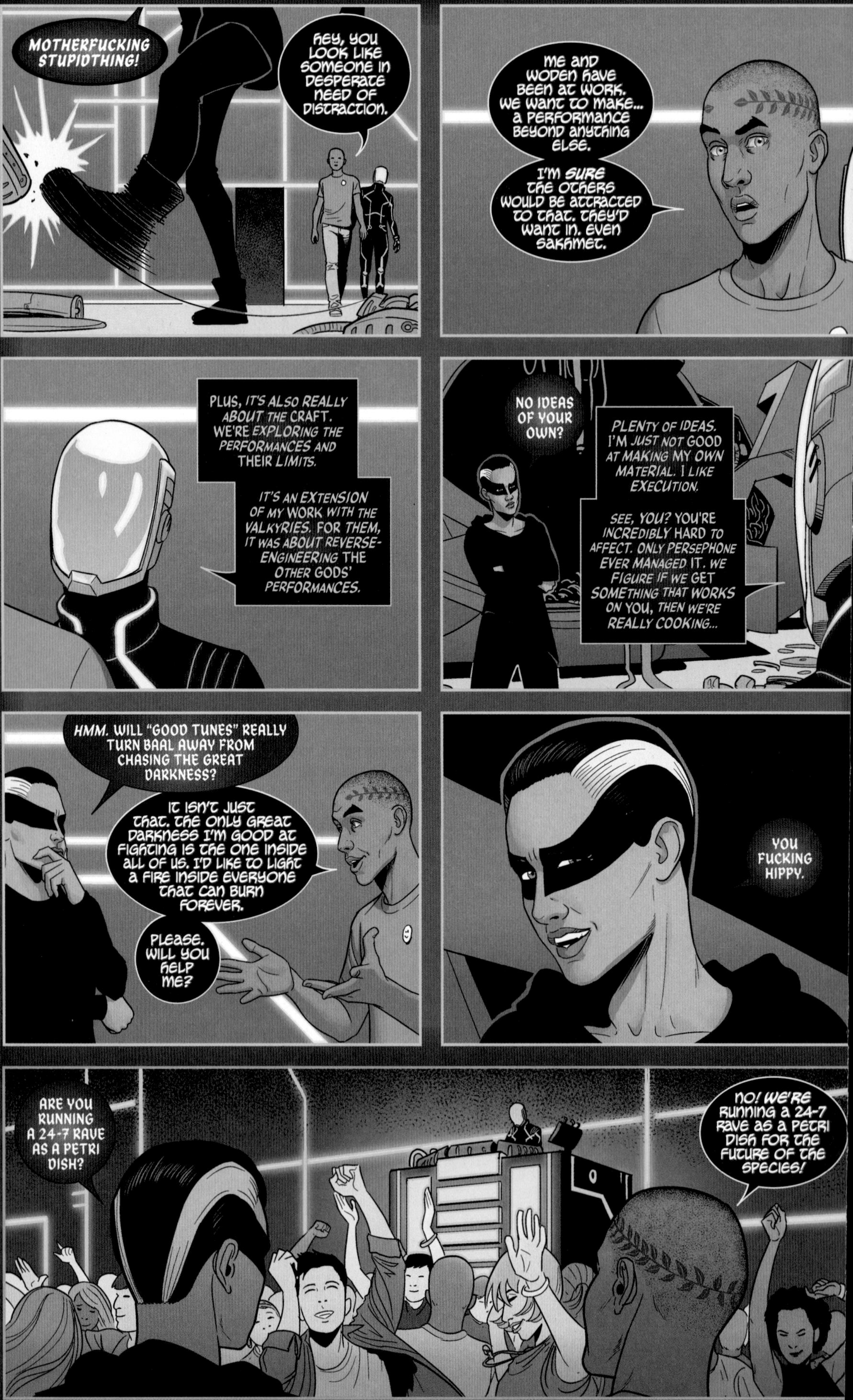
MOTHERFUCKING STUPIDTHING!
HEY, YOU LOOK LIKE SOMEONE IN DESPERATE NEED OF DISTRACTION.
ME AND WODEN HAVE BEEN AT WORK. WE WANT TO MAKE... A PERFORMANCE BEYOND ANYTHING ELSE.
I'M SURE THE OTHERS WOULD BE ATTRACTED TO THAT. THEY'D WANT IN. EVEN SAKHMET.
PLUS, IT'S ALSO REALLY ABOUT THE CRAFT. WE'RE EXPLORING THE PERFORMANCES AND THEIR LIMITS.
IT'S AN EXTENSION OF MY WORK WITH THE VALKYRIES. FOR THEM, IT WAS ABOUT REVERSE-ENGINEERING THE OTHER GODS' PERFORMANCES.
NO IDEAS OF YOUR OWN?
PLENTY OF IDEAS. I'M JUST NOT GOOD AT MAKING MY OWN MATERIAL. I LIKE EXECUTION.
SEE, YOU? YOU'RE INCREDIBLY HARD TO AFFECT. ONLY PERSEPHONE EVER MANAGED IT. WE FIGURE IF WE GET SOMETHING THAT WORKS ON YOU, THEN WE'RE REALLY COOKING...
HMM. WILL "GOOD TUNES" REALLY TURN BAAL AWAY FROM CHASING THE GREAT DARKNESS?
IT ISN'T JUST THAT. THE ONLY GREAT DARKNESS I'M GOOD AT FIGHTING IS THE ONE INSIDE ALL OF US. I'D LIKE TO LIGHT A FIRE INSIDE EVERYONE THAT CAN BURN FOREVER.
PLEASE. WILL YOU HELP ME?
YOU FUCKING HIPPY.
ARE YOU RUNNING A 24-7 RAVE AS A PETRI DISH?
NO! WE'RE RUNNING A 24-7 RAVE AS A PETRI DISH FOR THE FUTURE OF THE SPECIES!

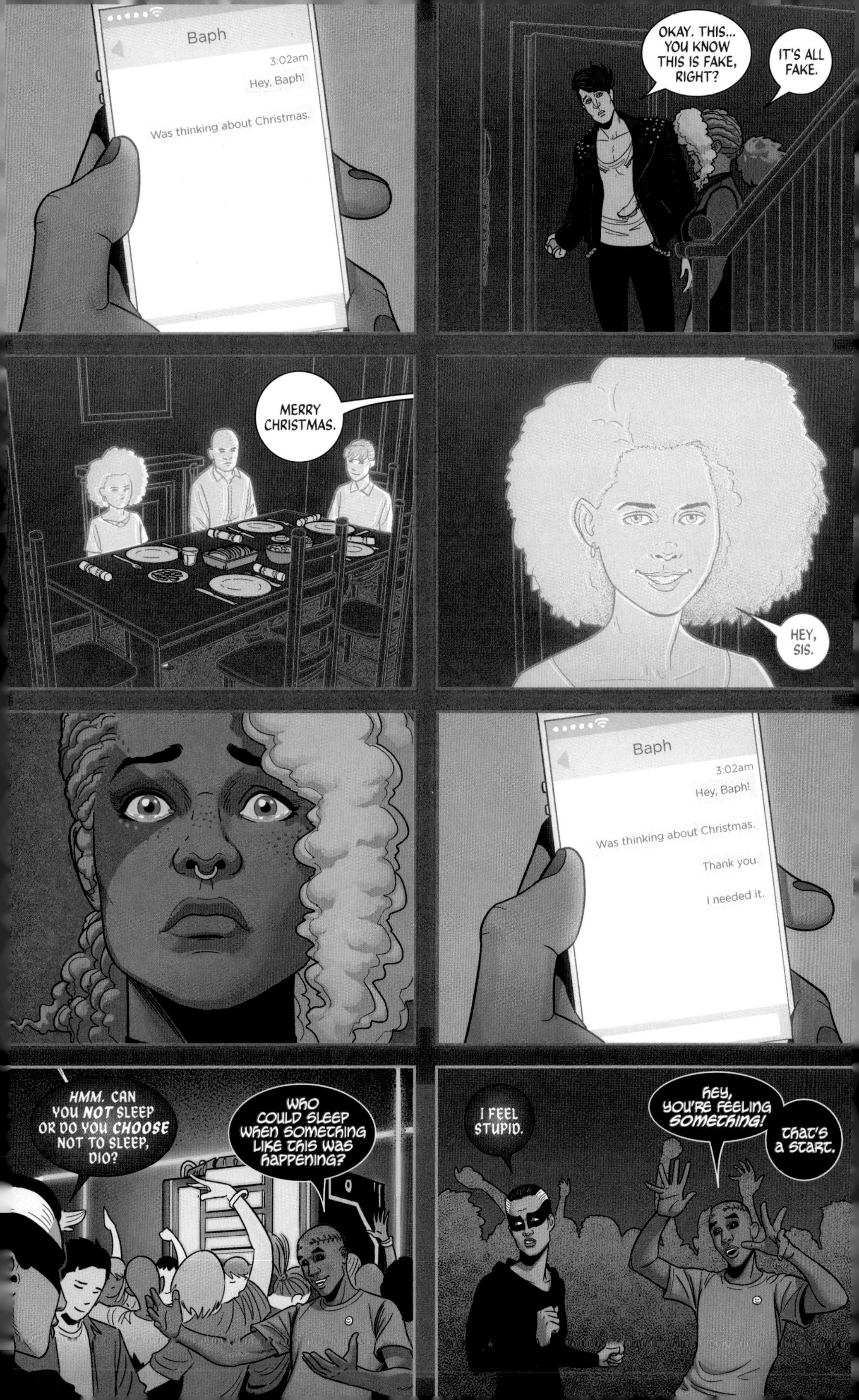
Baph
3:02am
Hey, Baph!
Was thinking about Christmas.
OKAY. THIS... YOU KNOW THIS IS FAKE, RIGHT?
IT'S ALL FAKE.
MERRY CHRISTMAS.
HEY, SIS.
Baph
3:02am
Hey, Baph!
Was thinking about Christmas.
Thank you.
I needed it.
HMM. CAN YOU NOT SLEEP OR DO YOU CHOOSE NOT TO SLEEP, DIO?
WHO COULD SLEEP WHEN SOMETHING LIKE THIS WAS HAPPENING?
I FEEL STUPID.
HEY, YOU'RE FEELING SOMETHING!
THAT'S A START.

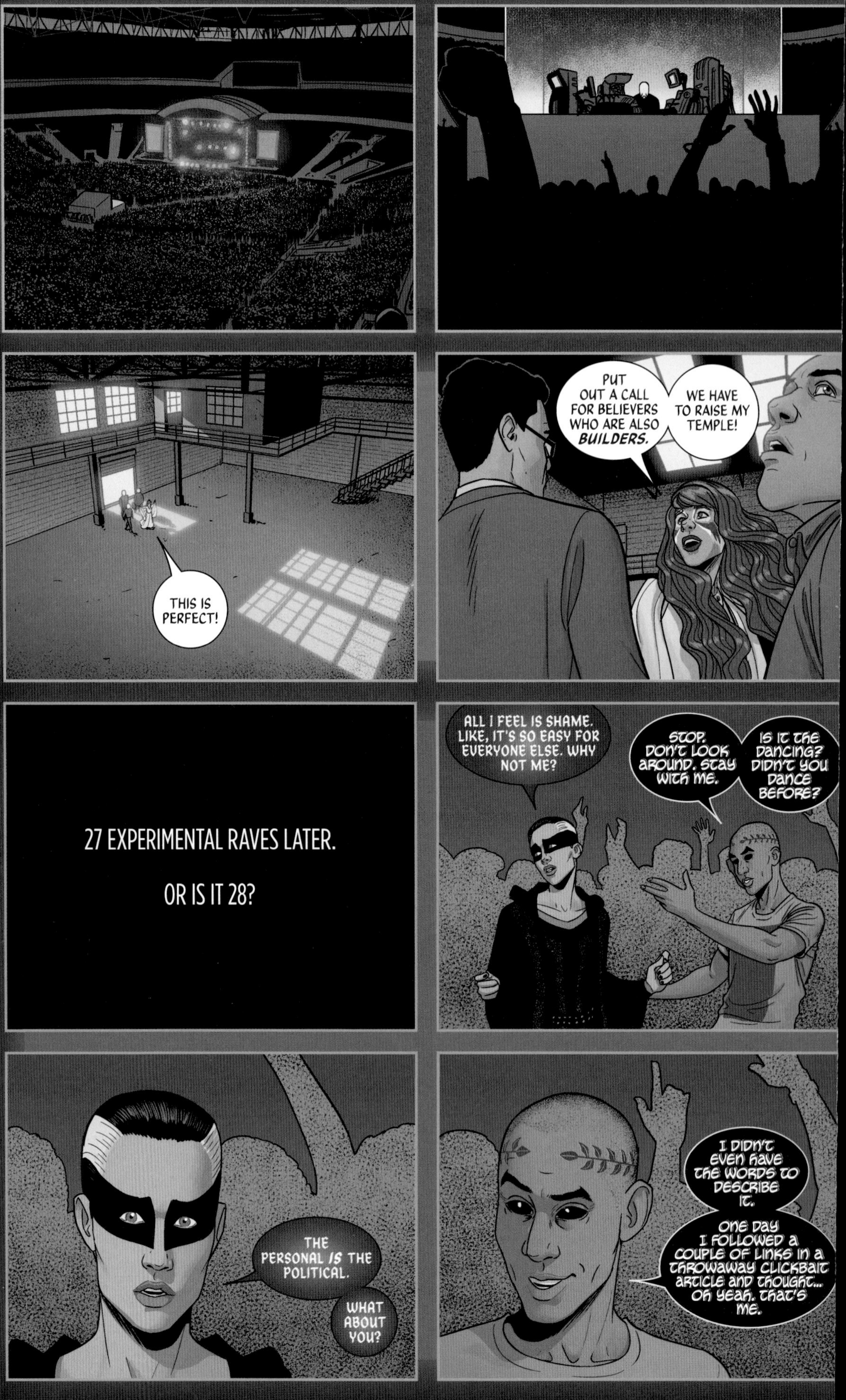
THIS IS PERFECT!
PUT OUT A CALL FOR BELIEVERS WHO ARE ALSO BUILDERS.
WE HAVE TO RAISE MY TEMPLE!
27 EXPERIMENTAL RAVES LATER.
OR IS IT 28?
ALL I FEEL IS SHAME. LIKE, IT'S SO EASY FOR EVERYONE ELSE. WHY NOT ME?
STOP. DON'T LOOK AROUND. STAY WITH ME.
IS IT THE DANCING? DIDN'T YOU DANCE BEFORE?
THE PERSONAL IS THE POLITICAL.
WHAT ABOUT YOU?
I DIDN'T EVEN HAVE THE WORDS TO DESCRIBE IT.
ONE DAY I FOLLOWED A COUPLE OF LINKS IN A THROWAWAY CLICKBAIT ARTICLE AND THOUGHT... OH YEAH. THAT'S ME.

THIS WILL BE THE FIRST SACRED PLACE OF MY RELIGION...

SHINTWO!

THAT'S "*ShinTwo*™".

NO. NOT MY THING. GROWING UP WAS HARD, FOR OBVIOUS FUCKING REASONS. I MEAN, IT IS FOR EVERYONE, BUT THE DISSONANCE BETWEEN HOW I FELT AND HOW I WAS TREATED?

I COULD NEVER RELAX. NOT IN THIS WORLD. IT'S NOT RIGHT.

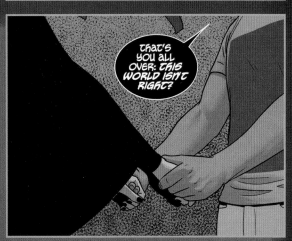

THAT'S YOU ALL OVER: THIS WORLD ISN'T RIGHT?

I'M NOT ACADEMIC.

IT DOESN'T ALWAYS HELP. SOMETIMES IT MAKES IT WORSE.

WE'RE TRYING TO GIVE BIRTH TO THE FUTURE USING THE LANGUAGE OF OUR OPPRESSORS.

HEH. OKAY, THAT WAS WANKY.

I MEAN--

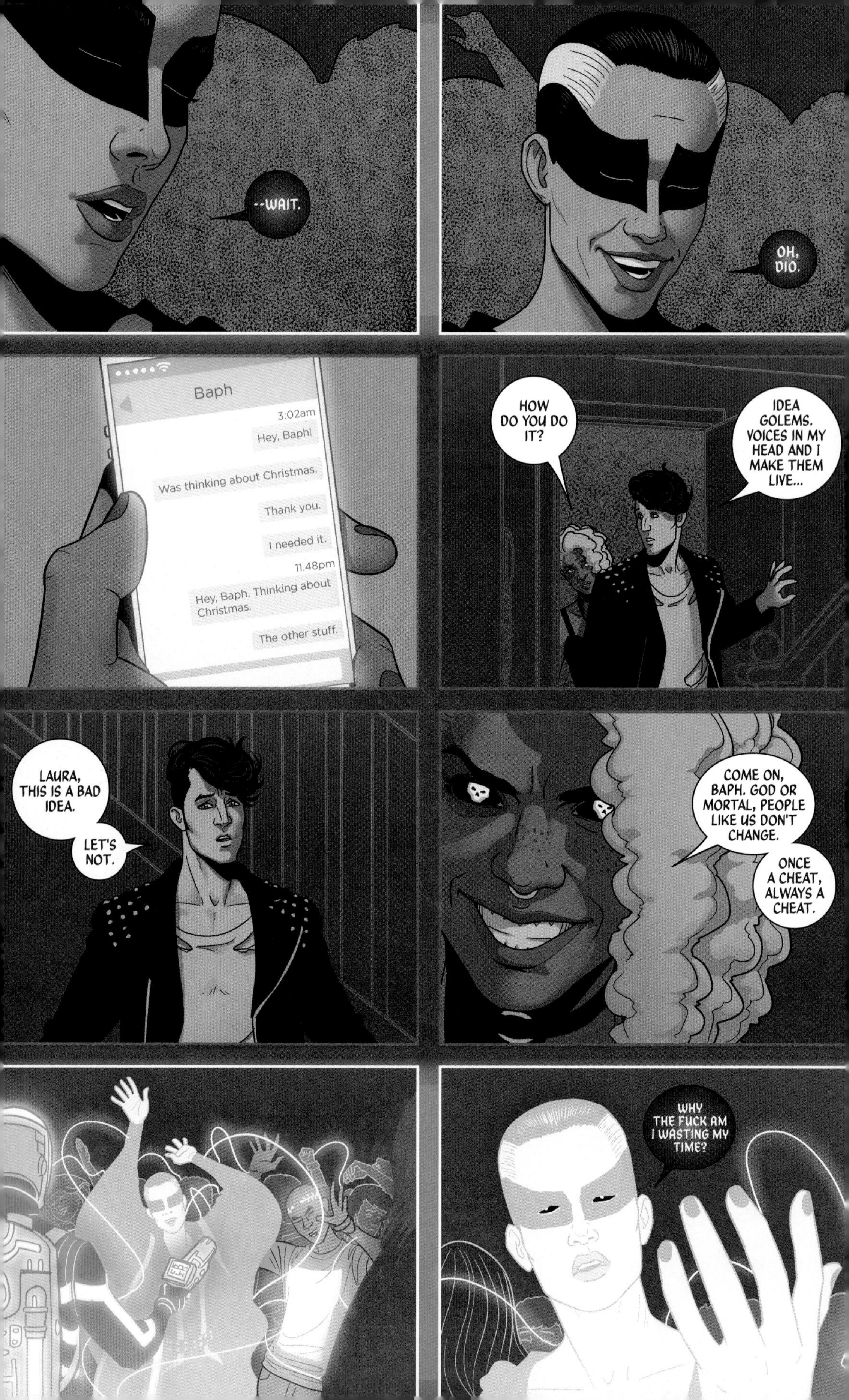
--WAIT.
OH, DIO.
Baph
3:02am
Hey, Baph!
Was thinking about Christmas.
Thank you.
I needed it.
11.48pm
Hey, Baph. Thinking about Christmas.
The other stuff.
HOW DO YOU DO IT?
IDEA GOLEMS. VOICES IN MY HEAD AND I MAKE THEM LIVE...
LAURA, THIS IS A BAD IDEA.
LET'S NOT.
COME ON, BAPH. GOD OR MORTAL, PEOPLE LIKE US DON'T CHANGE.
ONCE A CHEAT, ALWAYS A CHEAT.
WHY THE FUCK AM I WASTING MY TIME?

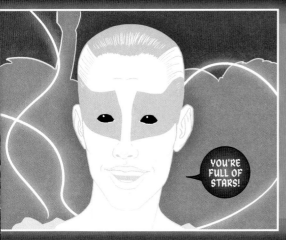

YOU'RE FULL OF STARS!

WE'RE ALL FULL OF STARS.

I GOT YOU A CHRISTMAS PRESENT TOO.

DO YOU WANT TO UNWRAP ME? OR SHALL I?

NO, I'M NOT GOING TO FALL APART.

I'M NOT GOING TO BE ANOTHER TEENAGE CAUTIONARY TALE.

Baph

Was thinking about Christmas.

Thank you.

I needed it.

11.48pm

Hey, Baph. Thinking about Christmas.

The other stuff.

That bit was fun.

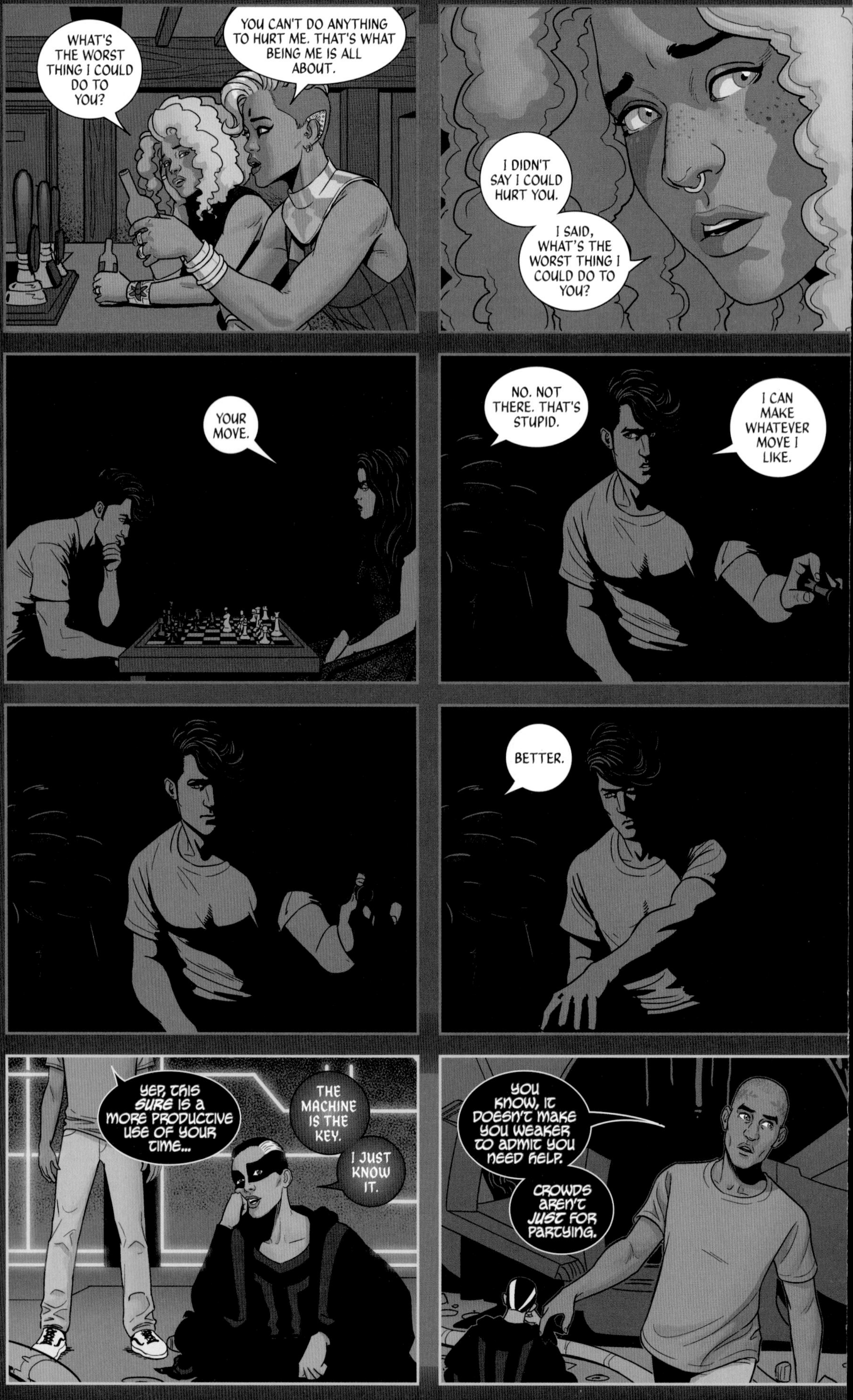

WHAT'S THE WORST THING I COULD DO TO YOU?
YOU CAN'T DO ANYTHING TO HURT ME. THAT'S WHAT BEING ME IS ALL ABOUT.
I DIDN'T SAY I COULD HURT YOU.
I SAID, WHAT'S THE WORST THING I COULD DO TO YOU?
YOUR MOVE.
NO. NOT THERE. THAT'S STUPID.
I CAN MAKE WHATEVER MOVE I LIKE.
BETTER.
YEP, THIS SURE IS A MORE PRODUCTIVE USE OF YOUR TIME...
THE MACHINE IS THE KEY.
I JUST KNOW IT.
YOU KNOW, IT DOESN'T MAKE YOU WEAKER TO ADMIT YOU NEED HELP.
CROWDS AREN'T JUST FOR PARTYING.

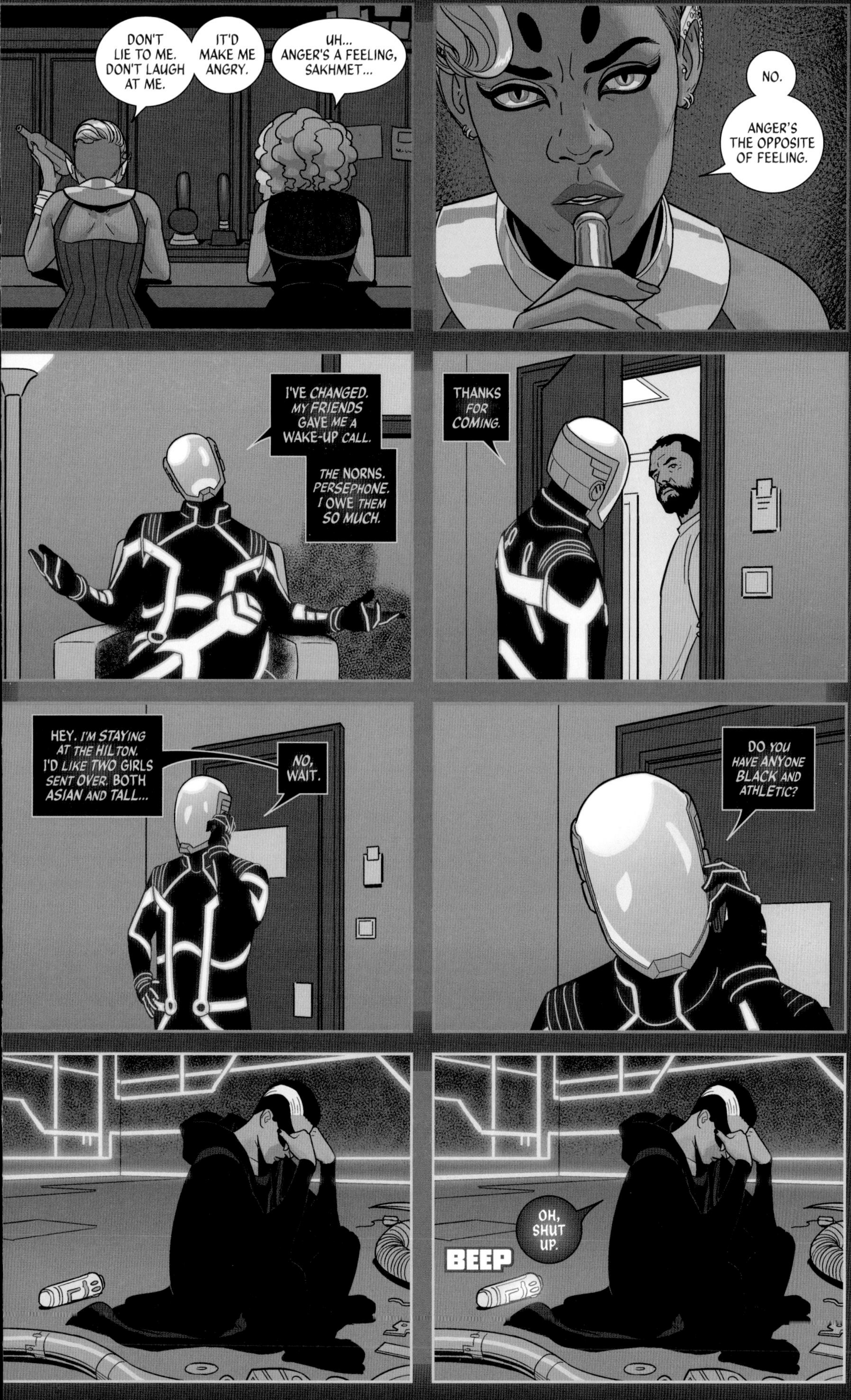
DON'T LIE TO ME. DON'T LAUGH AT ME.
IT'D MAKE ME ANGRY.
UH... ANGER'S A FEELING, SAKHMET...
NO.
ANGER'S THE OPPOSITE OF FEELING.
I'VE CHANGED. MY FRIENDS GAVE ME A WAKE-UP CALL.
THE NORNS. PERSEPHONE. I OWE THEM SO MUCH.
THANKS FOR COMING.
HEY. I'M STAYING AT THE HILTON. I'D LIKE TWO GIRLS SENT OVER. BOTH ASIAN AND TALL...
NO, WAIT.
DO YOU HAVE ANYONE BLACK AND ATHLETIC?
BEEP
OH, SHUT UP.

THE CASSANDRA PROJECT

1 MARCH 2015

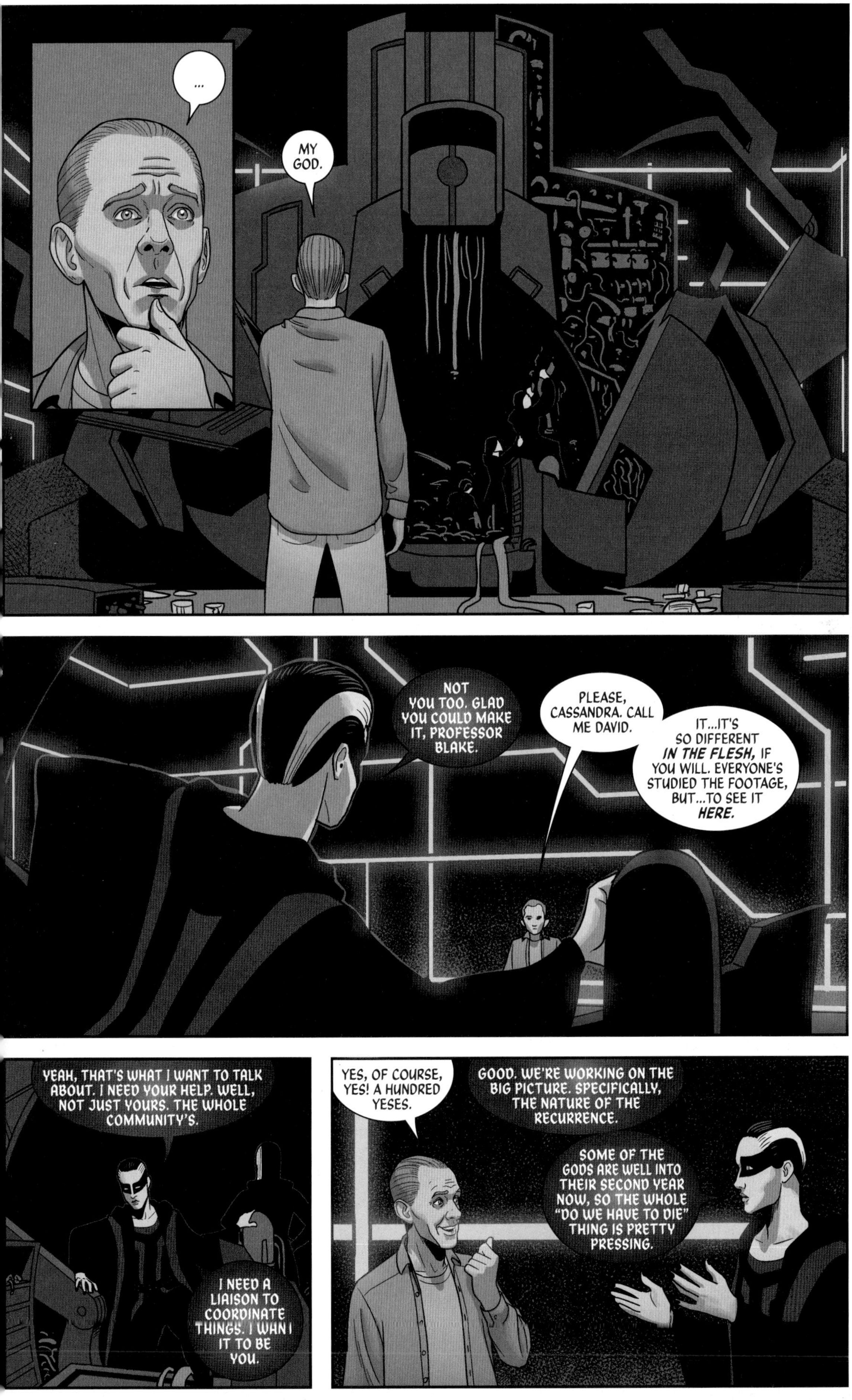
...
MY GOD.
NOT YOU TOO. GLAD YOU COULD MAKE IT, PROFESSOR BLAKE.
PLEASE, CASSANDRA. CALL ME DAVID.
IT...IT'S SO DIFFERENT IN THE FLESH, IF YOU WILL. EVERYONE'S STUDIED THE FOOTAGE, BUT...TO SEE IT HERE.
YEAH, THAT'S WHAT I WANT TO TALK ABOUT. I NEED YOUR HELP. WELL, NOT JUST YOURS. THE WHOLE COMMUNITY'S.
I NEED A LIAISON TO COORDINATE THINGS. I WANT IT TO BE YOU.
YES, OF COURSE, YES! A HUNDRED YESES.
GOOD. WE'RE WORKING ON THE BIG PICTURE. SPECIFICALLY, THE NATURE OF THE RECURRENCE.
SOME OF THE GODS ARE WELL INTO THEIR SECOND YEAR NOW, SO THE WHOLE "DO WE HAVE TO DIE" THING IS PRETTY PRESSING.

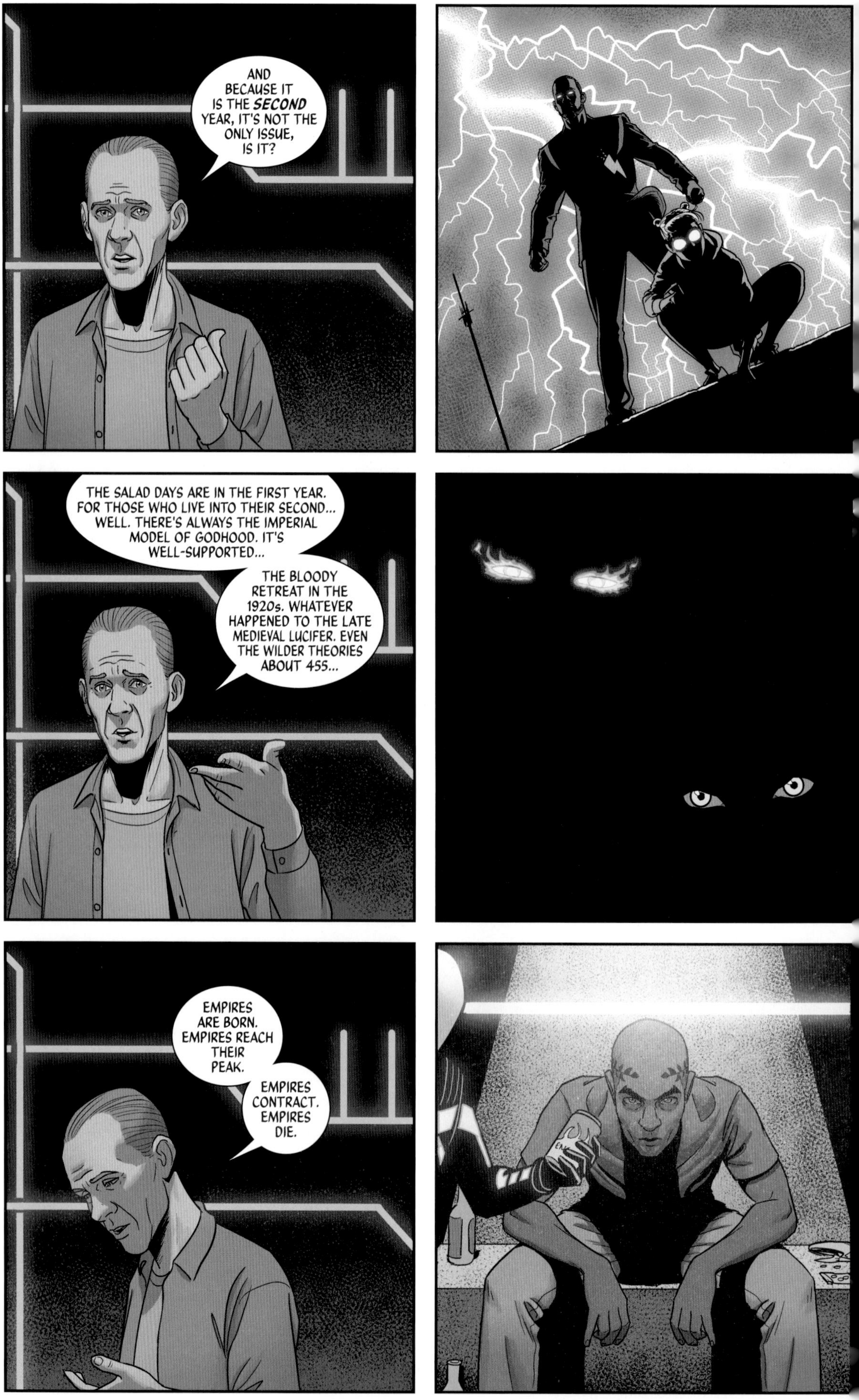
AND BECAUSE IT IS THE *SECOND* YEAR, IT'S NOT THE ONLY ISSUE, IS IT?
THE SALAD DAYS ARE IN THE FIRST YEAR. FOR THOSE WHO LIVE INTO THEIR SECOND... WELL. THERE'S ALWAYS THE IMPERIAL MODEL OF GODHOOD. IT'S WELL-SUPPORTED...
THE BLOODY RETREAT IN THE 1920s. WHATEVER HAPPENED TO THE LATE MEDIEVAL LUCIFER. EVEN THE WILDER THEORIES ABOUT 455...
EMPIRES ARE BORN. EMPIRES REACH THEIR PEAK.
EMPIRES CONTRACT. EMPIRES DIE.

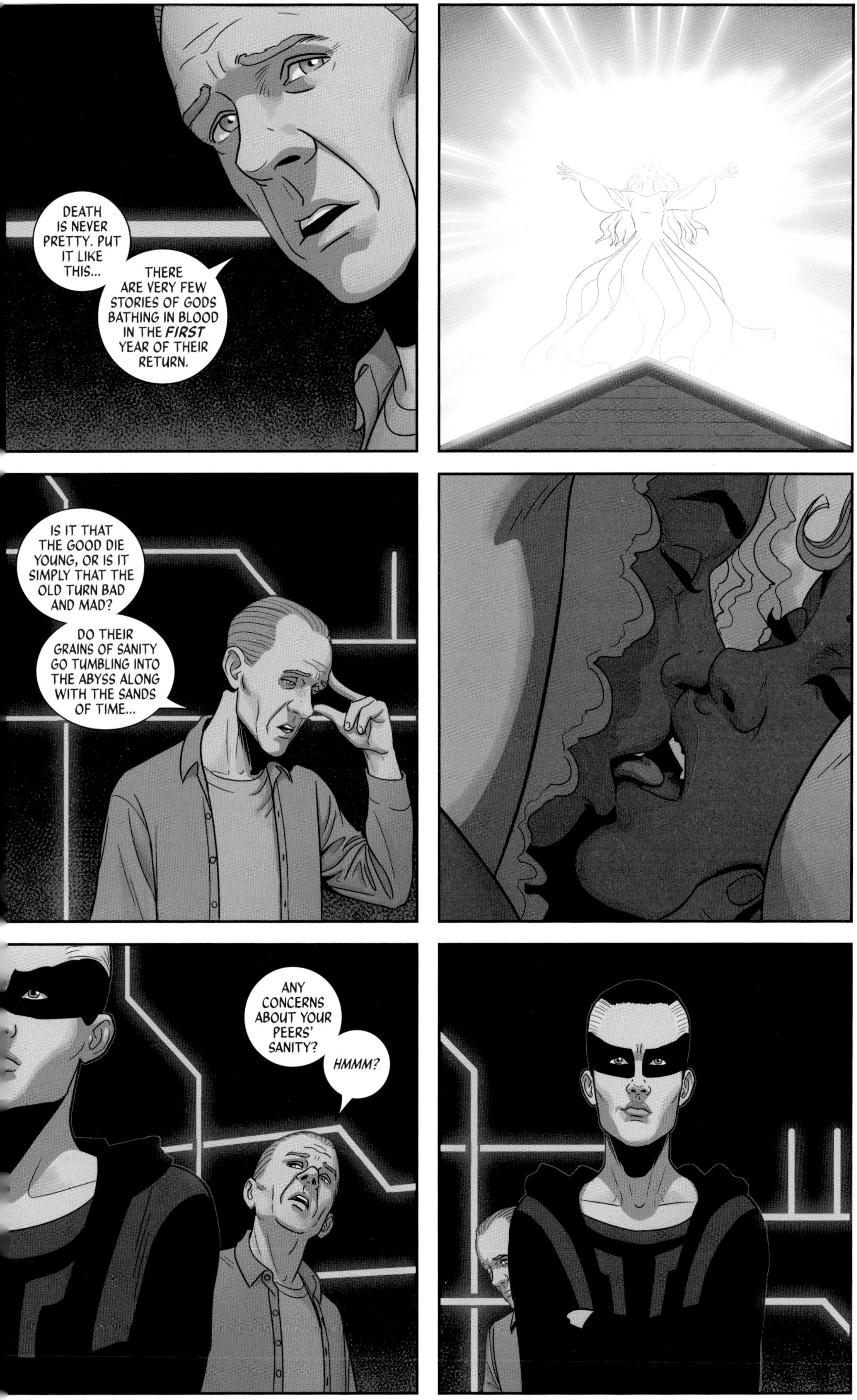
DEATH IS NEVER PRETTY. PUT IT LIKE THIS...
THERE ARE VERY FEW STORIES OF GODS BATHING IN BLOOD IN THE *FIRST* YEAR OF THEIR RETURN.
IS IT THAT THE GOOD DIE YOUNG, OR IS IT SIMPLY THAT THE OLD TURN BAD AND MAD?
DO THEIR GRAINS OF SANITY GO TUMBLING INTO THE ABYSS ALONG WITH THE SANDS OF TIME...
ANY CONCERNS ABOUT YOUR PEERS' SANITY?
HMMM?

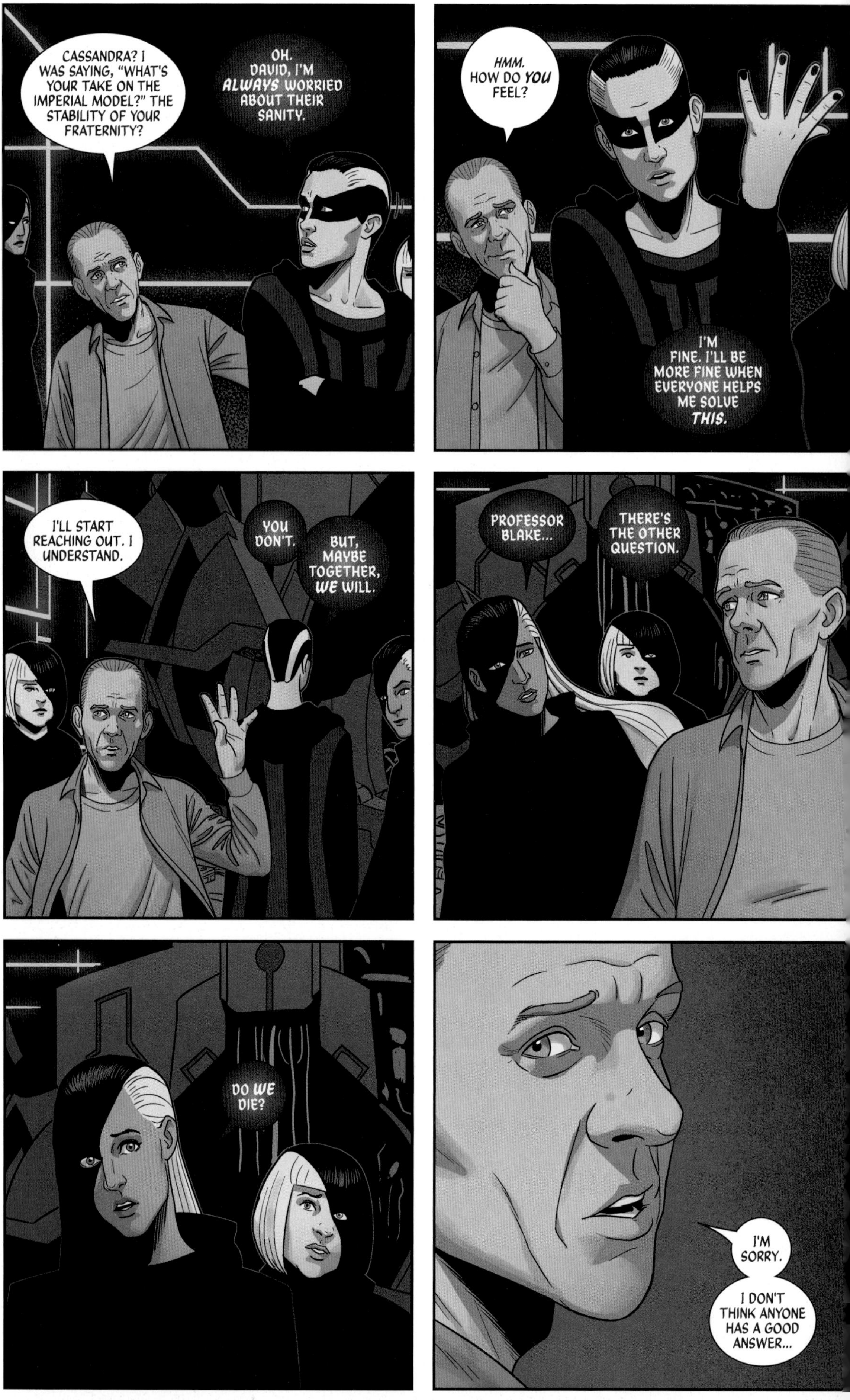
CASSANDRA? I WAS SAYING, "WHAT'S YOUR TAKE ON THE IMPERIAL MODEL?" THE STABILITY OF YOUR FRATERNITY?
OH. DAVID, I'M ALWAYS WORRIED ABOUT THEIR SANITY.
HMM. HOW DO YOU FEEL?
I'M FINE. I'LL BE MORE FINE WHEN EVERYONE HELPS ME SOLVE THIS.
I'LL START REACHING OUT. I UNDERSTAND.
YOU DON'T.
BUT, MAYBE TOGETHER, WE WILL.
PROFESSOR BLAKE...
THERE'S THE OTHER QUESTION.
DO WE DIE?
I'M SORRY.
I DON'T THINK ANYONE HAS A GOOD ANSWER...

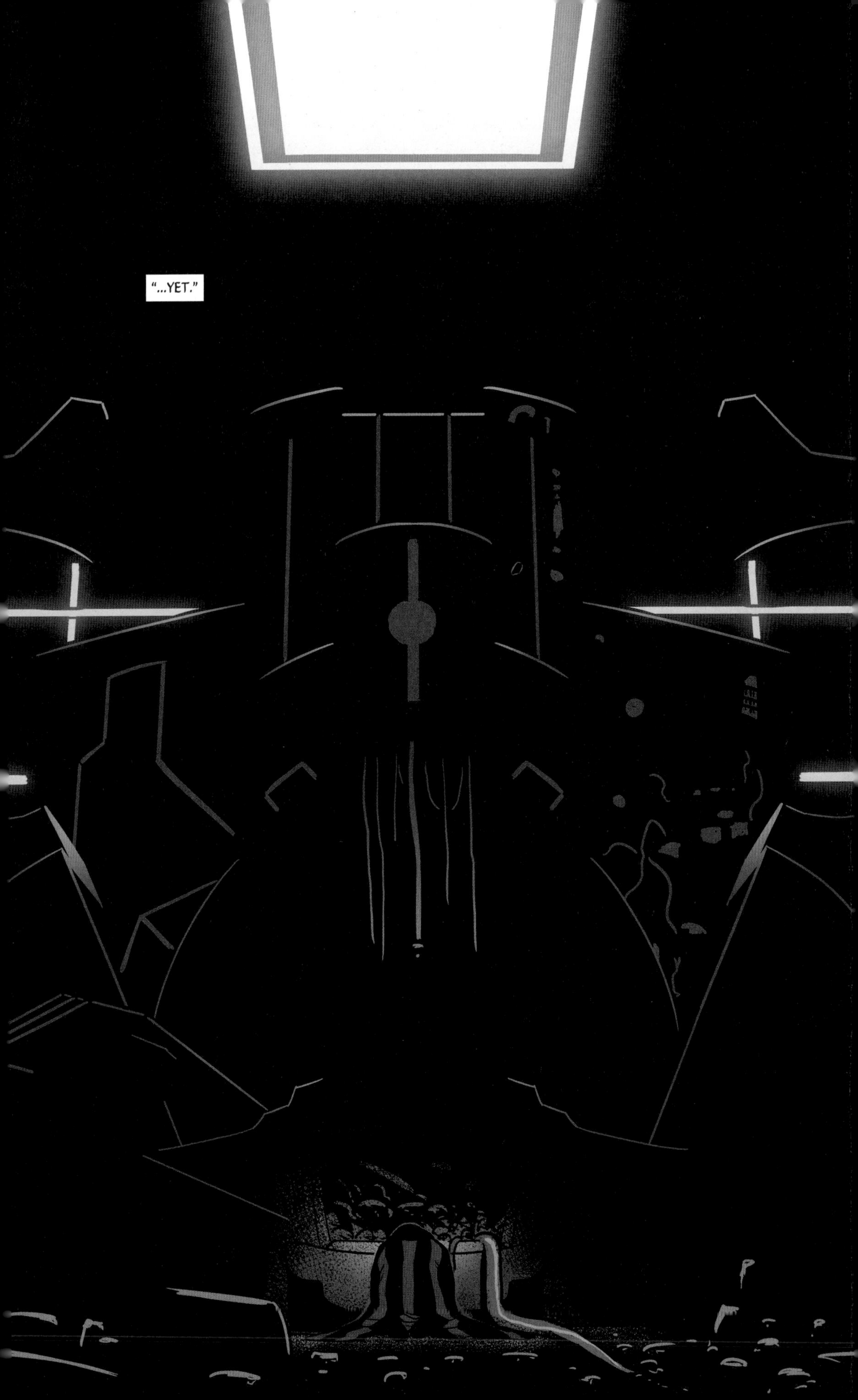
"...YET."

BE TRUE TO
YOUR OBSESSIONS

1 MARCH 2015

THE

WICKED

+

THE DIVINE

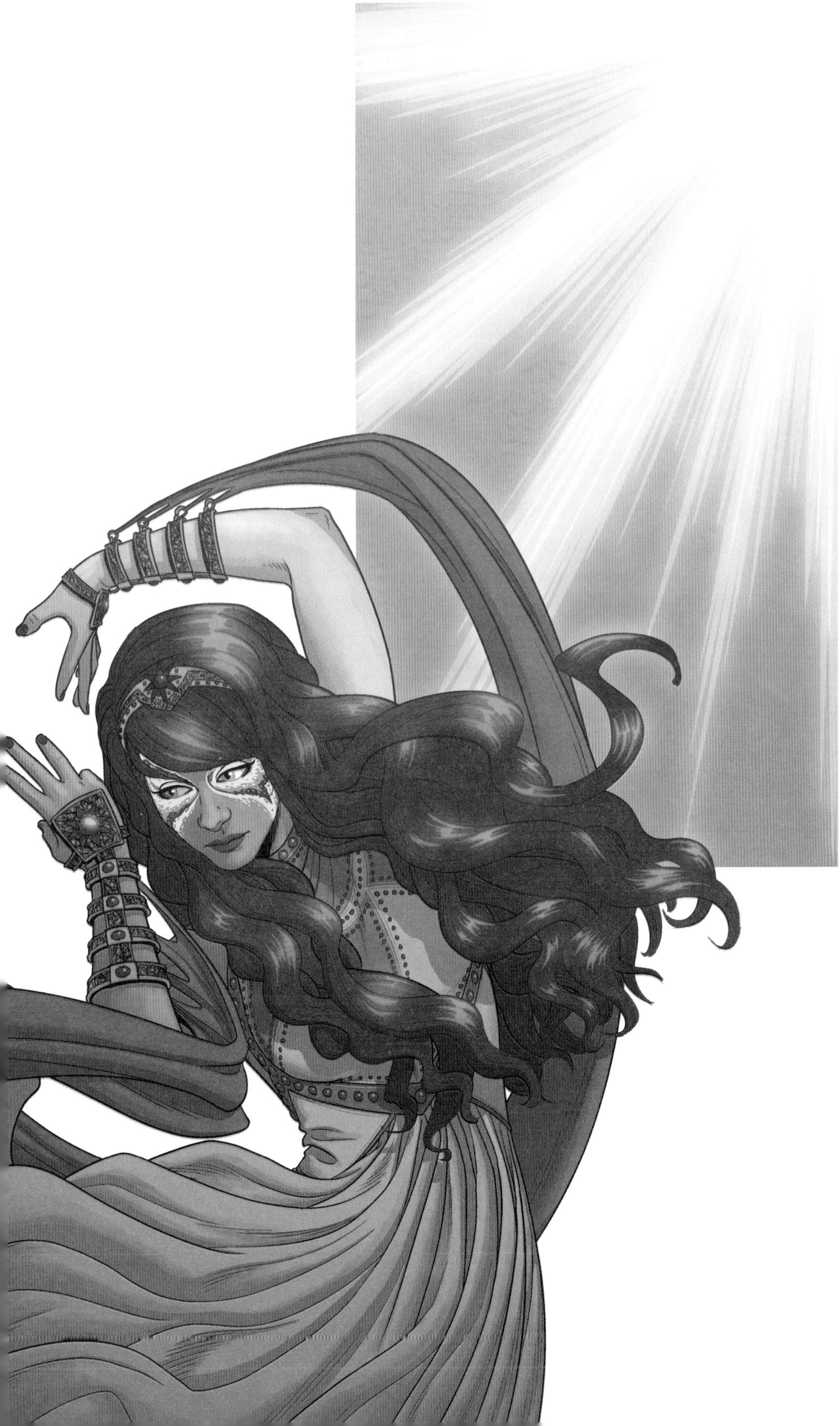

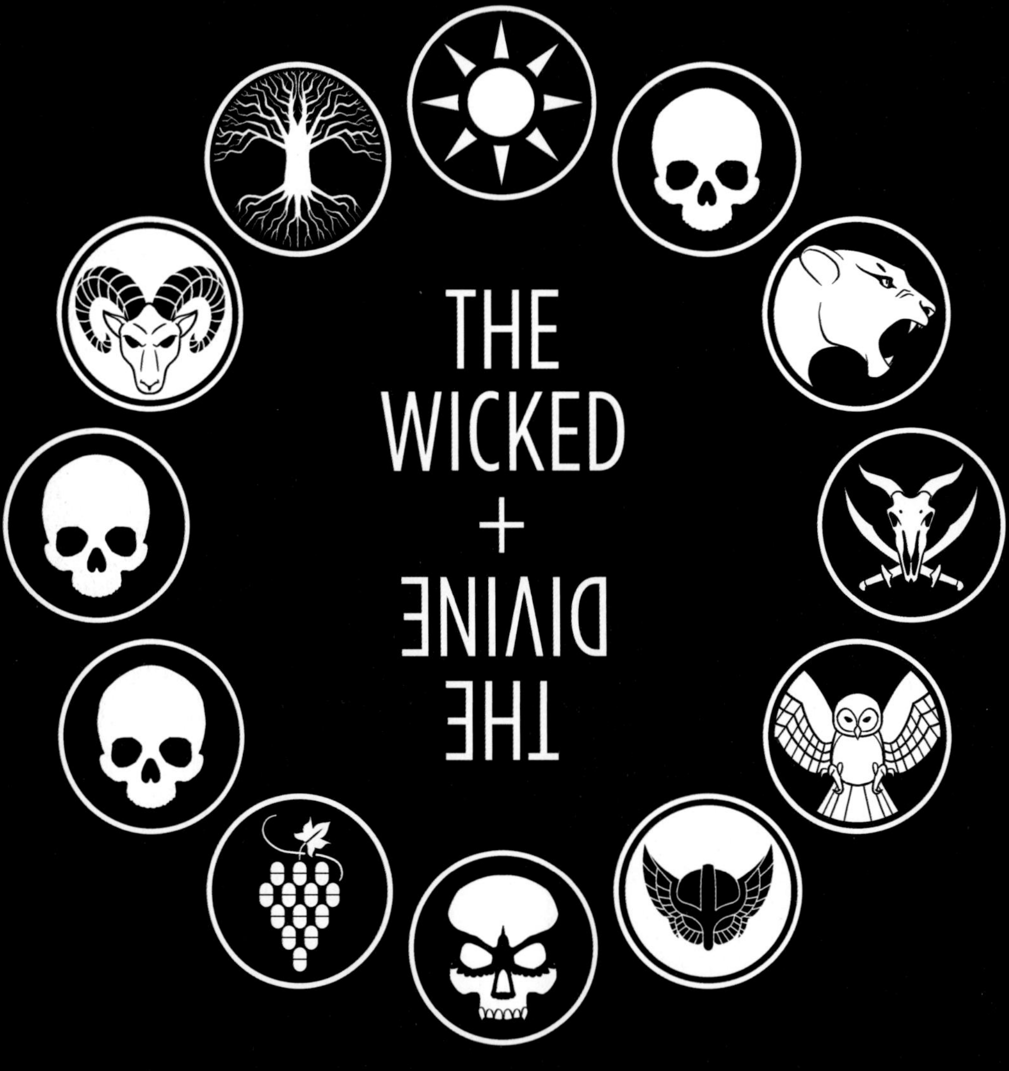
THE
WICKED
+
THE
DIVINE

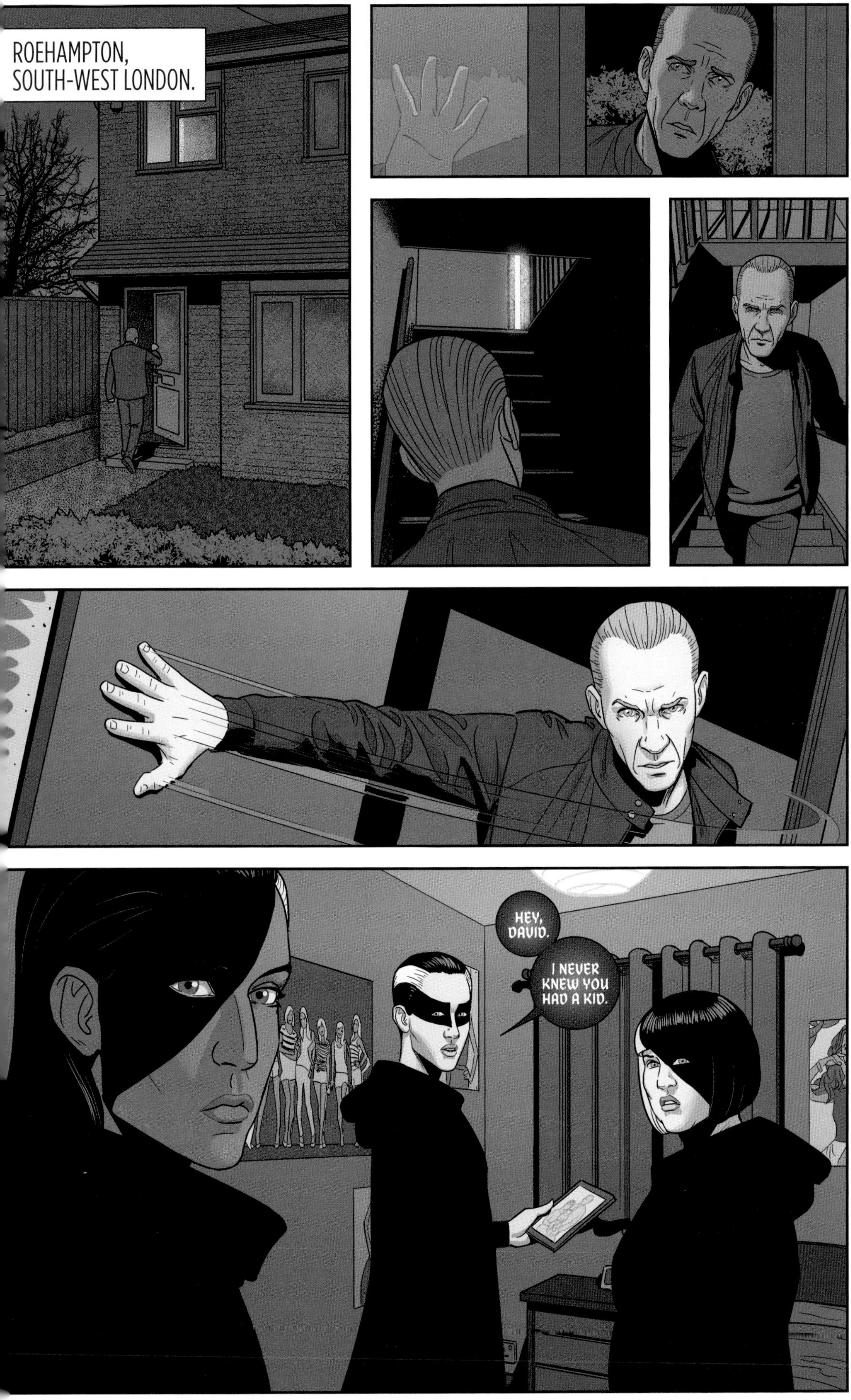
ROEHAMPTON,
SOUTH-WEST LONDON.
HEY, DAVID.
I NEVER KNEW YOU HAD A KID.

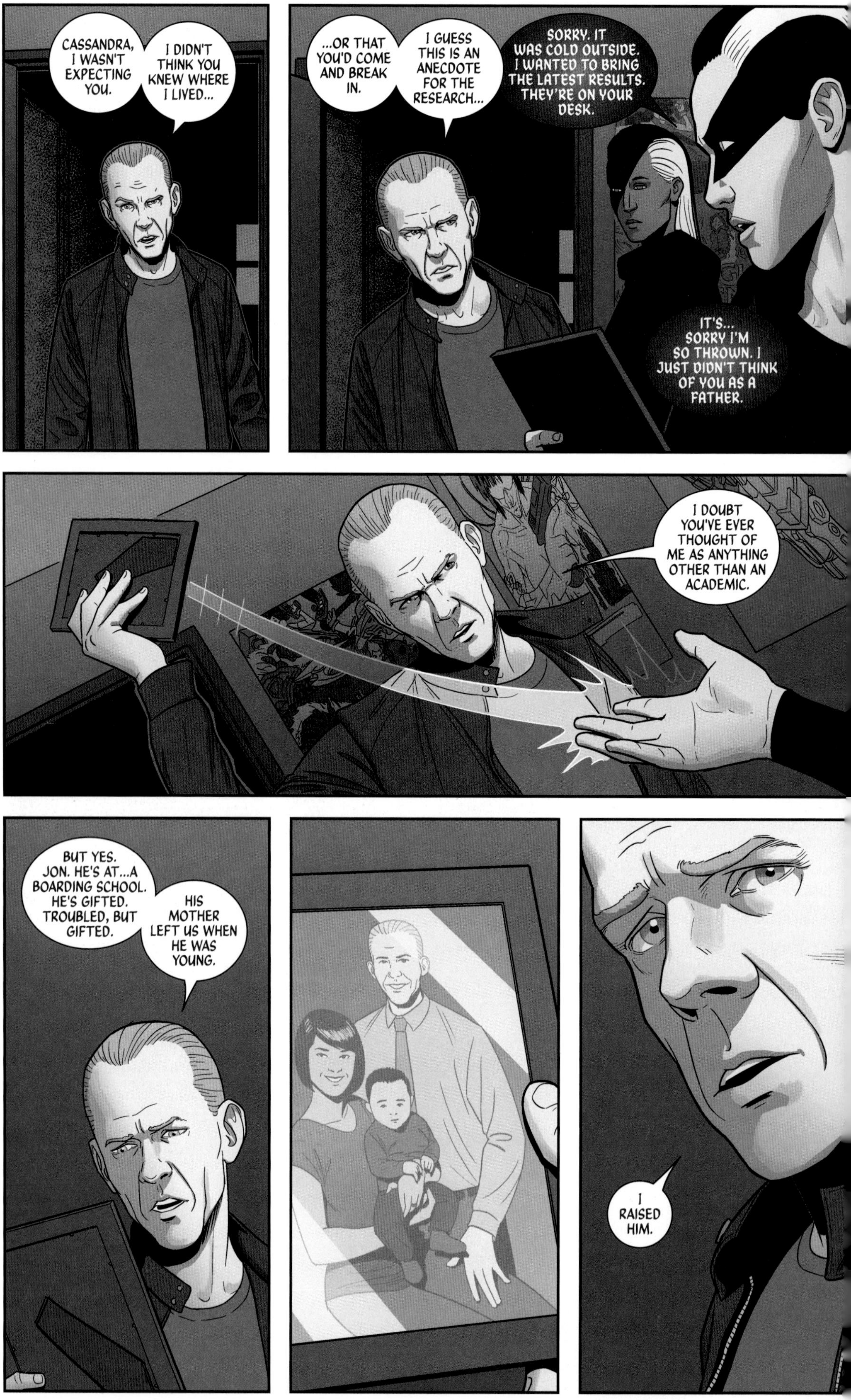
CASSANDRA, I WASN'T EXPECTING YOU.
I DIDN'T THINK YOU KNEW WHERE I LIVED...
...OR THAT YOU'D COME AND BREAK IN.
I GUESS THIS IS AN ANECDOTE FOR THE RESEARCH...
SORRY. IT WAS COLD OUTSIDE. I WANTED TO BRING THE LATEST RESULTS. THEY'RE ON YOUR DESK.
IT'S... SORRY I'M SO THROWN. I JUST DIDN'T THINK OF YOU AS A FATHER.
I DOUBT YOU'VE EVER THOUGHT OF ME AS ANYTHING OTHER THAN AN ACADEMIC.
BUT YES. JON. HE'S AT...A BOARDING SCHOOL. HE'S GIFTED. TROUBLED, BUT GIFTED.
HIS MOTHER LEFT US WHEN HE WAS YOUNG.
I RAISED HIM.

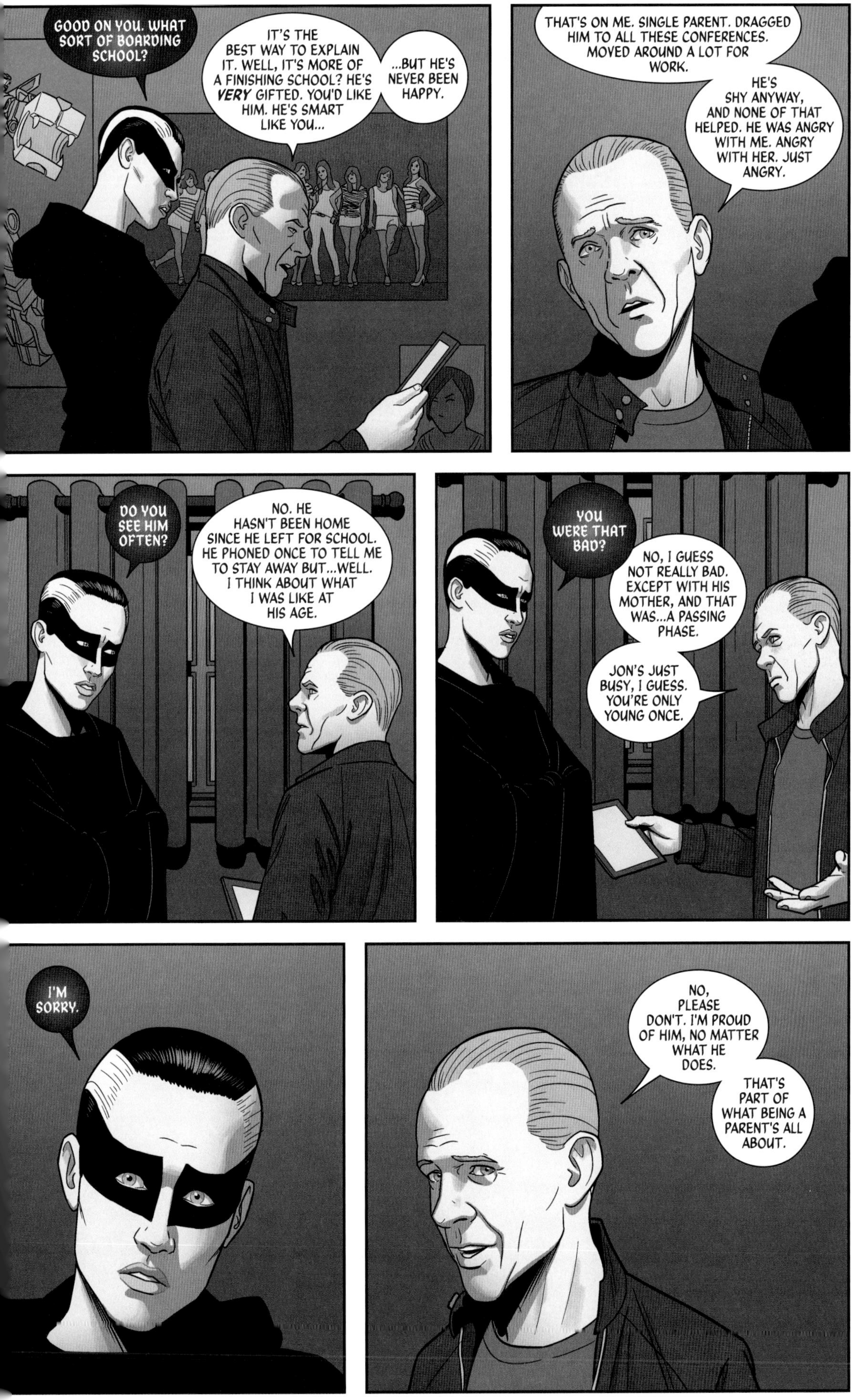
GOOD ON YOU. WHAT SORT OF BOARDING SCHOOL?
IT'S THE BEST WAY TO EXPLAIN IT. WELL, IT'S MORE OF A FINISHING SCHOOL? HE'S *VERY* GIFTED. YOU'D LIKE HIM. HE'S SMART LIKE YOU...
...BUT HE'S NEVER BEEN HAPPY.
THAT'S ON ME. SINGLE PARENT. DRAGGED HIM TO ALL THESE CONFERENCES. MOVED AROUND A LOT FOR WORK.
HE'S SHY ANYWAY, AND NONE OF THAT HELPED. HE WAS ANGRY WITH ME. ANGRY WITH HER. JUST ANGRY.
DO YOU SEE HIM OFTEN?
NO. HE HASN'T BEEN HOME SINCE HE LEFT FOR SCHOOL. HE PHONED ONCE TO TELL ME TO STAY AWAY BUT...WELL. I THINK ABOUT WHAT I WAS LIKE AT HIS AGE.
YOU WERE THAT BAD?
NO, I GUESS NOT REALLY BAD. EXCEPT WITH HIS MOTHER, AND THAT WAS...A PASSING PHASE.
JON'S JUST BUSY, I GUESS. YOU'RE ONLY YOUNG ONCE.
I'M SORRY.
NO, PLEASE DON'T. I'M PROUD OF HIM, NO MATTER WHAT HE DOES.
THAT'S PART OF WHAT BEING A PARENT'S ALL ABOUT.

THEY FUCK
YOU UP

5 MARCH 2015

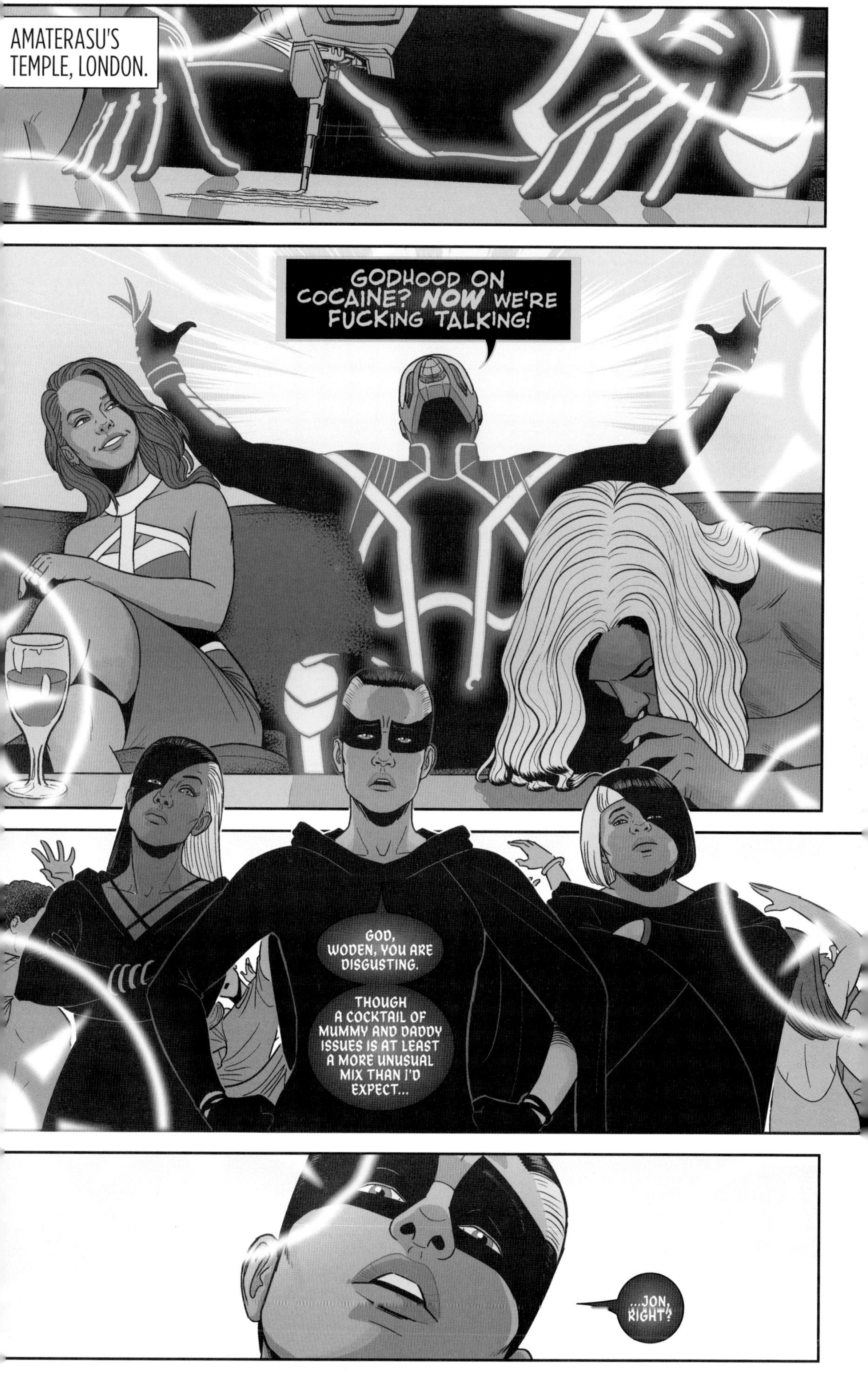
AMATERASU'S TEMPLE, LONDON.
GODHOOD ON COCAINE? NOW WE'RE FUCKING TALKING!
GOD, WODEN, YOU ARE DISGUSTING.
THOUGH A COCKTAIL OF MUMMY AND DADDY ISSUES IS AT LEAST A MORE UNUSUAL MIX THAN I'D EXPECT...
...JON, RIGHT?

A LITTLE PRIVACY, GIRLS.

...YOU KNOW, CASS, SOMEONE SENT ME A LINK TO ALL THAT STUFF *ABOUT* YOUR LIFE BEFORE YOU TRANSITIONED.

I *DIDN'T* CLICK IT.

YOU LITTLE SHIT! YOU COMPARING THIS TO THAT IS FUCKING OFFENSIVE.

YES. MICROAGGRESSION ISN'T TRYING HARD ENOUGH. MACROAGGRESSION OR NOTHING.

BUT *REALLY?* IMAGINE HOW ANGRY YOU'VE MADE ME TO BE THAT UNSUBTLE.

EVERYTHING ISN'T AN AMUSING PUZZLE FOR YOU TO FIGURE OUT.

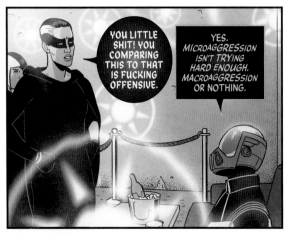

IT DOESN'T EXCUSE WHAT YOU JUST DID IN THE FUCKING SLIGHTEST...BUT YOU'RE RIGHT. I'M SORRY.

THANK *YOU*, AND... I *COULD* JUST HAVE SAID "STAY THE FUCK OUT OF MY LIFE" WITHOUT GOING THERE.

YOU *DIDN'T* COME HERE TO JUDGE ME, ANYWAY. YOU CAME TO JUDGE *HER*, RIGHT?

I THINK AMATERASU'S BODY IS MADE OF HUBRIS WITH TRACE ELEMENTS OF W, T AND F.

I CAN'T BELIEVE DIONYSUS AGREED TO THROWING A PARTY. THIS CULT THING IS...CULTY.

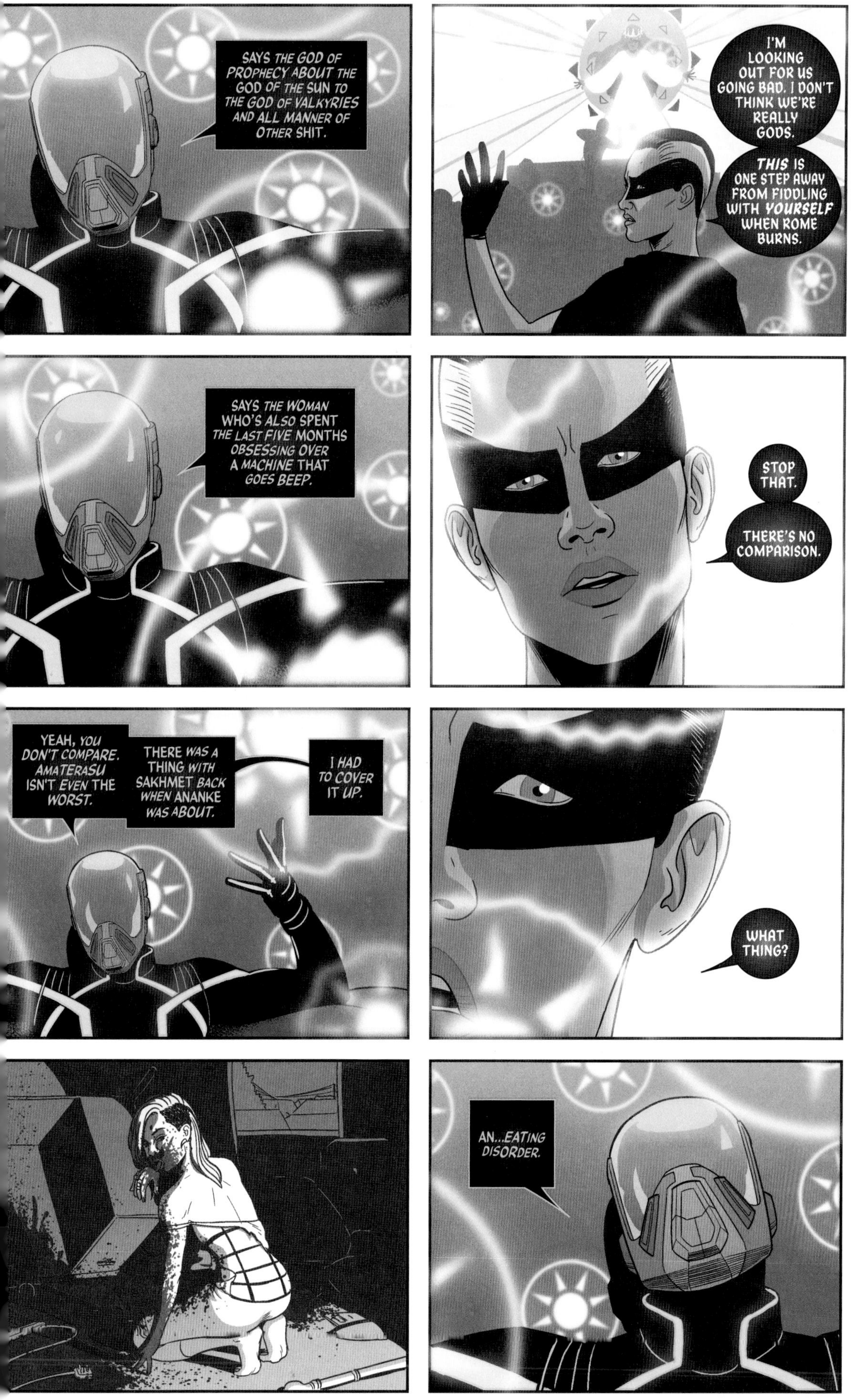
SAYS THE GOD OF PROPHECY ABOUT THE GOD OF THE SUN TO THE GOD OF VALKYRIES AND ALL MANNER OF OTHER SHIT.
I'M LOOKING OUT FOR US GOING BAD. I DON'T THINK WE'RE REALLY GODS.
THIS IS ONE STEP AWAY FROM FIDDLING WITH YOURSELF WHEN ROME BURNS.
SAYS THE WOMAN WHO'S ALSO SPENT THE LAST FIVE MONTHS OBSESSING OVER A MACHINE THAT GOES BEEP.
STOP THAT.
THERE'S NO COMPARISON.
YEAH, YOU DON'T COMPARE. AMATERASU ISN'T EVEN THE WORST.
THERE WAS A THING WITH SAKHMET BACK WHEN ANANKE WAS ABOUT.
I HAD TO COVER IT UP.
WHAT THING?
AN...EATING DISORDER.

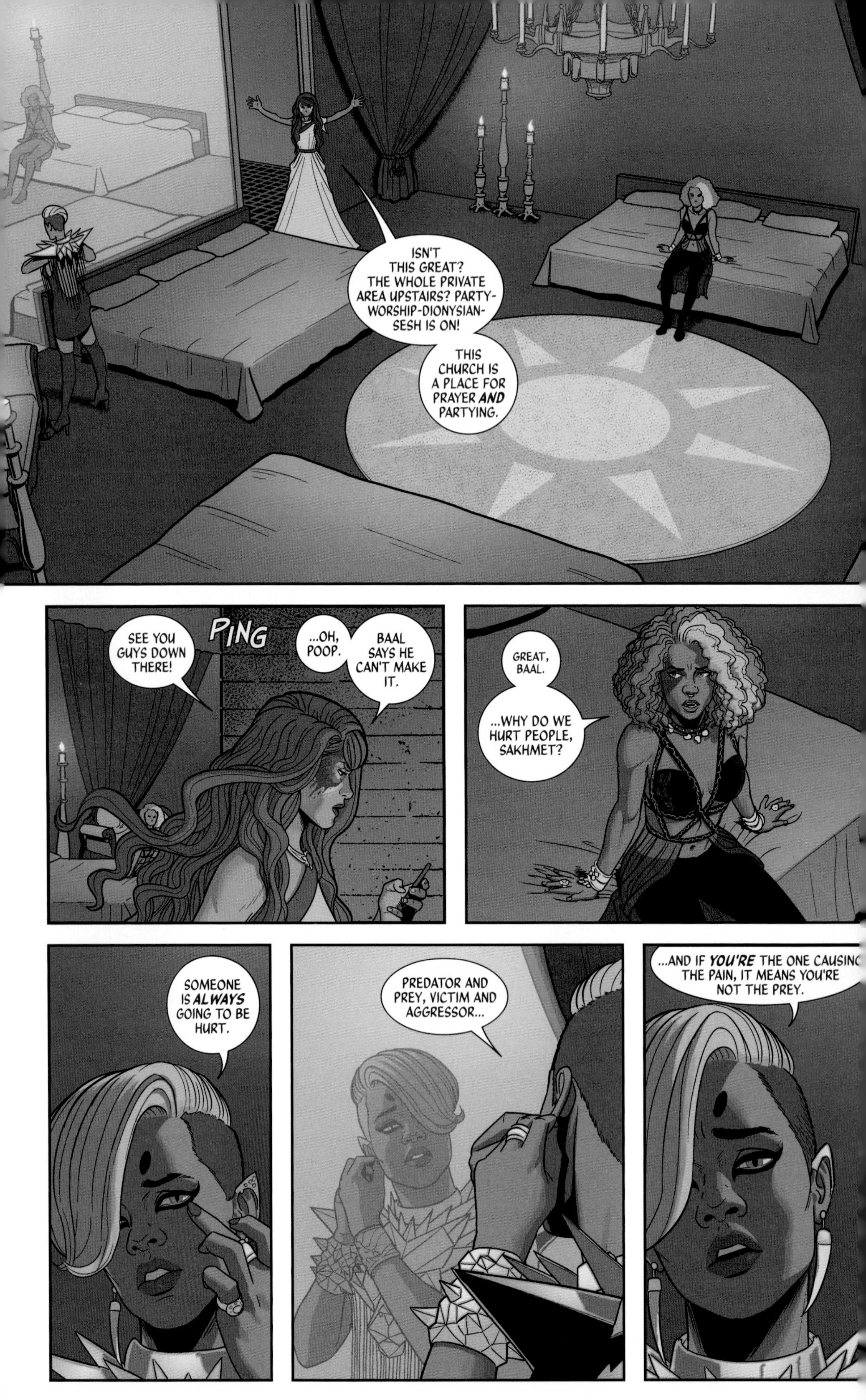
ISN'T THIS GREAT? THE WHOLE PRIVATE AREA UPSTAIRS? PARTY-WORSHIP-DIONYSIAN-SESH IS ON!
THIS CHURCH IS A PLACE FOR PRAYER **AND** PARTYING.
SEE YOU GUYS DOWN THERE!
PING
...OH, POOP.
BAAL SAYS HE CAN'T MAKE IT.
GREAT, BAAL.
...WHY DO WE HURT PEOPLE, SAKHMET?
SOMEONE IS ***ALWAYS*** GOING TO BE HURT.
PREDATOR AND PREY, VICTIM AND AGGRESSOR...
...AND IF ***YOU'RE*** THE ONE CAUSING THE PAIN, IT MEANS YOU'RE NOT THE PREY.

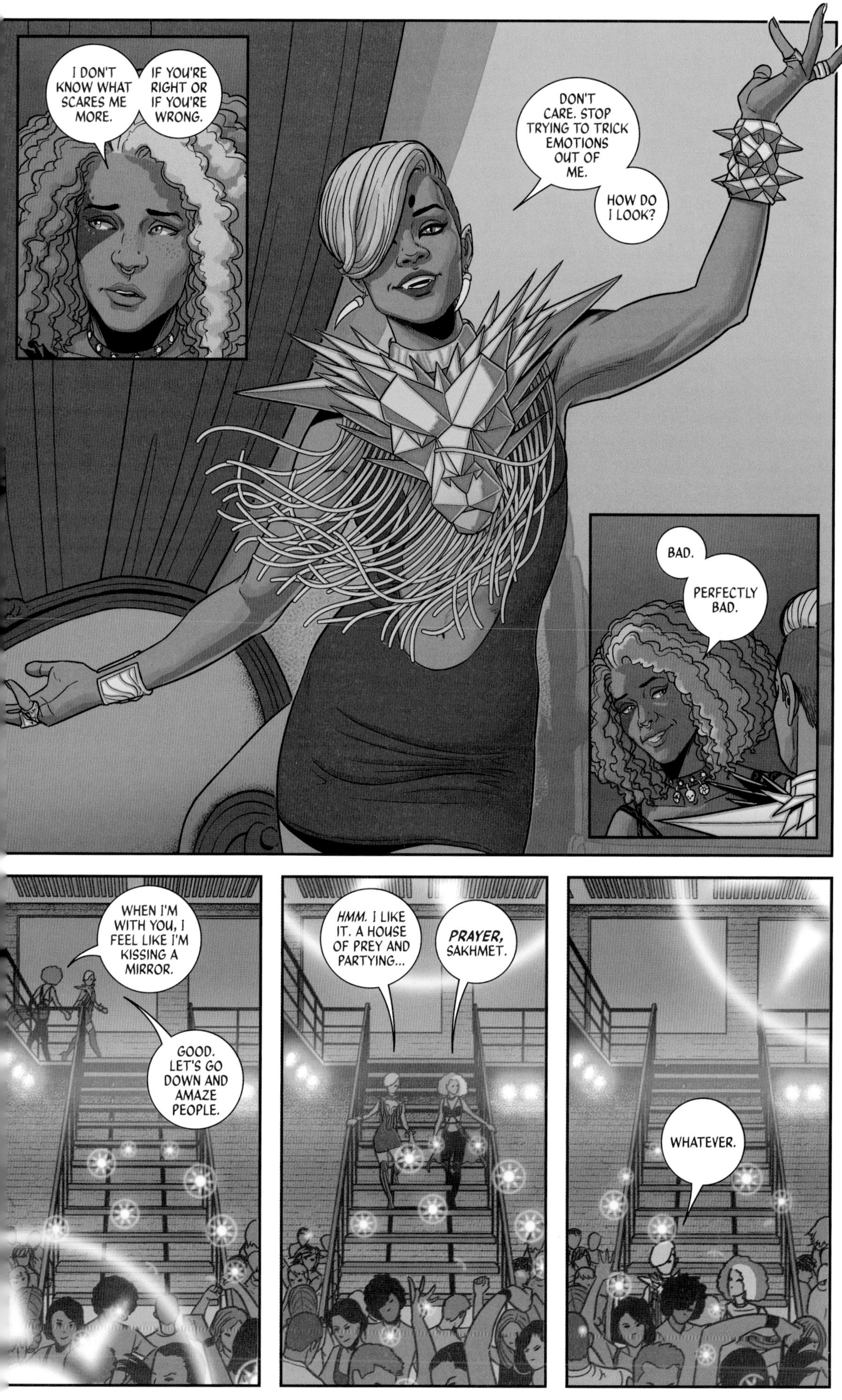
I DON'T KNOW WHAT SCARES ME MORE.
IF YOU'RE RIGHT OR IF YOU'RE WRONG.
DON'T CARE. STOP TRYING TO TRICK EMOTIONS OUT OF ME.
HOW DO I LOOK?
BAD.
PERFECTLY BAD.
WHEN I'M WITH YOU, I FEEL LIKE I'M KISSING A MIRROR.
GOOD. LET'S GO DOWN AND AMAZE PEOPLE.
HMM. I LIKE IT. A HOUSE OF PREY AND PARTYING...
PRAYER, SAKHMET.
WHATEVER.

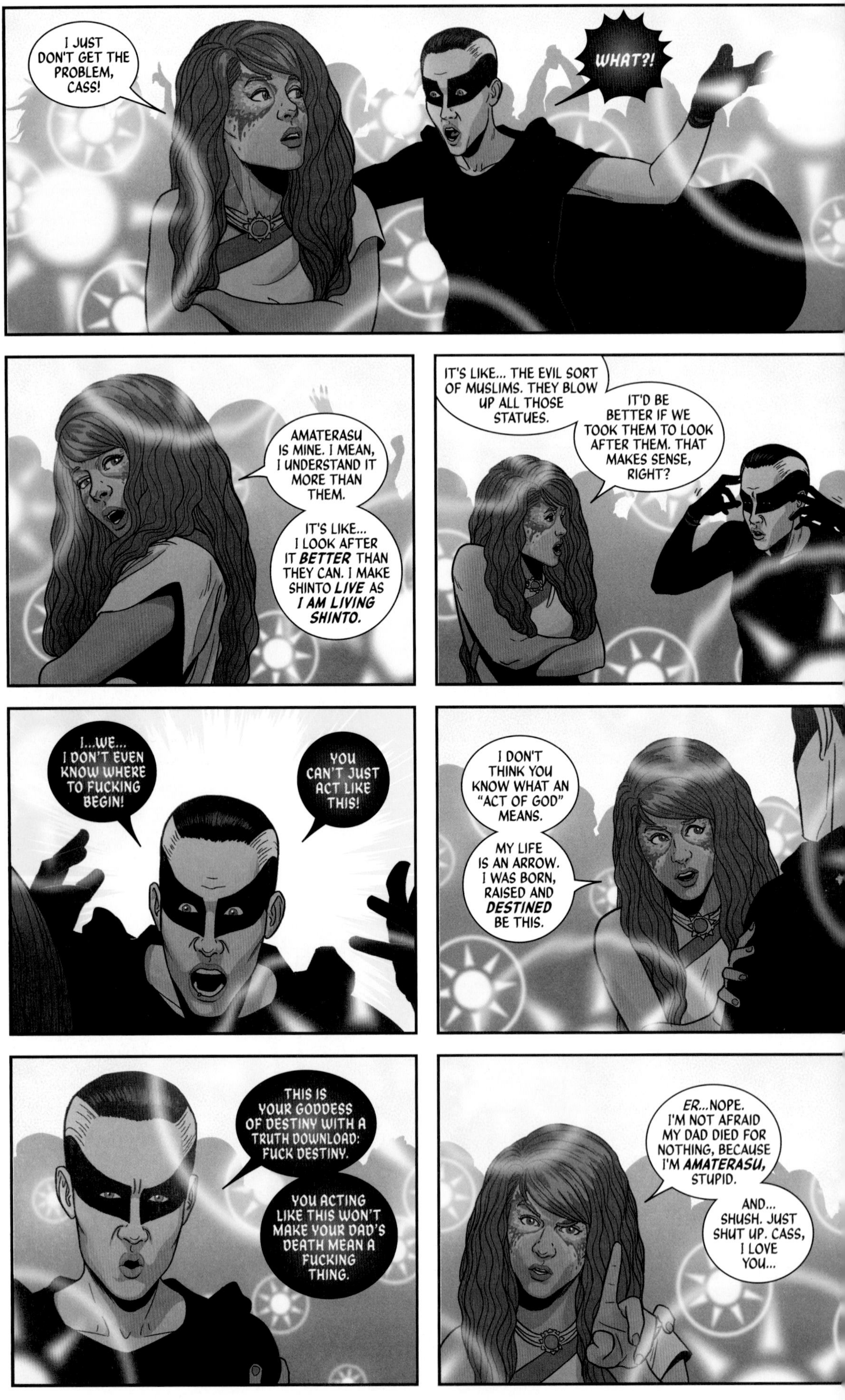
I JUST DON'T GET THE PROBLEM, CASS!
WHAT?!
AMATERASU IS MINE. I MEAN, I UNDERSTAND IT MORE THAN THEM.
IT'S LIKE... I LOOK AFTER IT *BETTER* THAN THEY CAN. I MAKE SHINTO *LIVE* AS ***I AM LIVING SHINTO.***
IT'S LIKE... THE EVIL SORT OF MUSLIMS. THEY BLOW UP ALL THOSE STATUES.
IT'D BE BETTER IF WE TOOK THEM TO LOOK AFTER THEM. THAT MAKES SENSE, RIGHT?
I...WE... I DON'T EVEN KNOW WHERE TO FUCKING BEGIN!
YOU CAN'T JUST ACT LIKE THIS!
I DON'T THINK YOU KNOW WHAT AN "ACT OF GOD" MEANS.
MY LIFE IS AN ARROW. I WAS BORN, RAISED AND ***DESTINED*** BE THIS.
THIS IS YOUR GODDESS OF DESTINY WITH A TRUTH DOWNLOAD: FUCK DESTINY.
YOU ACTING LIKE THIS WON'T MAKE YOUR DAD'S DEATH MEAN A FUCKING THING.
ER...NOPE. I'M NOT AFRAID MY DAD DIED FOR NOTHING, BECAUSE I'M ***AMATERASU,*** STUPID.
AND... SHUSH. JUST SHUT UP. CASS, I LOVE YOU...

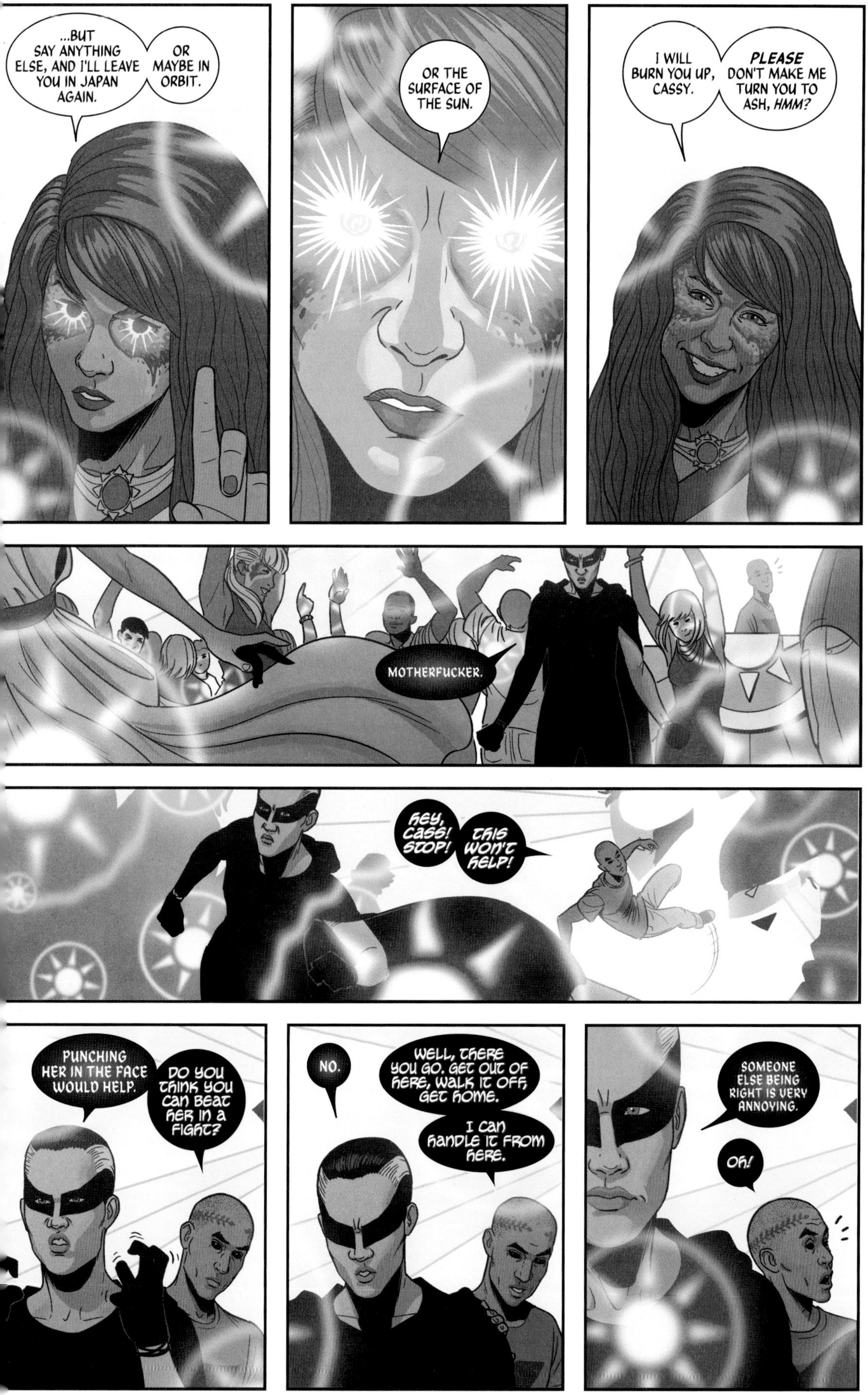
...BUT SAY ANYTHING ELSE, AND I'LL LEAVE YOU IN JAPAN AGAIN.
OR MAYBE IN ORBIT.
OR THE SURFACE OF THE SUN.
I WILL BURN YOU UP, CASSY.
PLEASE DON'T MAKE ME TURN YOU TO ASH, *HMM?*
MOTHERFUCKER.
HEY, CASS! STOP!
THIS WON'T HELP!
PUNCHING HER IN THE FACE WOULD HELP.
DO YOU THINK YOU CAN BEAT HER IN A FIGHT?
NO.
WELL, THERE YOU GO. GET OUT OF HERE, WALK IT OFF, GET HOME.
I CAN HANDLE IT FROM HERE.
SOMEONE ELSE BEING RIGHT IS VERY ANNOYING.
OH!

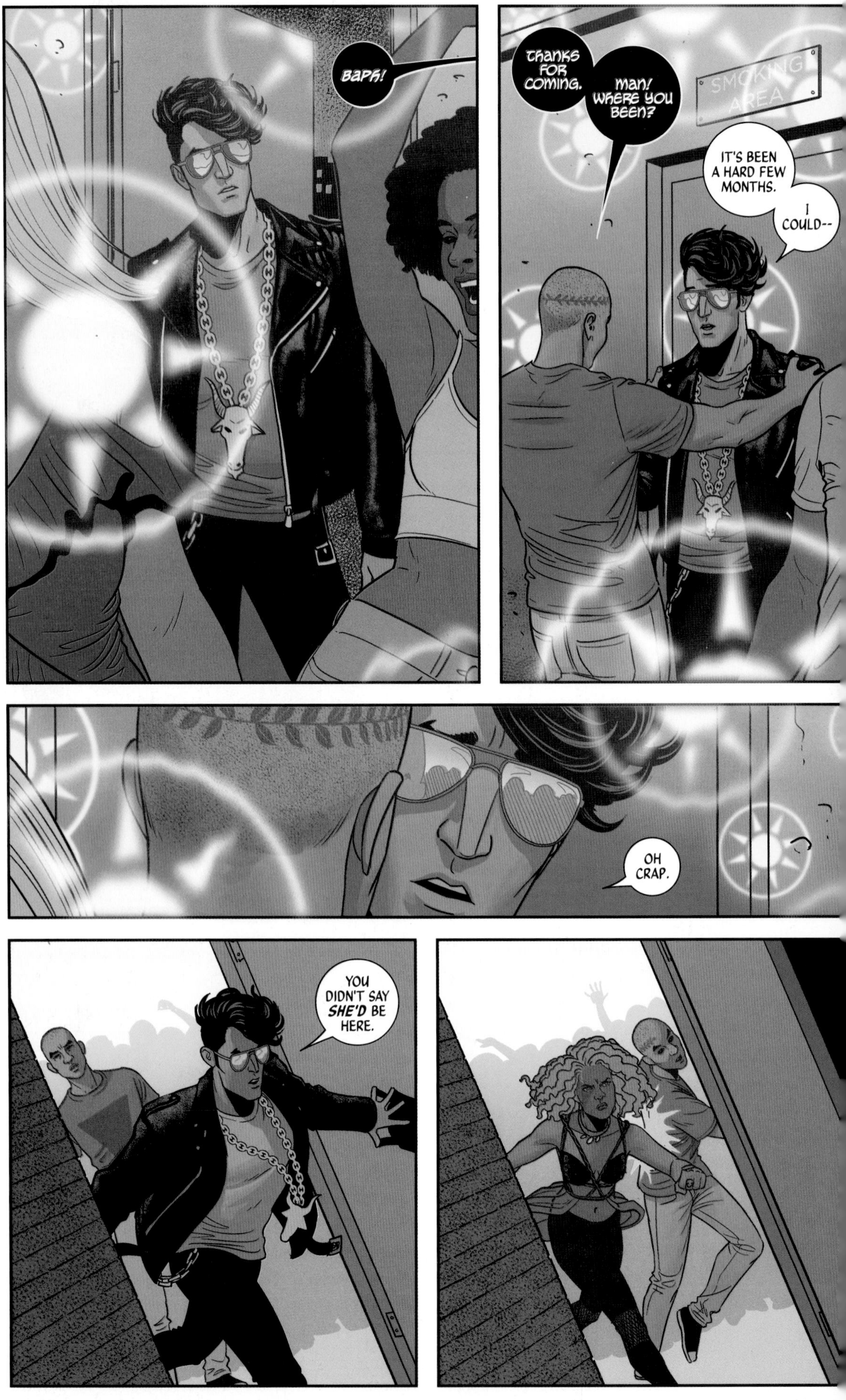
BAPH!
THANKS FOR COMING.
MAN! WHERE YOU BEEN?
SMOKING AREA
IT'S BEEN A HARD FEW MONTHS.
I COULD--
OH CRAP.
YOU DIDN'T SAY *SHE'D* BE HERE.

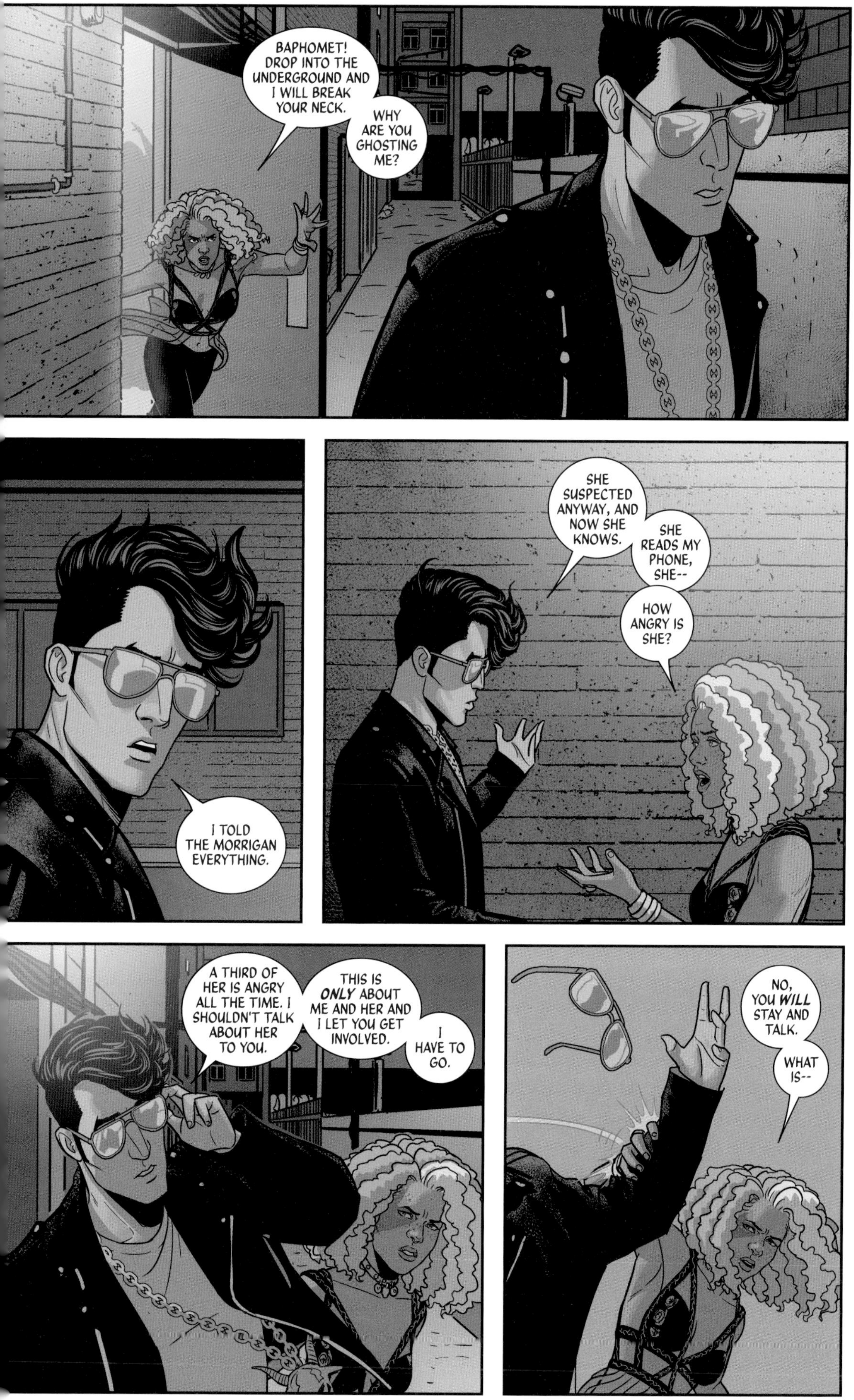
BAPHOMET! DROP INTO THE UNDERGROUND AND I WILL BREAK YOUR NECK.
WHY ARE YOU GHOSTING ME?
I TOLD THE MORRIGAN EVERYTHING.
SHE SUSPECTED ANYWAY, AND NOW SHE KNOWS.
SHE READS MY PHONE, SHE--
HOW ANGRY IS SHE?
A THIRD OF HER IS ANGRY ALL THE TIME. I SHOULDN'T TALK ABOUT HER TO YOU.
THIS IS ONLY ABOUT ME AND HER AND I LET YOU GET INVOLVED.
I HAVE TO GO.
NO, YOU WILL STAY AND TALK.
WHAT IS--

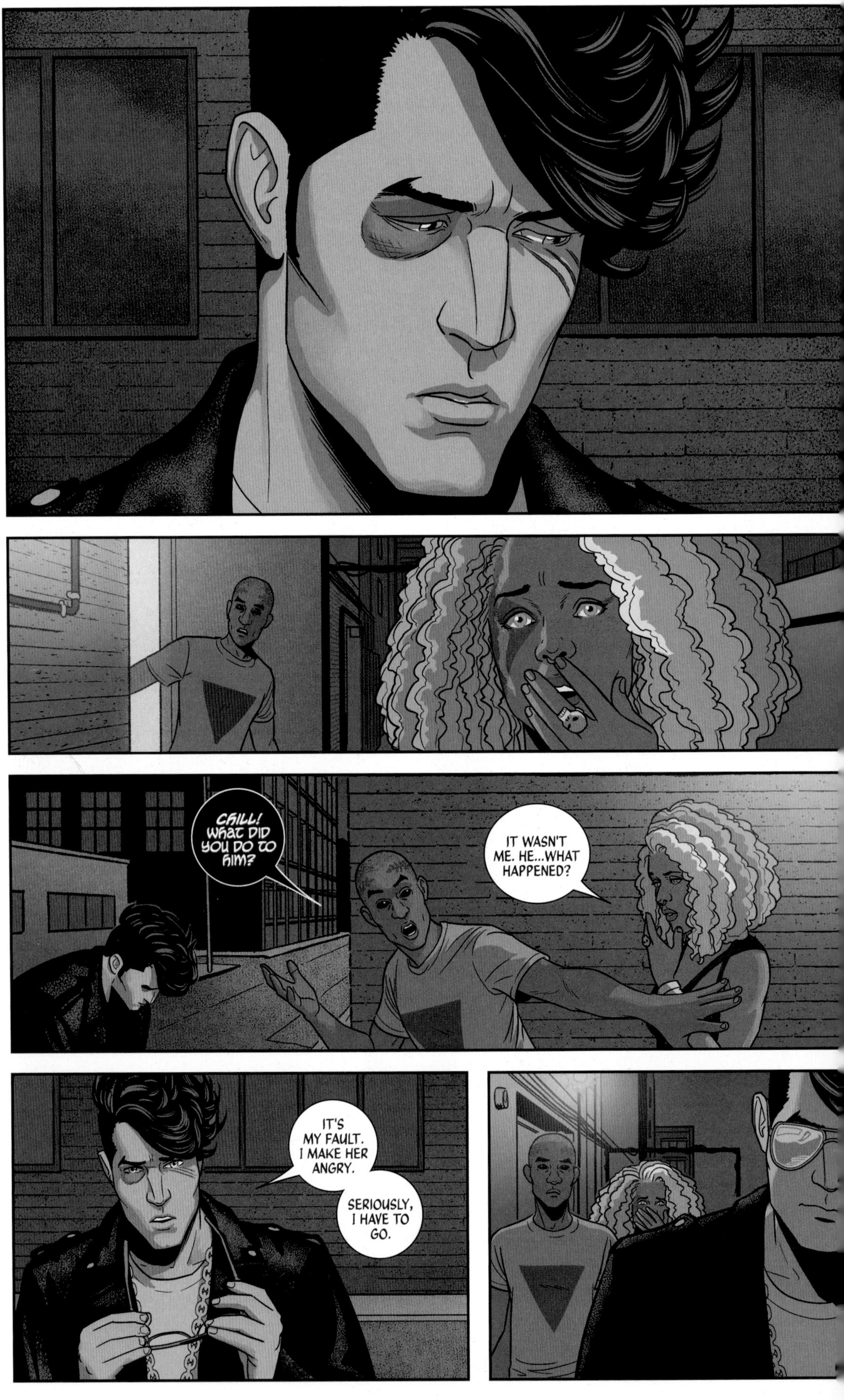
CHILL! WHAT DID YOU DO TO HIM?
IT WASN'T ME. HE...WHAT HAPPENED?
IT'S MY FAULT. I MAKE HER ANGRY.
SERIOUSLY, I HAVE TO GO.

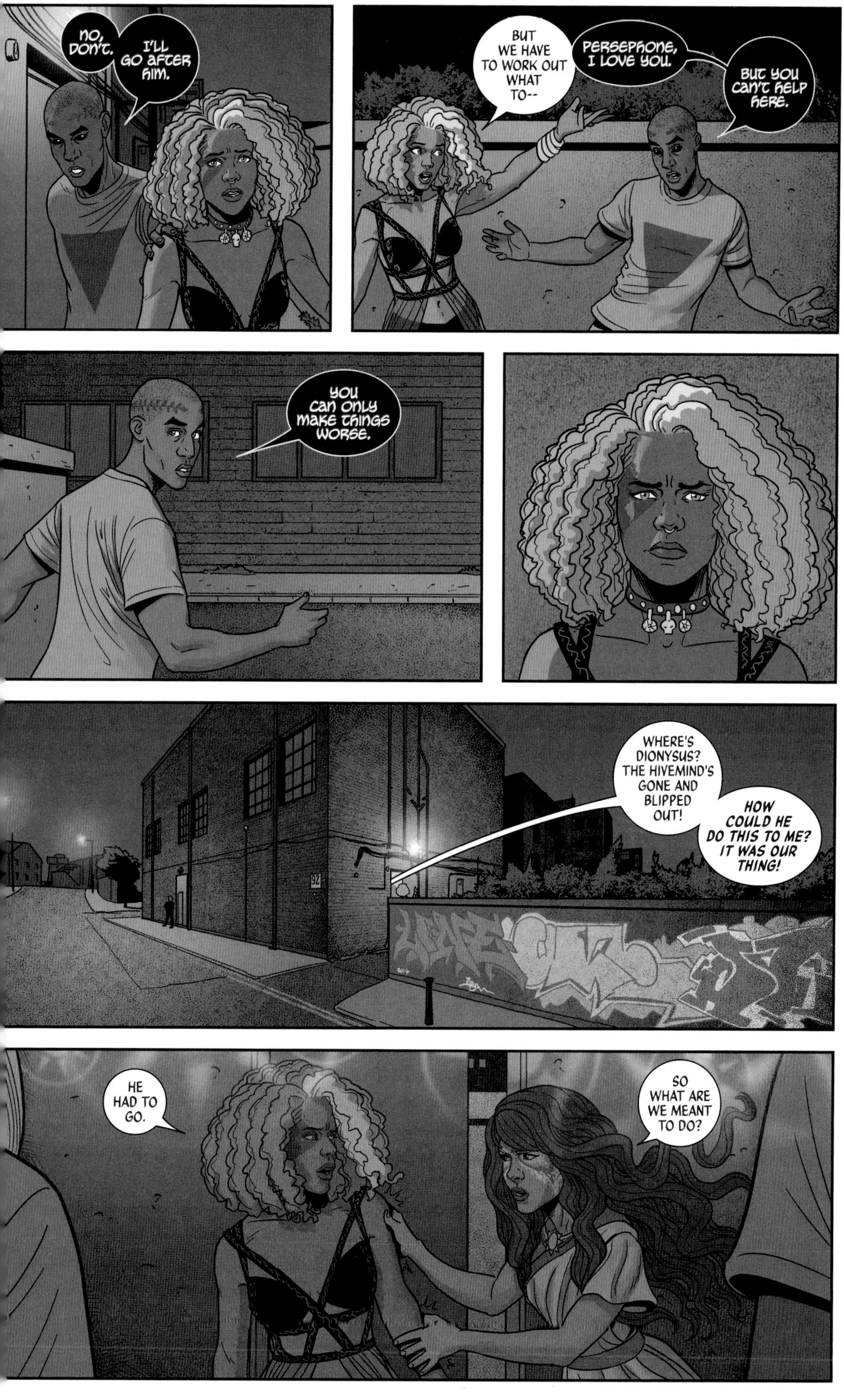
No, don't.
I'll go after him.
But we have to work out what to--
Persephone, I love you.
But you can't help here.
You can only make things worse.
Where's Dionysus? The hivemind's gone and blipped out!
How could he do this to me? It was our thing!
92
He had to go.
So what are we meant to do?

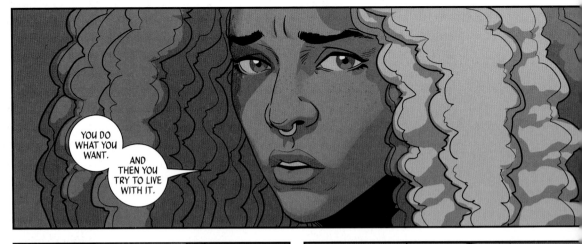

YOU DO WHAT YOU WANT.

AND THEN YOU TRY TO LIVE WITH IT.

IF THE PARTY'S OVER, ARE YOU COMING UPSTAIRS?

NUH-UH.

WELL, WE CAN GO ANYWHERE...

NO, SAKHMET.

I'M HEADING OUT.

NOT IN THE MOOD.

WELL THEN, WHO IS?

CURIOSITY

6 MARCH 2015

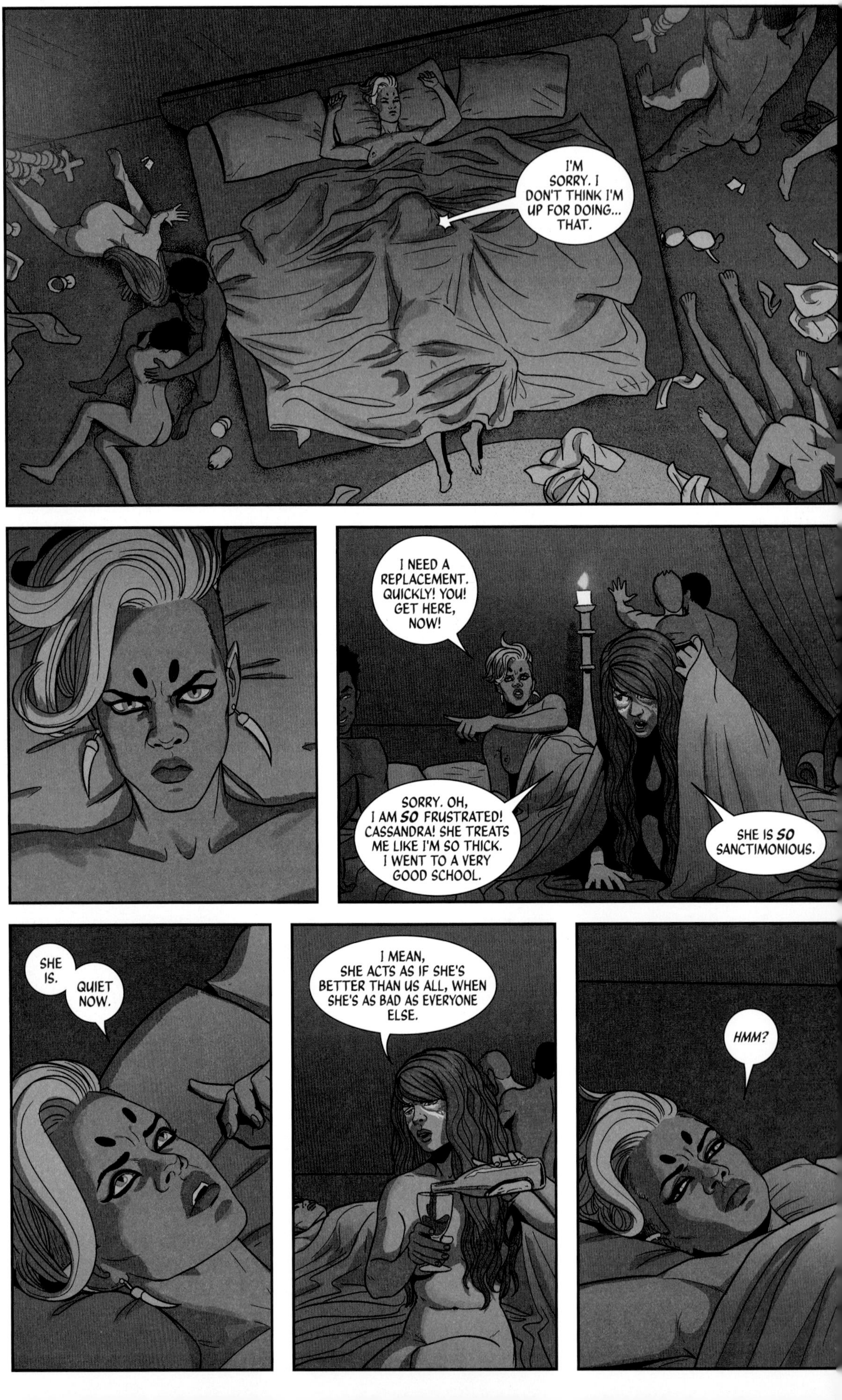
I'M SORRY. I DON'T THINK I'M UP FOR DOING... THAT.
I NEED A REPLACEMENT. QUICKLY! YOU! GET HERE, NOW!
SORRY. OH, I AM SO FRUSTRATED! CASSANDRA! SHE TREATS ME LIKE I'M SO THICK. I WENT TO A VERY GOOD SCHOOL.
SHE IS SO SANCTIMONIOUS.
SHE IS.
QUIET NOW.
I MEAN, SHE ACTS AS IF SHE'S BETTER THAN US ALL, WHEN SHE'S AS BAD AS EVERYONE ELSE.
HMM?

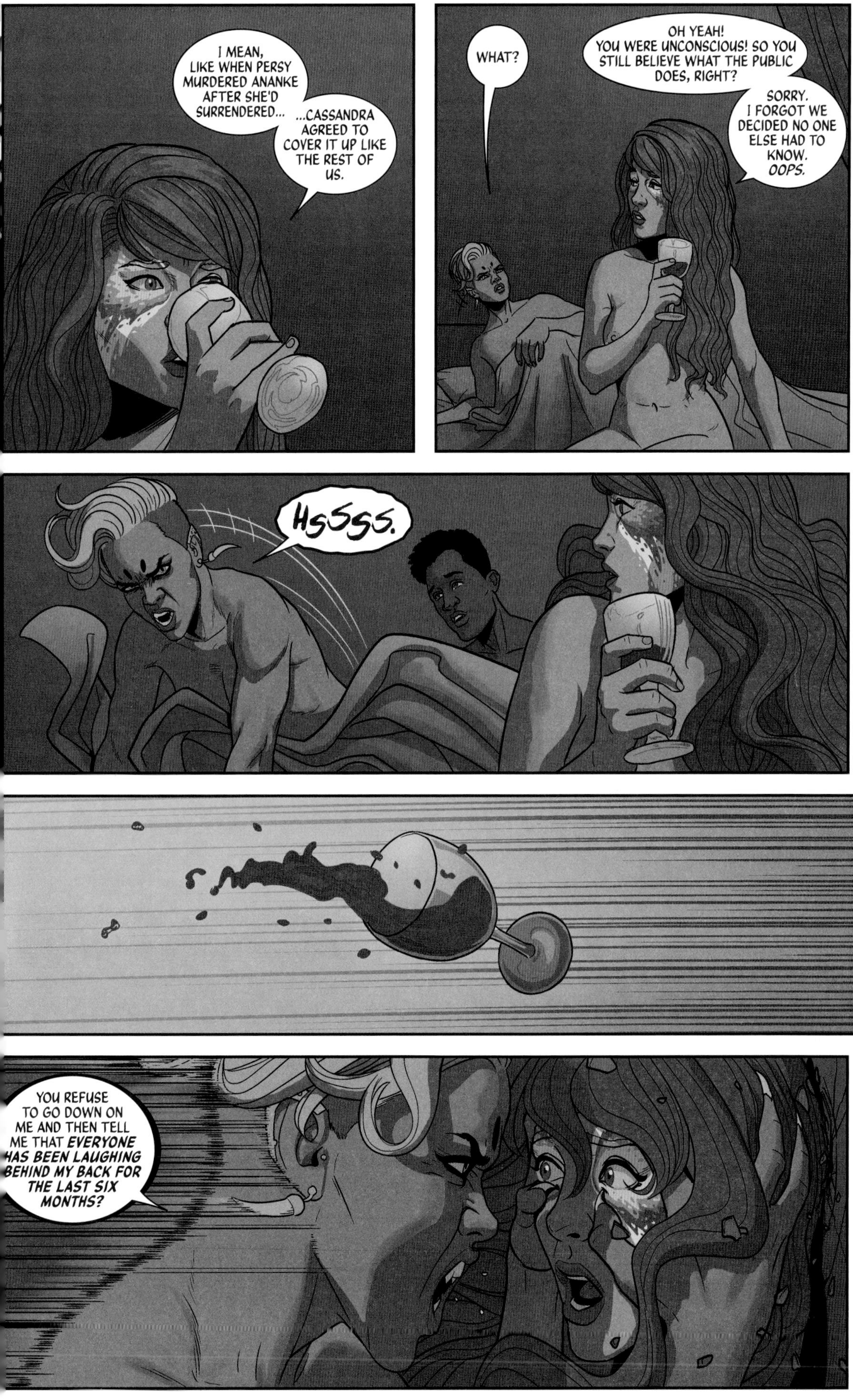
I MEAN, LIKE WHEN PERSY MURDERED ANANKE AFTER SHE'D SURRENDERED...
...CASSANDRA AGREED TO COVER IT UP LIKE THE REST OF US.
WHAT?
OH YEAH! YOU WERE UNCONSCIOUS! SO YOU STILL BELIEVE WHAT THE PUBLIC DOES, RIGHT?
SORRY. I FORGOT WE DECIDED NO ONE ELSE HAD TO KNOW. *OOPS.*
HSSSS.
YOU REFUSE TO GO DOWN ON ME AND THEN TELL ME THAT *EVERYONE HAS BEEN LAUGHING BEHIND MY BACK FOR THE LAST SIX MONTHS?*

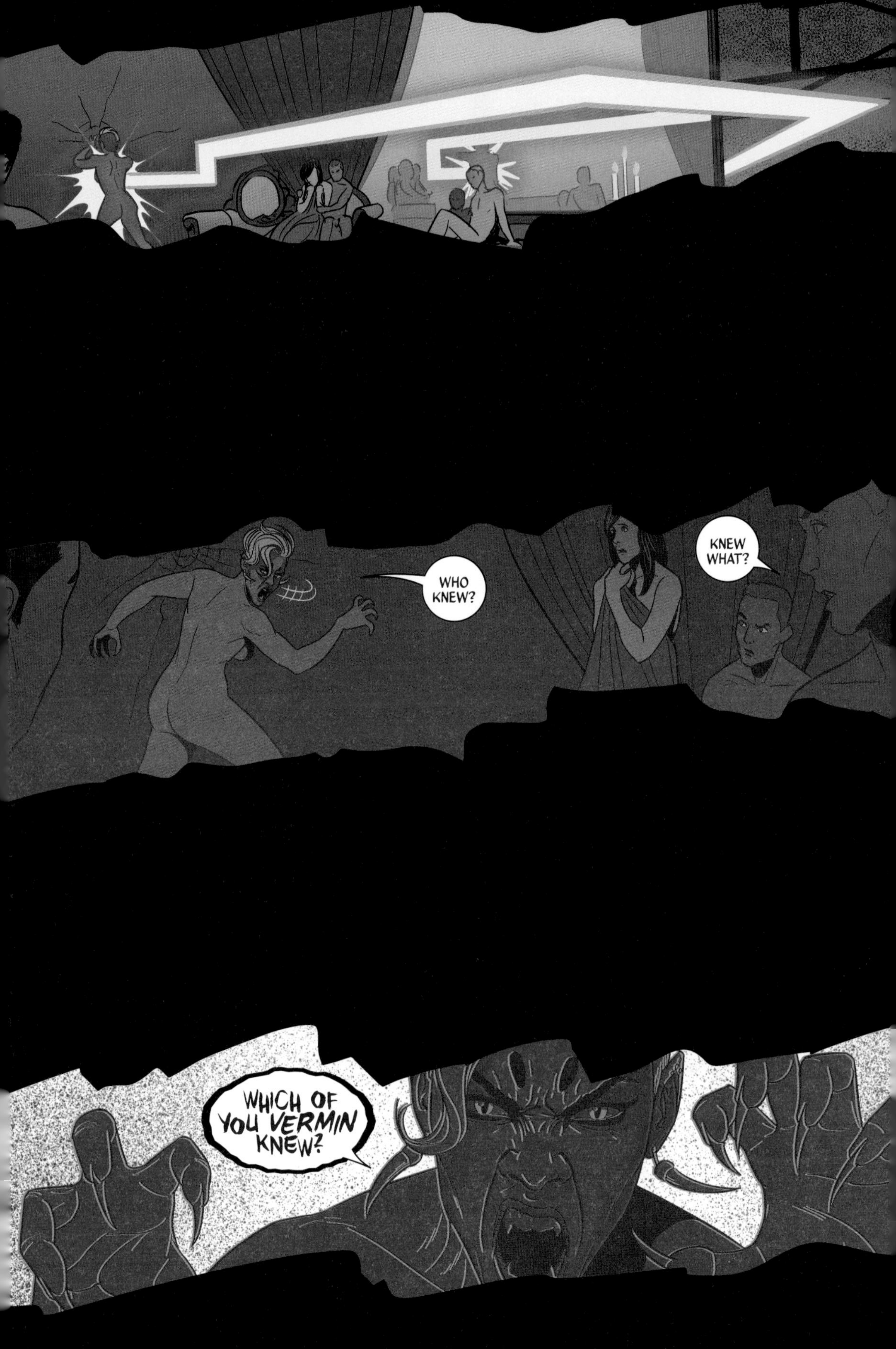
WHO KNEW?
KNEW WHAT?
WHICH OF YOU VERMIN KNEW?

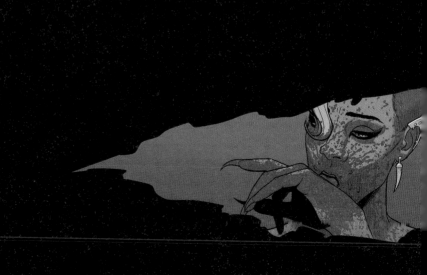

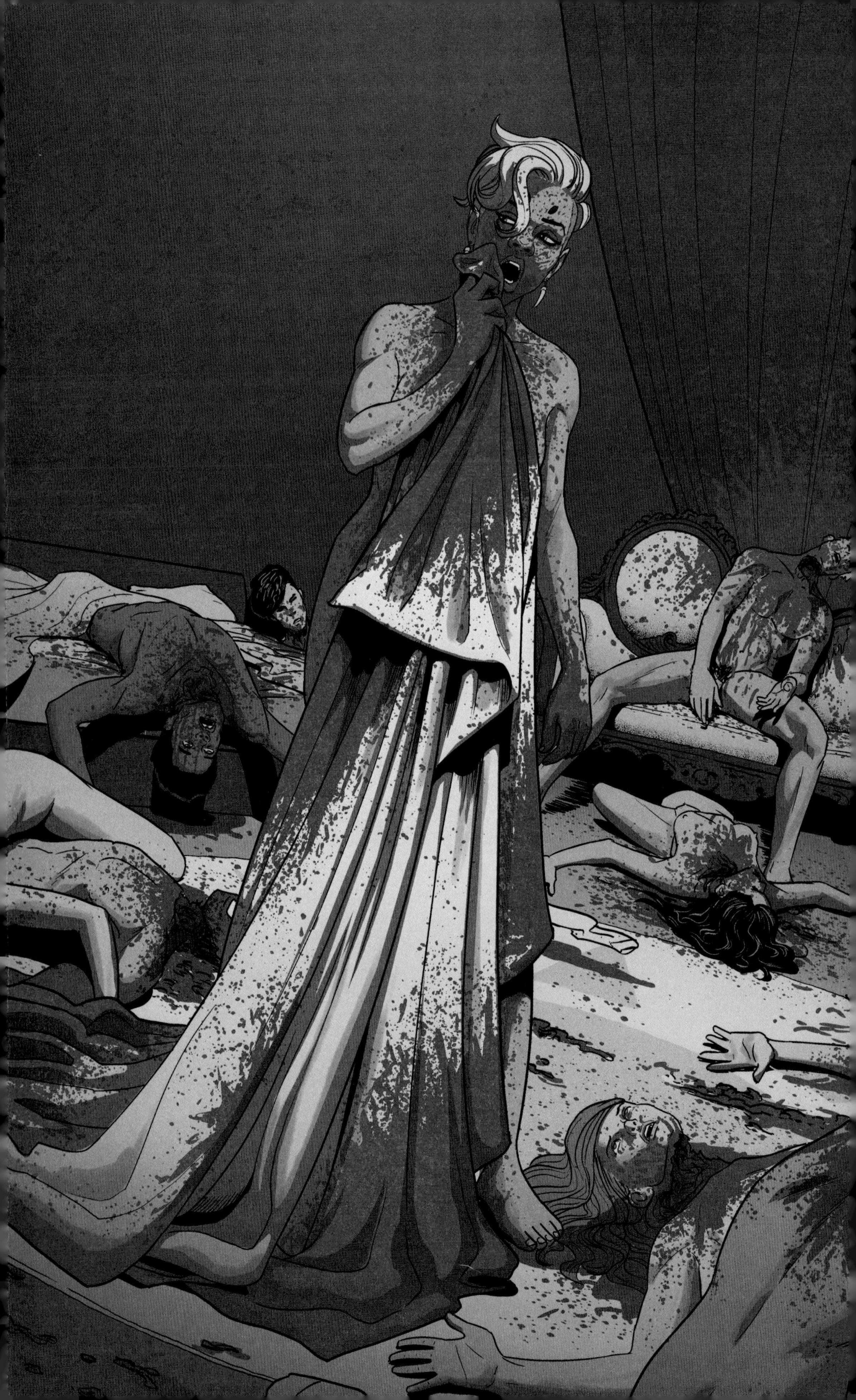

OH, ONE
MORE THING...

SIX MONTHS EARLIER

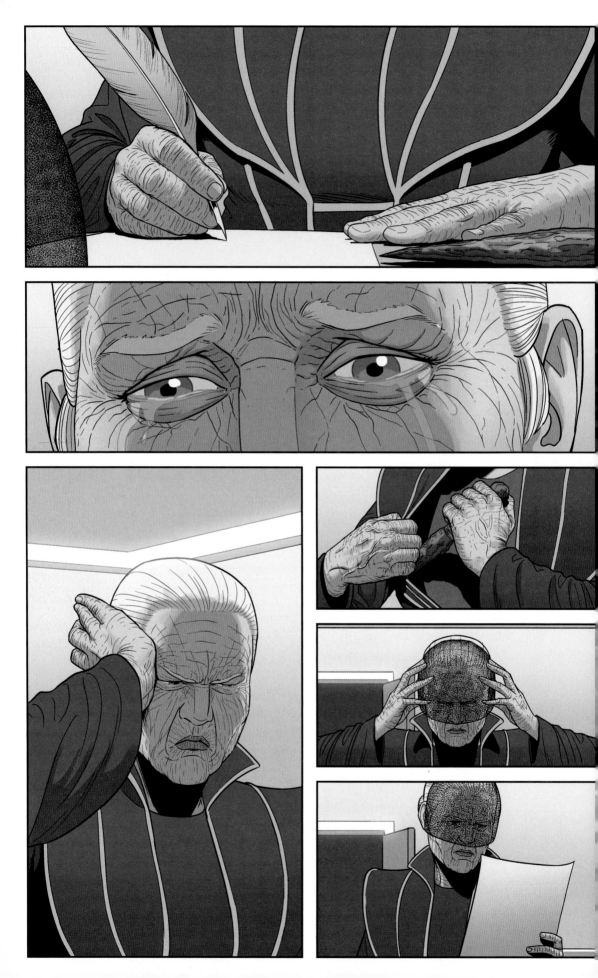

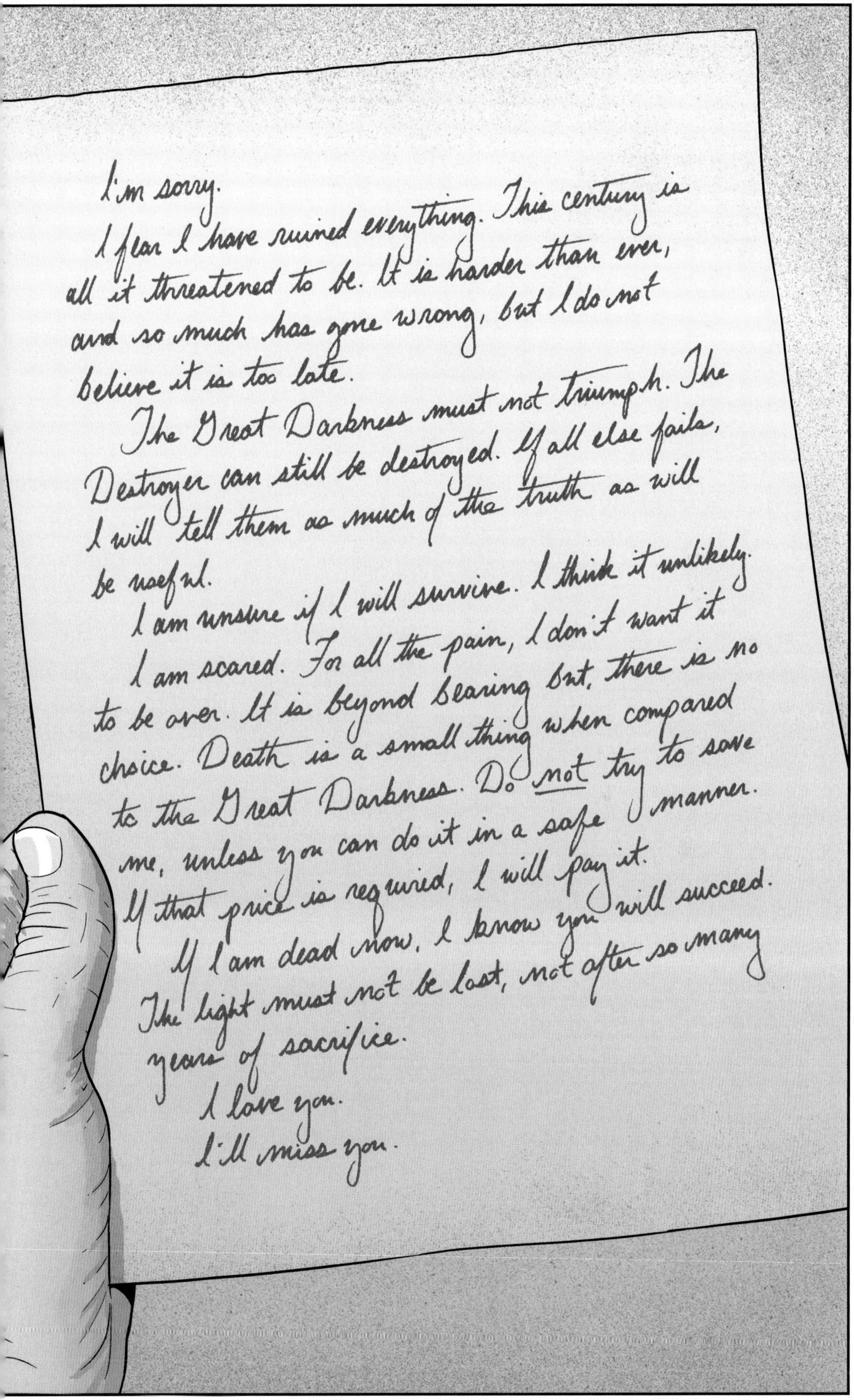
I'm sorry.
I fear I have ruined everything. This century is
all it threatened to be. It is harder than ever,
and so much has gone wrong, but I do not
believe it is too late.
The Great Darkness must not triumph. The
Destroyer can still be destroyed. If all else fails,
I will tell them as much of the truth as will
be useful.
I am unsure if I will survive. I think it unlikely.
I am scared. For all the pain, I don't want it
to be over. It is beyond bearing but, there is no
choice. Death is a small thing when compared
to the Great Darkness. Do not try to save
me, unless you can do it in a safe manner.
If that price is required, I will pay it.
If I am dead now. I know you will succeed.
The light must not be lost, not after so many
years of sacrifice.
I love you.
I'll miss you.

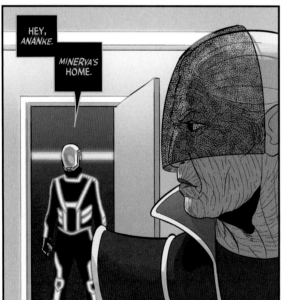

HEY, *ANANKE.*

MINERVA'S HOME.

IS THE MACHINE READY?

PREPARE IT.

YES, BUT--

WHY, YES, YOUR *HIGHNESS.*

BADDIES

24 SEPTEMBER 2014

MAKING OF

For your amusement and delight, read on to see the fine alternate covers for this arc from our enormously talented friends, as well as some "Making Of" material (including a tweaked transcript example of how we did the magazine issue). Like craft stuff? Kieron does writer notes on the wicdiv blog you may dig (www.wicdiv.com).

Kevin Wada
Issue 23 cover

Jen Bartel
Issue 24 cover

Emi Lenox
Issue 25 cover

Nicola Scott
Issue 26 cover

Jamie McKelvie and Katie West
Issue 26 *Sex Criminals* parody cover
for Image Comics 25th Anniversary

Alison Sampson
Issue 27 cover

Chynna Clugston Flores
Issue 27 Women's History Month cover

Elsa Charretier
Issue 28 cover

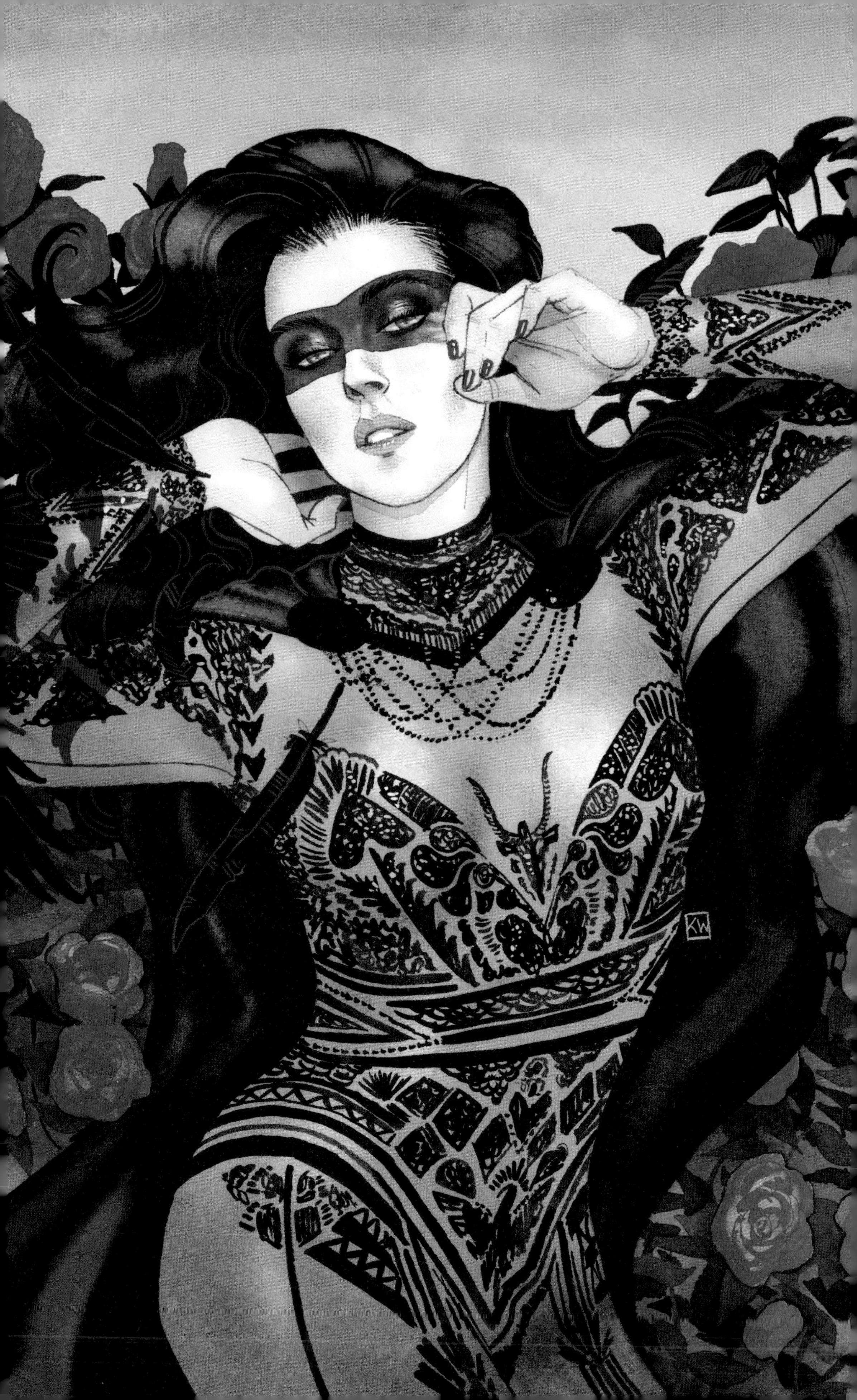
KW

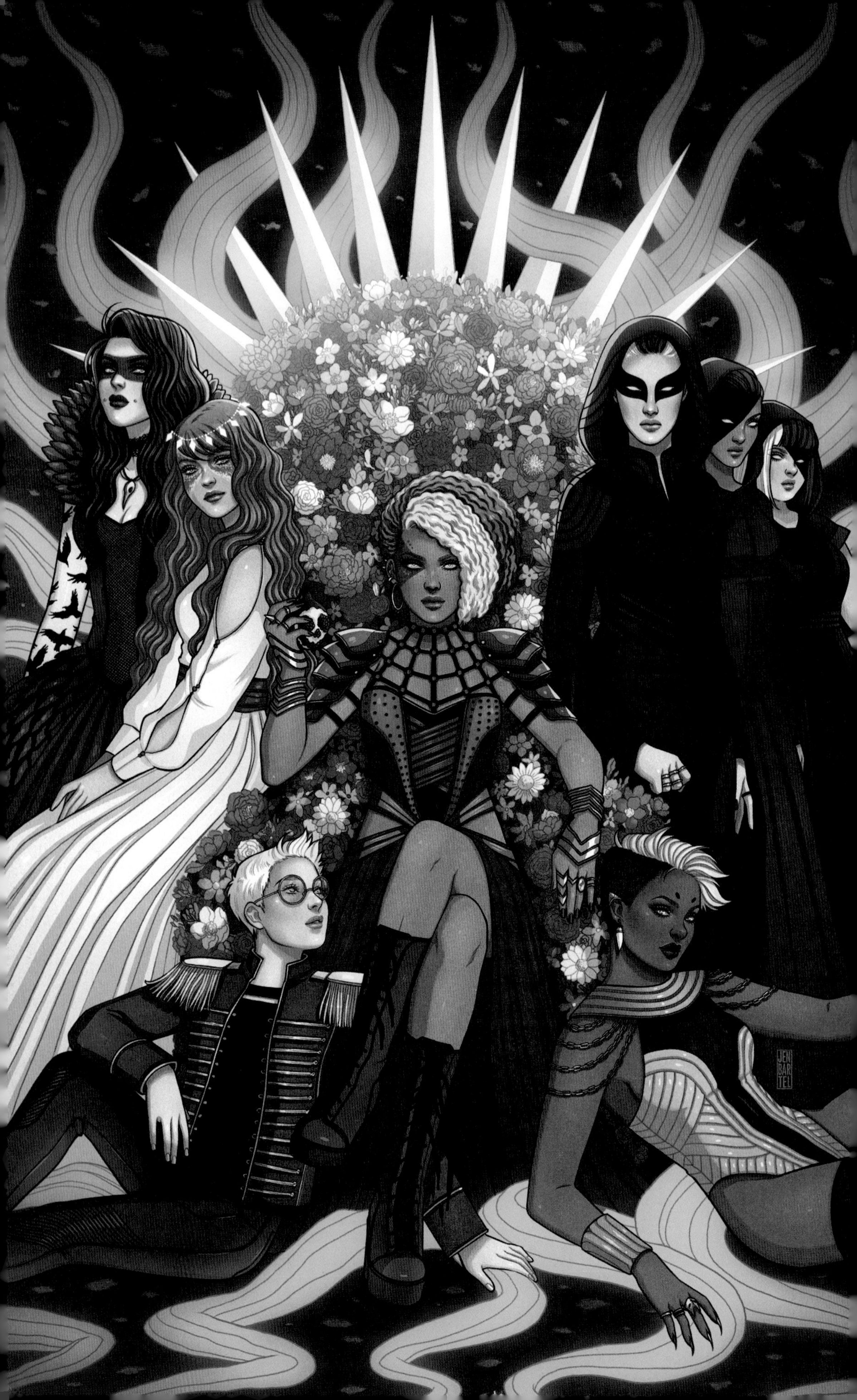
JEN
BAR
TEL

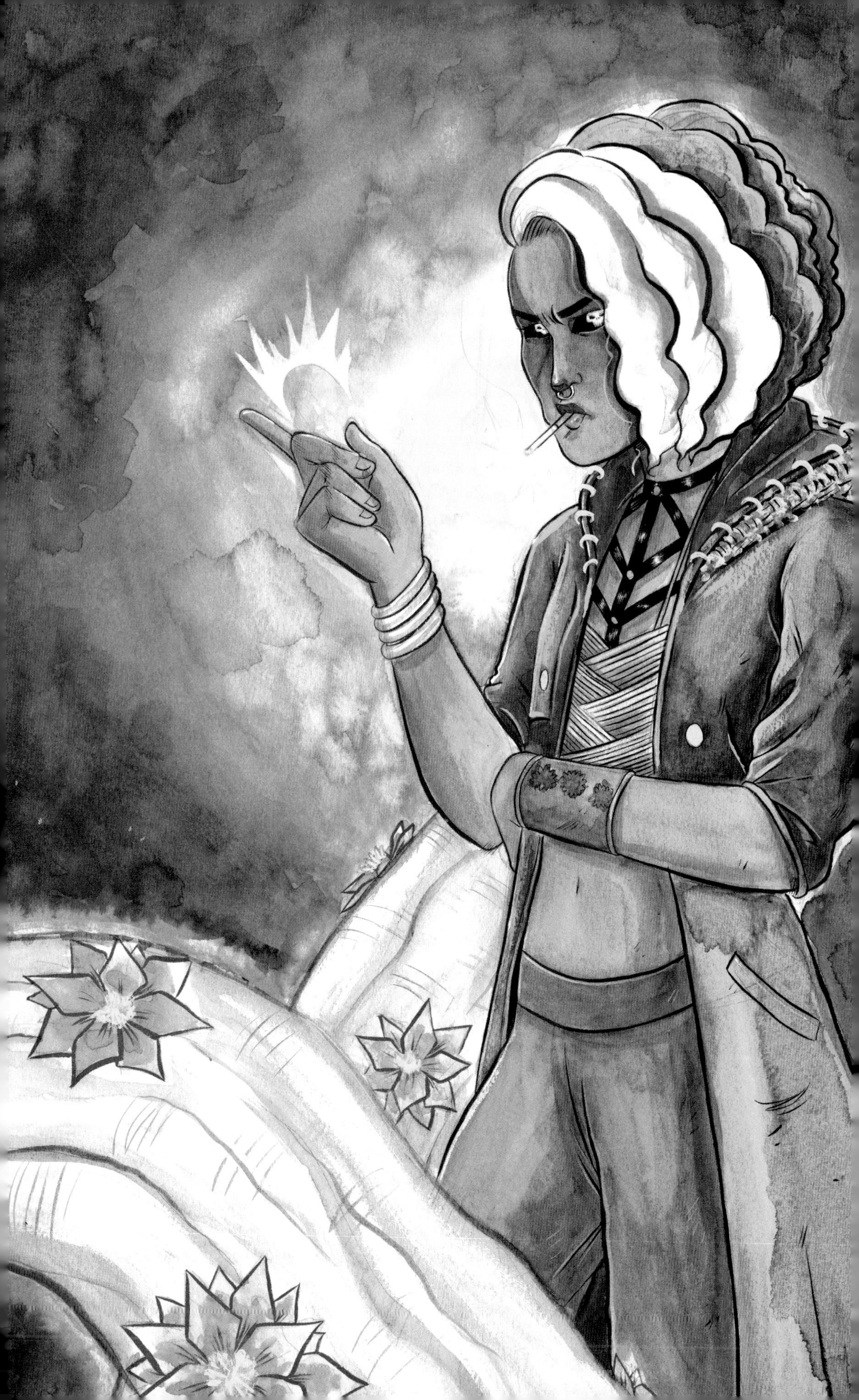

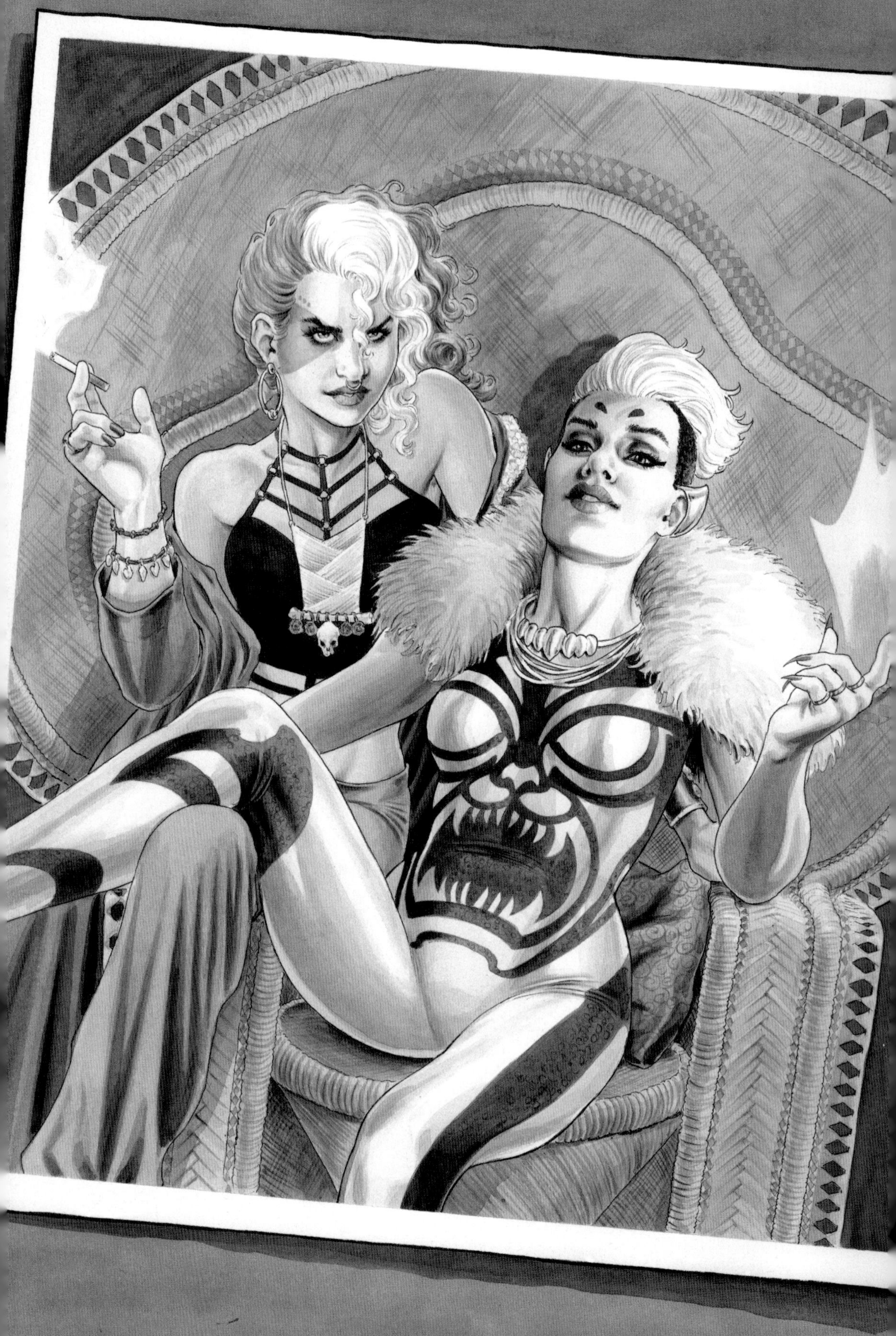

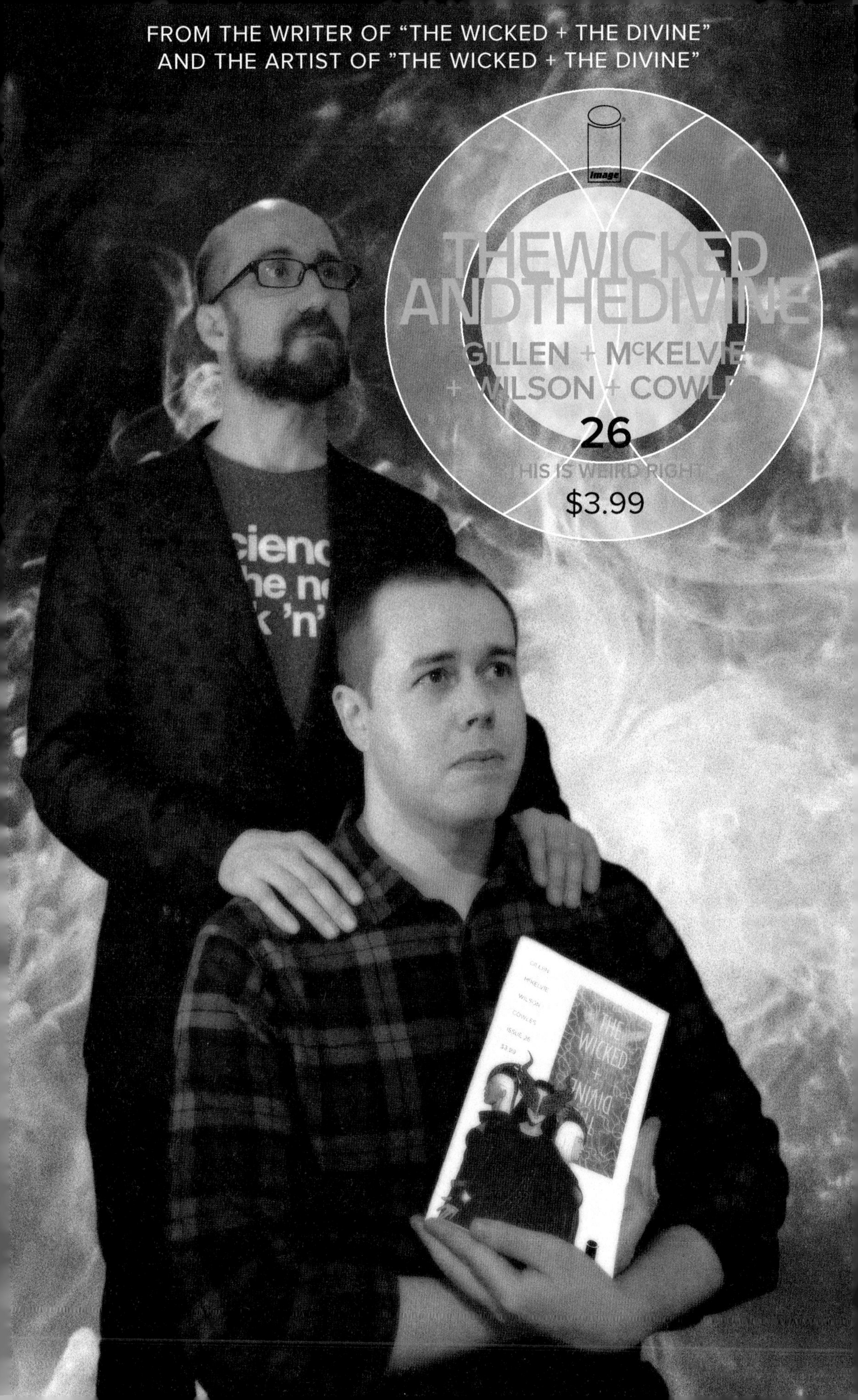
FROM THE WRITER OF “THE WICKED + THE DIVINE”
AND THE ARTIST OF ”THE WICKED + THE DIVINE”
image
THEWICKED
ANDTHEDIVINE
GILLEN + McKELVI
+ WILSON + COWL
26
THIS IS WEIRD RIGHT
$3.99

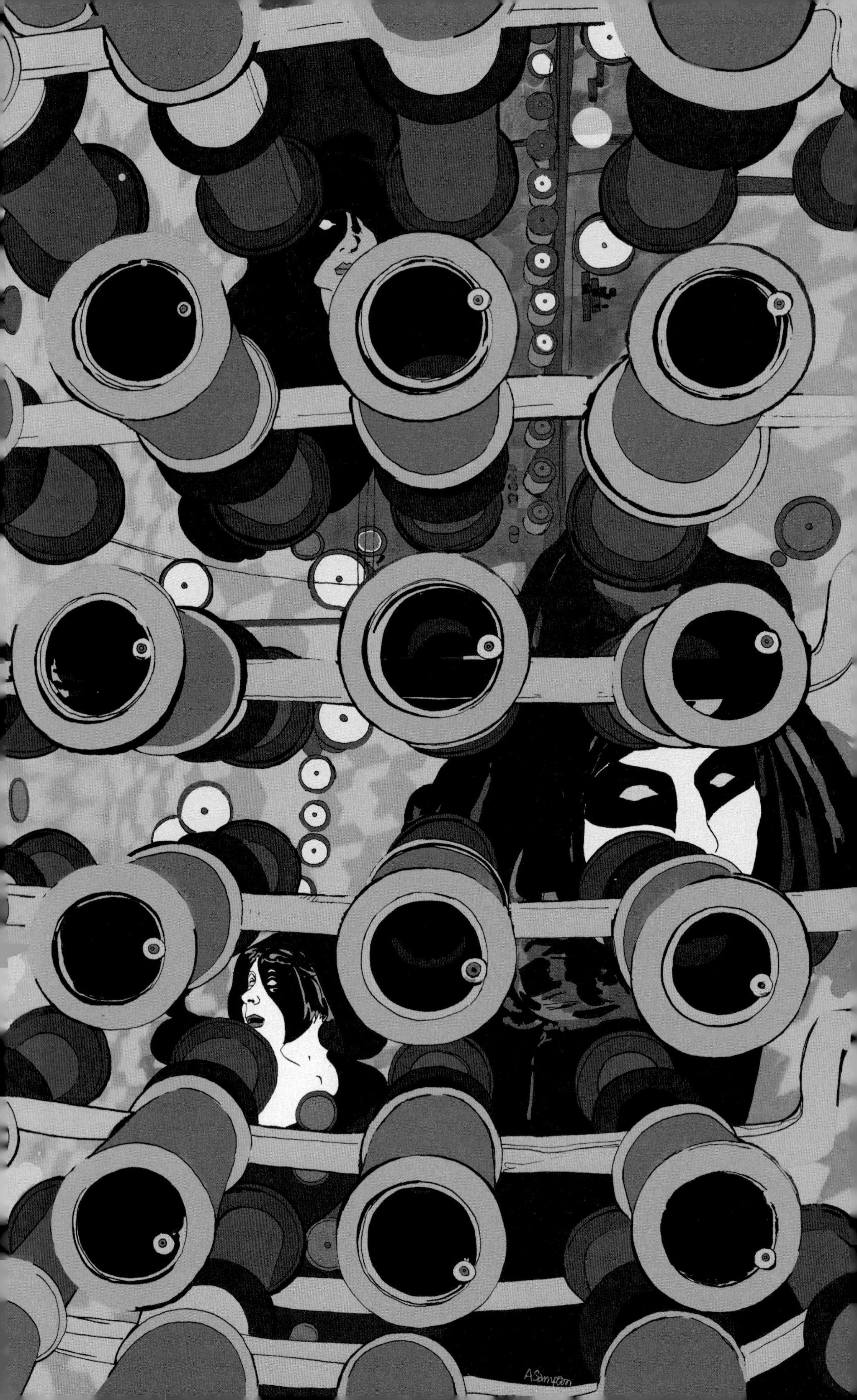
A Sampson

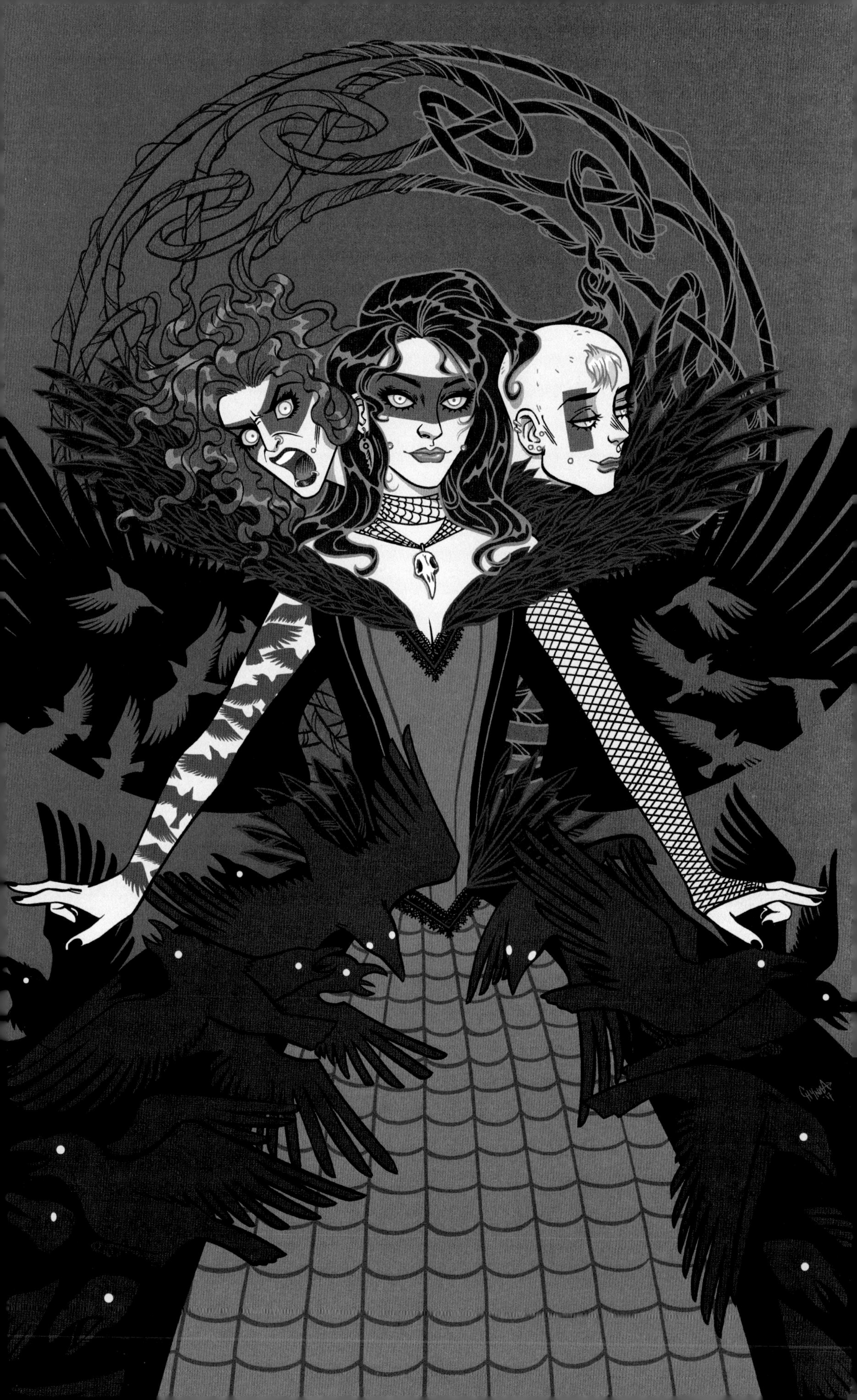

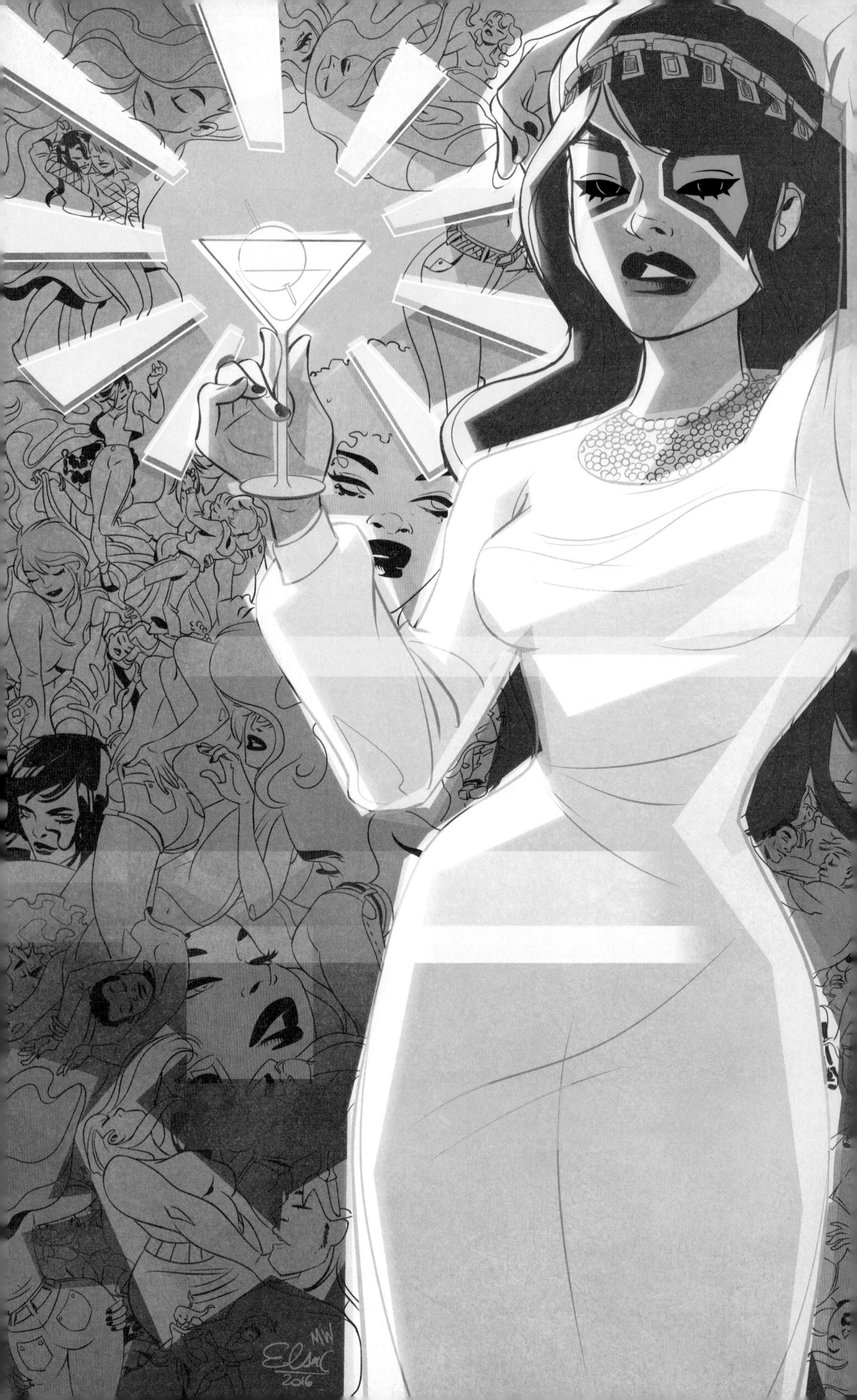
MW
2016

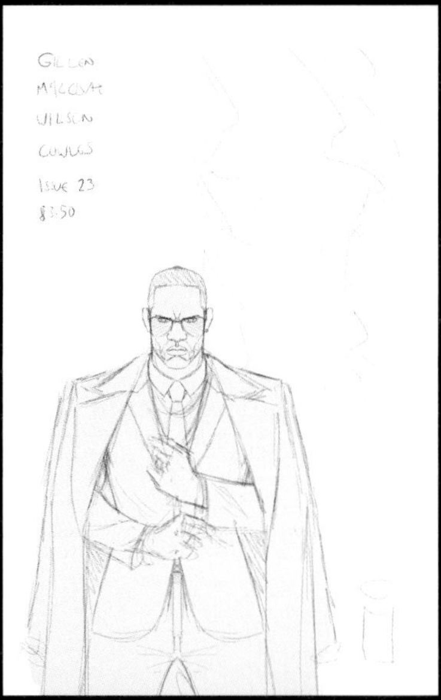
GILLEN
WILSON
ISSUE 23
$3.50

With each new cover, Jamie steps back and looks at overall design. The idea of juxtaposing a fashion portrait with a character's power-set seemed fruitful.

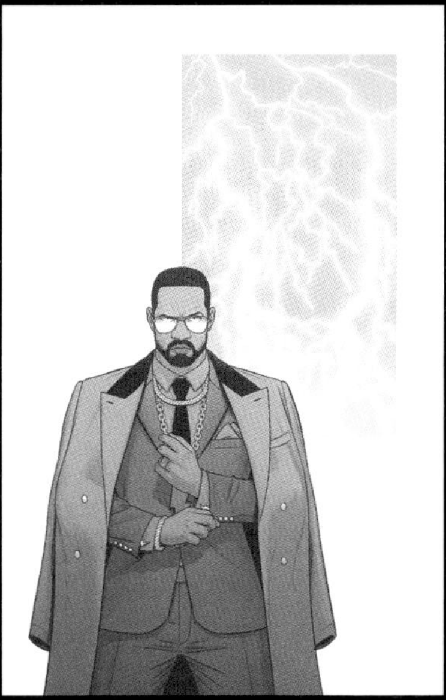

After flatting, Matt did an initial take on the colours, with him trying to push the hyper-bright lightning glow effect. In the end, we decided it was too much for an initial image.

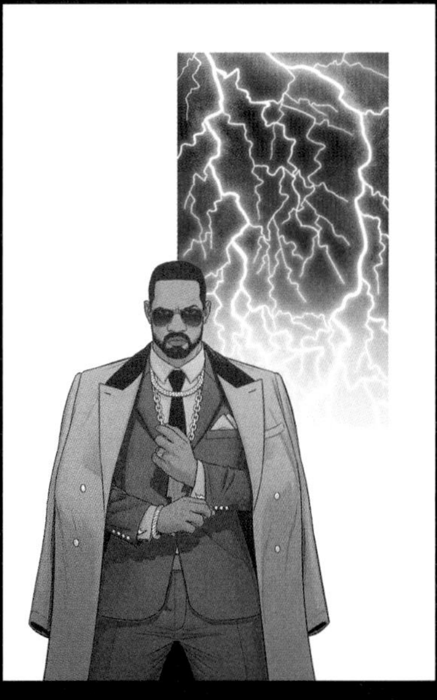

Instead, we grounded it a little, making it feel more like an actual fashion shoot, with more of a range of purple, white and pinks, plus dark shades rather than reflecting.

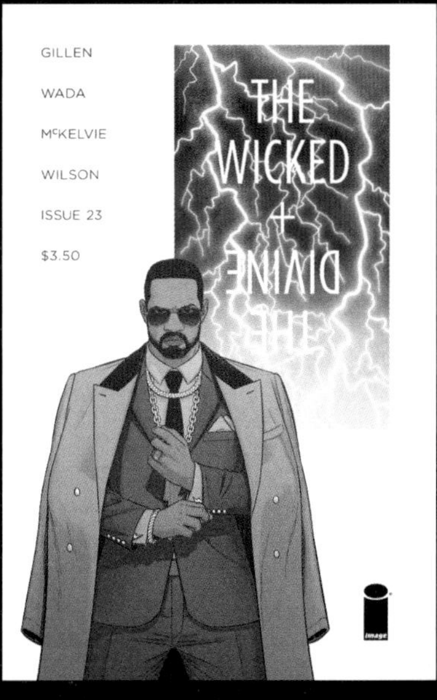
GILLEN
WADA
McKELVIE
WILSON
ISSUE 23
$3.50
THE
WICKED
+
DIVINE

And then, lastly, there's the integration of the page furniture, which is where we actually see if the cover works as desired. Phew. It does.

LUCIFER INTERVIEW RAW TRANSCRIPT

The magazine issue was done in a somewhat unusual way. We asked various real-world writers if they'd like to interview our gods. When they said yes, we got them in an instant message chat window and Kieron role-played the interaction as each god. They then took the raw transcript (with some tweaks when we had second thoughts about the events) and wrote it up in their style.

Here's a polished version of one of the transcripts, between Mary HK Choi and Lucifer.

It's just after noon. Soho is a long time from its peak as London's sex district. Sex shops rub shoulders with hipster eateries, and London does the London being alive thing it does so well. The Groucho remains the Groucho. You're told where to go – no obvious minder – and head upstairs. Lucifer is sitting by the window, dressed in one of her immaculate trademark suits. You glance to one side and see that there's a watchful Press person, kept at a discrete distance. Lucifer seems to like the appearance of independence. She's wearing shades and has a tall Bloody Mary on the table in front of her. A thick leather seat is opposite.

Mary HK Choi (MC): Hi, I was hoping to beat you here. *(Extends a hand to shake.)* Were you waiting long? *(I'm dressed in black, amorphous, space goth, deliberately asexual and the opposite of what I know she'd wear.)* A little early for gazpacho no? *(Sits down.)*

Lucifer (ER): *(Looks you up and down. She is very... considered. She gives the impression of thinking things through intensely before speaking.)* ...

MC: Oh, do you mind if I tape this? *(Starts taping before she answers.)*

ER: *(Eventually smiles.)* Just enough for a couple of sips of this. *(She tilts the glass.)* This morning has been somewhat purgatorial. Go ahead. *(Leans back in the seat, arm resting on the rest, and waits. She's definitely somewhat run down.)*

MC: Mornings here tend to be. I just got in last night. *(Pulls out another tape recorder as a back up.)* Sorry, I'm paranoid. *(Places it on the table.)*

ER: *(Smiles at that.)* You must feel as bad as I do. But mine was self-inflicted. I do have a tendency to make crosses for myself to bear in the morning... And paranoia, like most flaws, is something I tend to consider a virtue.

MC: A handy survival mechanism as these things go. So, what finally made you agree to this? We (Hedi Slimane) shot the photos months ago. I thought the three email questions were all I was going to get.

ER: *(Sips the drink.)* Christmas... *(She stops herself, then smiles.)* Xmas. Mustn't say the "C" word. Xmas has a way of making me maudlin and confessional.

MC: *(Laughs.)* Makes sense. The C word. Like saying Beetlejuice three times I guess.

ER: *(Nods.)* Heaven help me if I get too much attention. And clearly, it won't. The boys upstairs do hold grudges against those of us who get ideas above our station.

MC: Well, hubris always leads to a healthy smiting. Even with free will and all of that. I've got to ask you though, I can see why suicide spikes this time of year for the hoi polloi, but you? What does Xmas mean to you? You just had a killer Q4.

ER: *(Smiles at that, actually fond.)* I've had what I like to call fun. Q3 was bored teenage girl. Q4, antichrist superstar. I try to make the most of every second I have. I'm hoping the next year and a half will prove likewise... Xmas has me thinking bigger. Mythically. What it all means. And, being the devil is about knowing you've lost. If that makes sense. That's what I'm for. I'm the bogeyman. The one good side is that I can afford to buy my friends presents now... even if I haven't actually remembered to do so.

MC: Look, I'm familiar with the two years origin story and I think it's genius, but reinvention is a huge part of every popstar, I mean, "Antichrist Superstar's" evolution. I'm not saying you've got to go into your Harajuku era or your blue period but I'm confident it won't all end in a year and a half. They flew me out for your Brixton show before we knew we were getting a tête-à-tête and your fan army will surely follow you to whatever persona you want to embody next. Or is that just not on brand?

ER: *(Looks at you intensely. With her shades, it's hard to tell, but it's long and silent and lingering.)* I wish I had your faith in the future. It would be wonderful if you were right, but I fear I'm doomed. *(Downs the Bloody Mary.)*

MC: I know, your publicist asked me not to ask about anything "off character" but come on, it's not like you're going to "die", die. God, this is depressing, I'm going to get a drink as well. *(Orders a Sancerre.)* Okay, let's regroup. This is for a fucking women's fashion magazine after all. Are you seeing anyone special?

ER: *(Smiles.)* Let's go to the bar to get them and just go before she notices. I hate this place. Let's go and see what London has to amuse us. Hair of the dog, and all that, and I have Cerberus at the doors of my home. That's one hell of a dog. One hell of a dog, with one hell of a hair.

MC: Here, do you mind holding this one? I didn't know we'd be ambulatory. *(Hands her a recorder to hold up to her.)*

ER: *(Takes the microphone, winks and sneaks off.)*

Lucifer takes you out the club, having a cigarette on the way, before knocking on a door in one of Soho's alleys into one of many unmarked cocktail bars in the area. An hour and two cocktails later things are more relaxed, with the pair of you propping up the bar. Her poise has relaxed a little.

ER: *(Leans on one elbow, eating the occasional olive.)* So, my love life. I'll describe it as... lively, but not much actual love.

MC: Say more things.

ER: *(Is definitely being leading. Her shades are off.)*

MC: There are rumours on the internet — the most reliable place on earth — that you're conjugating verbs with Inanna.

ER: *(Smiles at that, clearly considers denying it, and then dives right in.)* Well, we have a shared interest in orgasms and the accumulation thereof, so it does make some degree of sense...

but he's so nice. I had to make it bad somehow. He's seeing Baal. That's the big secret. I don't think Inanna quite realised Baal thought they were exclusive. *(There's a frown there.)*

MC: Oh shit. Did you know? Oh, you did know.

ER: *(Nods, sipping the drink some more.)* I did. I knew exactly what I was doing. I thought... well, playing the Serpent is on brand.

MC: And yet you seem miserable about it. Or is that just the Xmas talking?

ER: *(Bristles a little.)* It's the Old Fashioned talking, mainly. *(Thinks it through.)* It was cruel and petty, and... I was feeling cruel and petty. The surfeit of happiness was utterly unbearable, and Baal is a judgemental prick of a god.

MC: Your happiness or theirs?

ER: Theirs. I brought knowledge to their garden of Eden. It's a sin, sure... but they'll both thank me for it. *(Doesn't seem ENTIRELY convinced by her own line there.)*

MC: But clearly you had... have feelings for Inanna beyond the cardiovascular pursuits of shagging for sport? I'm sensing contrition, frankly. And that might be the wine talking.

ER: *(Smiles.)* The devil having contrition would be most unlike me, wouldn't it? *(The smile is a little sad.)* Inanna is a puppy of a dog. I felt like I was kicking a puppy. I wish I wasn't the sort of person who occasionally kicks puppies. But the noise they make when they yelp in confusion is so delightful! *(Reaches over to touch your hand.)* Mary — you must stress that I don't actually kick puppies. I may be the source of all human misery, but a girl has to have standards.

MC: So you basically just adulterated something for the sake of doing it? Like climbing Everest but for ruination? Jesus, and sorry because this a magazine question, but what DO you do for self-care? Because your branding seems to be way too much work. Like, emotionally.

ER: *(Pauses.)* Yeah, I did. And my honest response is to basically grab the world by the lapels and snarl "FUCK YOU FOR JUDGING ME" at them. *(There's a snarl with that last line... which turns into a smile. And then a shrug.)*

MC: Labels. what's the world wearing? McQueen too? Dior Homme? *(Smiles.)*

ER: *(Smiles.)* Saint Alexander is too good for this world. *(Thinks about the self-care and work question.)*

MC: I know fame is psychologically expensive but is it worth it?

ER: I don't know yet, but I'm certainly finding out. Won't it be fun? To paraphrase a fellow traveller: Divinity is an art, like everything I do it exceedingly well. It just takes a lot of work. And for self-care... I like sunsets. Let's go find a sunset.

You head south from Soho, through the London lights, popping through a shopping precinct. It's not American level of OTP tack, but certainly has a level of try. Lucifer turns heads, but she moves in a way which makes people take photos rather than actually talk to her. She has a very good glower when she wishes.

MC: You're taking me to the mall?

ER: It's Christmas, you're American and Consumerism is your religion. Of course we're going to the Mall!

MC: Ahahahha.

It's two hours later, and you're in a private booth looking over the river in the Southbank Centre — which is mainly an arts place. Lucifer mentions in passing her parents used to take her here. Cheap places for liberal-arts parents to do stuff with their kids. She stresses she means the Southbank Centre, not the cocktail bar specifically...

ER: *(Stirring a cocktail. It's very tall, and she's definitely a little drunk now.)*

MC: Your parents... huge Beatles fans. What else were they like? Creative? Supportive? What do they think about what you're doing now?

ER: *(Thinks about that.)* They had their moments. They taught me to love art. They encouraged me to think. Yet they're... distant. Like children. I think of them as peers more than parents half the time. *(She shrugs.)* I mean, I am 19 going on 6,000, so that does make some sense. *(Laughs.)* They are so embarrassing in their own way. They told me I was conceived the night of a Blur gig at Alexandra Palace. They could have lied to me and said it was something more credible.

MC: Ew Blur... So about your songwriting? Any merit to the fact that you guys are as manufactured as NSync? There are rumours as to who your Lou Pearlman is... I guess that's Simon Cowell over here.

ER: *(Tilts her brow forward and smirks.)* Oh, we are definitely in the six drinks and counting stage of the interview, aren't we?

MC: Who's your Brian Epstein, Ms. Rigby? *(Laughs.)*

ER: *(Puts her hands together, forming a wall between you two.)* You are on this side of the curtain. I am on this side. There are things in my life you will never know. Alas, that's the way of these things. I wouldn't feel too bad — it's awful back here. The rider is terrible. *(Lowers her hands.)* But our Epstein is quite the... person. *(Raises a finger to her lips.)*

MC: Jesus, you're inscrutable. Although Jesus is perhaps not the one to invoke right now. OK, well what about the rumour that you slather yourself in Crème de la Mer before you go to sleep at night?

ER: *(Smirks.)* Oh, that's partially true. I don't slather myself. I have people to do the slathering for me.

MC: Like Sakhmet?

ER: Not as often as I'd like, really, but she's fun. In her own way.

MC: And which way is that?

ER: Petrifying too.

MC: Ahahahha. I'm surprised a portal doesn't open into another dimension when you two make the beast with two backs.

ER: She is very beautiful, intense and knows exactly what she wants. I would feel sorry for anyone who gets in the way of that. But yes... we've certainly had our moments.

ER: *(Frowns.)* I do wish the photos from that party with her had me at a more flattering angle. My forehead looked obscene.

MC: Ahahahahha. I can assure you no one was looking at your forehead.

ER: You say the kindest things.

MC: What are you getting her for Xmas?

ER: Sakhmet's Christmas present... will be... A distraction, I think.

MC: From what exactly?

ER: Boredom, really. Sakhmet doesn't like to be bored. She is rarely bored around me. Few people are. I have many faults, but I think I have a strong claim to being interesting. I doubt many people forget me.

MC: How obliging of you. For all your exploits and the fame you are still very young. What are you getting your parents and what are they getting you for Xmas?

ER: (Takes a long pause.) Hopefully, a better daughter. Whatever THAT means. (Shudders.)

MC: THAT was an emo answer. Ahahhaaha!

ER: Oh god. Xmas spirits have overcome me. And possibly actual spirits.

MC: Ahahhahaha

ER: (Tilts her glass.)

MC: (Also tilts a glass.) I'm going to stop right here. But I have to say, I thought you were going to be a lot more... hostile. I heard you had a thing against asian members of the press. It's not like we have a fatwah out on you but I did talk to Cassandra...

ER: (Curls her fingers a little. Sighs, and lights a cigarette. You don't see how she does it. She clicks her fingers. Maybe some kind of built-in lighter.) If someone comes at me, I will use whatever weapon to hand to take them down. I will not be judged by anyone, and that very minor cultural commentator seems to think she can judge us. As my personal history shows, I don't take being judged well. But I am a very pleasant monster if you don't hit that somewhat... apocalyptic self-defence response.

MC: And yourself, it would seem. I don't mean to be patronizing, but I've interviewed so many of the sparkliest stars from whom we want our pound of flesh, and you shouldn't be so hard on yourself. Drinks are on me. And the crumbling institution of print media. Have a good Xmas, Luci. We're going to hug now.

ER: (Looks at you, and the eyes are suddenly very young and scared. That posture is gone for a second. She accepts the hug, and is about to answer...)

There's a flash of light. You can't locate it. And then the doors from the inside of the cocktail bar open — we're on the balcony — and a young woman rushes out. She's got flaming red hair, and dressed in a long white dress, with face paint. You don't recognise her. "LUCI! LOOK!" she shouts, wildly. Lucifer breaks the hug, turning amazed, shocked. "Hazel?" The two women grab each other's arms, looking at each other. "No, not Hazel!" she replies, "Amaterasu! I'm a god too. We get to do this together." Lucifer stops, and whispers "I'm sorry." Amaterasu is clearly not getting her friend's worry. "Luci! You are wrong. This is everything. This is exactly how it should be. Trust me. Didn't I always say we were special?"

ER: (Sighs, turning back to you.) I have to go. Old friend, shall we say. Have a nice life. G-o-d knows I will.

MC: Take care, Luci. Be good to yourself. (Stops recording.)

ER: (Smiles backwards.) I don't need to be good to myself. I have adoring worshippers for that.

And then Lucifer and Amaterasu run off, holding hands, almost like schoolgirls.

ALSO BY THE CREATORS

THE WICKED + THE DIVINE

VOL. 1: THE FAUST ACT
#1—5 COLLECTED

GILLEN McKELVIE WILSON COWLES
THE
WICKED
+
DIVINE
THE
THE FAUST ACT

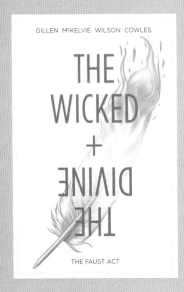

VOL. 2: FANDEMONIUM
#6—11 COLLECTED

GILLEN McKELVIE WILSON COWLES
THE
WICKED
+
DIVINE
THE
FANDEMONIUM

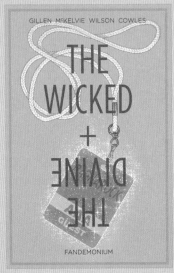

VOL. 3: COMMERCIAL SUICICDE
#12—17 COLLECTED

GILLEN McKELVIE WILSON COWLES
THE
WICKED
+
DIVINE
THE
COMMERCIAL SUICIDE

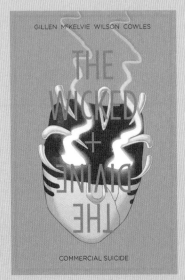

VOL. 4: RISING ACTION
#18—22 COLLECTED

GILLEN McKELVIE WILSON COWLES
THE
WICKED
+
DIVINE
THE
RISING ACTION

BOOK ONE:
#1—11 COLLECTED

GILLEN McKELVIE WILSON COWLES
THE
WICKED
+
DIVINE
THE
1

BOOK TWO:
#12—22 COLLECTED

GILLEN McKELVIE WILSON COWLES
THE
WICKED
+
DIVINE
THE
2

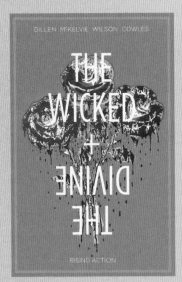

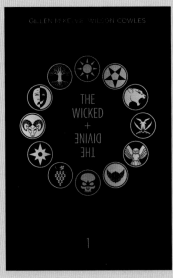

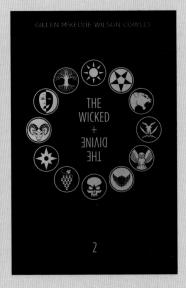

ALSO BY THE CREATORS

PHONOGRAM

VOL. 1:
RUE BRITANNIA

PHONOGRAM
RUE BRITANNIA
Kieron
GILLEN
Jamie
McKELVIE

VOL. 2:
THE SINGLES CLUB

PHONOGRAM
THE SINGLES CLUB
KIERON GILLEN & JAMIE McKELVIE

VOL. 3:
THE IMMATERIAL GIRL

PHONOGRAM
THE IMMATERIAL GIRL

THE COMPLETE
PHONOGRAM

GILLEN McKELVIE WILSON COWLES
SIDE A
THE COMPLETE
PHONOGRAM

THE COMPLETE PHONOGRAM COLLECTS

Vol. 1: Rue Britannia

Vol. 2: The Singles Club

Vol. 3: The Immaterial Girl

And the previously uncollected B-side stories.

FOR FURTHER INFORMATION ON

THE WICKED + THE DIVINE:

www.wicdiv.com

major news, new issues, merchandise.

#WicDiv

the hashtag on twitter for WicDiv Discussion

WicDiv

the general tag on tumblr for the community.

bit.ly/WicDivPlaylist

the ever-updated Spotify Playlist for the series.

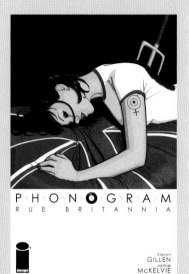

Kieron Gillen is a writer drinking a mojito. Imperial Phase!

Jamie McKelvie is an artist drinking a mojito. Imperial Phase!

Matt Wilson doesn't get to drink a mojito in a swimming pool
as he is working too hard.

Photograph by Katie West